18 - 99

D1100862

CONTEMPORARY POLITICAL STUDIES SERIES

Series Editor: John Benyon, *University of Leicester*

Published

DAVID BROUGHTON
Public Opinion and Political Polling in Britain

CLYDE CHITTY
Education Policy in Britain

MICHAEL CONNOLLY
Politics and Policy Making in Northern Ireland

DAVID DENVER
Elections and Voters in Britain

JUSTIN FISHER
British Political Parties

ROBERT GARNER
Environmental Politics: Britain, Europe and the Global Environment; 2nd edn

ANDREW GEDDES
The European Union and British Politics

WYN GRANT
Pressure Groups and British Politics

WYN GRANT
Economic Policy in Britain

DEREK HEATER and GEOFFREY BERRIDGE
Introduction to International Politics

DILYS M. HILL
Urban Policy and Politics in Britain

ROBERT LEACH
Political Ideology in Britain

ROBERT LEACH and JANIE PERCY-SMITH
Local Governance in Britain

PETER MADGWICK
British Government: The Central Executive Territory

ANDREW MASSEY and ROBERT PYPER
Public Management and Modernisation in Britain

PHILIP NORTON
Parliament and British Politics

MALCOLM PUNNETT
Selecting the Party Leader

ROBERT PYPER
The British Civil Service

Forthcoming

RAYMOND KUHN
Politics and the Media in Britain

Political Ideology in Britain

Robert Leach

palgrave

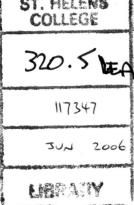
First published 2002 by
PALGRAVE
Houndmills, Basingstoke, Hampshire RG21 6XS and
175 Fifth Avenue, New York, N. Y. 10010
Companies and representatives throughout the world

PALGRAVE is the new global academic imprint of
St. Martin's Press LLC Scholarly and Reference Division and
Palgrave Publishers Ltd (formerly Macmillan Press Ltd).

ISBN-13: 978-0-333-96350-0 hardback
ISBN-10: 0-333-96350-4   hardback
ISBN-13: 978-0-333-96353-1 paperback
ISBN-10: 0-333-96353-9   paperback

This book is printed on paper suitable for recycling and
made from fully managed and sustained forest sources.

A catalogue record for this book is available
from the British Library.

Library of Congress Cataloging-in-Publication Data
Leach, Robert, 1941–
    Political ideology in Britain/Robert Leach.
       p. cm. — (Contemporary political studies)
    Includes bibliographical references and index.
    ISBN 0–333–96350–4
    1. Political science — Great Britain. 2. Ideology — Great Britain.
3. Right and left (Political science) I. Title. II. Contemporary political
studies (Palgrave (Firm))

JA84.G7 L395 2002
320.5'0941–dc21   2001059839

10 9 8 7 6 5 4 3 2
11 10 09 08 07 06 05

Printed in China

Contents

List of Figures and Tables

Figures

Tables

Preface

Political Ideology in Britain effectively replaces an earlier title in the Contemporary Political Studies series. *British Political Ideologies* went through two editions (1991, 1996) under its former publisher, and although both editions sold gratifying well in an increasingly crowded market, the time seemed ripe for a more fundamental rethink of the structure and content of the book than was compatible with a further edition of the original. This rethinking was assisted by the transfer of the series to Palgrave, which entailed some refreshing new ideas on format and content. Thus *Political Ideology in Britain* is a new book which differs markedly from its predecessors, as readers of the old book will readily appreciate.

Two decisions were reached at an early stage of planning the new book. One was to maintain the distinctive British focus, which allows full scope to relate ideologies to political practice. The other was to add to the new book a more explicitly contemporary focus, in keeping with the title of the series. Those studying ideologies expect to encounter ideas and controversies at the heart of modern politics.

Accordingly, while I have continued to devote substantial chapters to the evolution of the mainstream ideologies of liberalism, conservatism and socialism, I have also included separate chapters on the New Right and New Labour, while fully recognizing and exploring the elements of continuity with traditional Conservative and Labour thinking. I have also provided a more extended discussion of the implications of varieties of nationalist thinking within Britain, and the implication for the future of the United Kingdom. In keeping with a contemporary debate over multiethnic Britain I have chosen to devote a chapter to ideas associated with racism and multiculturalism, rather than one restricted to British fascism and neo-fascism. I have also rethought as well as updated my approach to feminism and Green thinking, and have sought to relate this both to contemporary issues and controversies.

I am grateful to Leeds Metropolitan University for awarding me a sabbatical semester, which has enabled me to complete this book. I should acknowledge a debt to the colleagues with whom I have worked over the years and to my students, both past and present. Both have sharpened my ideas. I must also express my thanks to John Benyon, the series editor, for his continuing warm encouragement, and to Steven Kennedy for his highly committed hands-on approach to publishing. However, my greatest debt, as always, is to my wife Judith, without whom this book would certainly not have been written.

ROBERT LEACH

1

Introduction: Ideology in British Politics

Political ideas and ideologies

Serious study of political ideas goes back at least as far as Greece of the fifth and fourth centuries BC. when thinkers such as Socrates, Plato and Aristotle speculated about the best system of government and the meaning of terms like 'justice' 'equality', 'freedom'. The modern study of political theory or political philosophy has focused on the writings of major political thinkers and the key concepts and theories which they examined. The study of political ideologies draws on this very old study of ideas but is of more recent origin. The term 'ideology' is itself problematic and contested (see below) but for the present may be loosely defined as 'any system of ideas and norms directing political and social action' (Flew, 1979, p. 150). The key words here are 'system' and 'action'. An ideology involves firstly an interconnected set of ideas which form a perspective on the world – what the Germans call *weltanschauung*. Secondly, ideologies have implications for political behaviour – they are 'action-oriented.'

Most of the ideologies which are examined under this heading, such as liberalism, socialism, nationalism or feminism are themselves relatively new and have developed over the last two hundred or so years, products of the eighteenth-century enlightenment, industrialization and the French revolution, although their inspiration may often be traced back earlier. While conservative habits of thought are perhaps as old as humanity, conservatism as a coherent political perspective was only articulated more systematically in response to radical political doctrines which sought to change the world, such as liberalism and socialism. Some ideologies, including fascism and green thinking, were essentially products of the twentieth century, although again their core ideas developed out of and in opposition to mainstream political thinking from the enlightenment onwards.

This book explores these ideologies with particular reference to British politics. While there are many good texts on ideologies in general, there are few which explicitly relate ideologies to a particular political system. If ideologies are not 'pure theory' but 'action-oriented' they should be related to practical politics. The British focus allows greater scope for examining the impact of ideology on policy, and the effect of the latter in turn on the development of ideological thinking. A study grounded in the realities of British politics can avoid some of the more abstract accounts of ideologies inevitably involved in ostensibly international texts.

Political ideas in Britain have been influenced by distinctive features of the economic, social and cultural background, and have developed against a distinctive history. Key domestic developments which have shaped political thinking include the English and Scottish reformations of the sixteenth century, the political upheavals in Britain and Ireland of the seventeenth century, the evolution of the British state and constitution following the 1688 revolution and the 1707 Act of Union, industrialization and urbanization from the late eighteenth century onwards, and the parallel growth (and subsequent rapid decline) of the British empire. These developments, some far back in time, have shaped enduring cleavages in British politics and society and continue to influence the way in which the British (or English, Scottish and Welsh) think about politics, and help to explain some significant differences between political ideas in Britain and its near neighbours across the Channel (to say nothing of the greater differences between countries further away in distance and culture).

Yet these differences can only be understood if the study of ideology in British politics is located within a broader comparative context. Thus although our primary focus is on Britain, the approach here is not narrowly insular. British political thinking has been extensively influenced by events and ideas from the wider world, and British variants of ideologies need relating to wider currents of thought. The distinctive features of British liberalism or socialism can only by understood with reference to the experience of liberalism and socialism elsewhere. As Vincent (1995, p. 19) rightly warns us, 'All ideologies are internally complex, intermixed and overlapping. There is no *one* pure socialist and liberal view of the world.'

Ideas, power and interests

How important are political ideas? Ideas, it might be urged, are the lifeblood of politics. There is nothing so powerful as an idea whose time has come. Thus the ideas expressed in the American Declaration of

Independence or the French revolutionary slogan 'Liberty, Equality, Fraternity' transformed the world. 'The Communist Manifesto' of Marx and Engels inspired a revolution in Russia and an economic and political system which shaped the lives and work of a third of the globe. More recently the rediscovery of the free market has stimulated political and economic change over the western, former Communist and third world.

From another perspective, politics is essentially about power and interests rather than ideas. As Thrasymachus in Plato's *Republic* (tr. Cornford, 1945, p. 18) argues, 'just or right means nothing but what is to the interest of the stronger party.' Ideas of what is right involve rationalizations of interest. Those in power can ensure that the ideas which are widely accepted are those which are in accordance with their own interest, or, as Marx put it much later, 'The ruling ideas of every age are the ideas of the ruling class.'

Marx was concerned with the source of ideas. How and why do ideas originate? One of his targets was idealism, the philosophical approach derived ultimately from Plato but featuring especially Kant and Hegel which suggested that ideas are the ultimate reality, and the motive force in human history. Against this, Marx presented his own materialist conception of history in which ideas derive from the material circumstances of humanity. 'Life is not determined by consciousness, but consciousness by life' (Marx, ed. McLellan, 1977, p. 164). Our experience of the world shapes our outlook, not the other way round.

Thus ideas reflect social and economic circumstances. Marx, moreover, saw society as deeply divided, so that the moral and political ideas expressed at any time reflect conflicting class interests. Such an approach provides rich insights into the mainstream ideologies of the western world. Thus traditional conservatism may be linked with the landed interest, liberalism with financial and industrial capital, and socialism with the industrial working class. Conservatives, liberals and many non-Marxist socialists would deny that that their creeds exclusively reflected specific class interests, but claim instead that they had a universal relevance, and draw support across classes. Nevertheless, analysis of the membership, electoral support and policies of political parties associated with these ideologies suggests some significant correlations with class interests.

However, if, as Marxists suggest, political ideologies essentially articulate class interests, where does that leave perspectives which reflect other divisions in society, such as those based on religion, ethnicity or gender? In practice, Marxists have viewed some such divisions (for example nation, race and religion) as artificially fostered to weaken working class unity, and other divisions (such as gender) as essentially subordinate to more fundamental class divisions. Yet for some people issues of race, gender, religion or nationhood are real and fundamental rather than secondary, and inform their whole perspective on politics, power, decision-making and public policy. Thus feminism or nationalism are as much ideologies as political outlooks which can be related more plausibly to class divisions, such as conservatism, socialism or liberalism.

Relating political ideas to material interests is certainly a fruitful approach, whether ideologies are linked exclusively to class interests in the Marxist sense, or associated more broadly with other interests in society. It does make sense to ask who is putting forward particular doctrines and why, and whose interests they serve. Answers to such questions can be very illuminating. Even so, there are ideologies such as ecologism (or green thinking) which are less easily equated with specific interests within human society. Moreover, while most ideologies may be strongly associated with material interests, this does not necessarily entail that they are just rationalizations of interest, and have no intrinsic validity.

Marx himself generally employed the term 'ideology' in a pejorative (or negative) sense, and identified ideology with illusion. The prevailing ideas in any society, he suggested, will reflect the existing power structure, the current pattern of domination and subordination, partly because those with economic and political power will be well-placed to control the dissemination and legitimation of ideas, through, for example, education and the mass media. It follows that subordinate classes will not necessarily recognize the real basis of society, nor their own exploitation, but will hold a distorted, mistaken view of reality. Marx commonly used the term 'ideology' to describe this distorted view that a social class, such as the industrial working class, might have of its own position in society as a whole. Much of the prevailing wisdom of his day, including the ideas of the classical economists Smith, Malthus and Ricardo, Marx regarded as ideological rather than scientific: their theories served the interests of capitalism. By contrast, Marx thought his own method provided a powerful tool for penetrating below the surface and understanding the real economic and social forces which shape change. Thus Marxism was science rather than ideology.

This identification of ideology with illusion and distortion and what Engels later called 'false consciousness' (McLellan, 1995, p. 20) is of course highly pejorative. However, Marx sometimes used the term in a more neutral sense, and later Marxists such as Lenin, Gramsci and Lukacs assumed a need to actively promote a working-class socialist ideology to counter the dominant ruling-class ideology.

Ideology as dogmatism – the 'end of ideology'

Some modern, particularly American, social scientists have also, like Marx, employed the term ideology in a highly pejorative and restricted manner, but in a quite opposite sense to his. Thus non-Marxist economists, sociologists and political scientists emphasized the need for detached, value-free, rigorous empirical research – which they saw as the essence of the social science method. Marxist analysis was regarded, by contrast, as dogmatic, unscientific and 'ideological'. Ideology was identified particularly with closed 'totalitarian' systems of thought, including both fascism and Marxist-inspired Communism. Ideology was the enemy of western pluralist democracy. The future lay with non-ideological thinking, pragmatism rather than ideology, and preconceived ideas and all-embracing theories were useless or positively dangerous.

Just as many Marxists did not think their own political ideas were 'ideological', so these western political thinkers did not consider that the liberal pluralist or conservative ideas they held were ideological either. An ideology was the political outlook of someone else. The liberal pluralist ideas on which postwar western society rested were scientific and non-ideological. Thus the triumph of pluralist liberal democracy involved the 'end of ideology' (Bell, 1960). More recently, in an echo of Bell's thesis, the fall of the Berlin wall and soviet communism marked the victory of liberal capitalism and the 'end of history' (Fukuyama, 1992).

Meanwhile, in Britain and western Europe ideological conflict apparently gave way to an ideological consensus in the post-Second World War era. In Britain it appeared that leading Labour and Conservative politicians increasingly shared the same assumptions, and often the same remedies. The term 'Butskellism' was coined (from the names of Labour and Conservative Chancellors, Gaitskell and Butler) to describe the similar approach of both major parties to economic management. Over western Europe generally there was a similar 'social democratic' consensus around the welfare state and managed capitalism.

The extent of ideological consensus in the post-Second World War has arguably been exaggerated. However, a widely prevailing consensus does not necessarily imply the 'end of ideology' in Bell's sense, but rather the dominance of a particular ideology, the acceptance by the political establishment, and perhaps the bulk of the masses also, of a set of ideas which may become for a time the ruling political orthodoxy. Indeed, as some twentieth-century Marxists like Gramsci have argued, the dominance of such a single 'hegemonic' ideology may be more the norm than the exception. It may become so widely accepted and unchallenged that it is not even perceived as ideological, but simply 'common sense' or 'the way things are', to which 'there is no alternative'. It is only when the assumptions behind such a dominant orthodoxy are eventually challenged that its ideological character is acknowledged.

Contemporary approaches towards the study of ideologies

As McLellan (1995, p. 1) has ironically observed, 'Ideology is someone *else's* thought, seldom our own,' underlining the pejorative interpretation of ideology both by Marxists and leading anti-Marxists, such as Oakeshott (1962) or Minogue (1985). An alternative approach assumes that all political thinking, including our own, is ideological. The use of the term 'ideology' does not by itself imply any kind of judgement on the validity of the ideas discussed. Ideology is not necessarily to be identified with illusion or unreflecting dogma, nor should it be contrasted with 'truth' or 'science'. Moreover, while ideologies may be employed to legitimate existing systems or regimes, they can also be used to justify their overthrow. Ideologies may thus be conservative, reformist or revolutionary, moderate or extremist. They may be associated with conflicting interests in society, but also with a system of belief which appears to command general assent. This more inclusive approach to the study of ideology (Seliger, 1976, pp. 91–121), has now become sufficiently common to be described as mainstream, and implicitly or explicitly underpins a burgeoning literature surveying modern political ideologies (for example, Eccleshall *et al.*, 1994; Vincent, 1995; Adams, 1993, 1998; Heywood, 1997; Eatwell and Wright, 1999).

While not neglecting the importance of social context, power and interests, some exponents of this modern approach to the study of ideology also draw more freely on the older study of political theory and philosophy, which treats political ideas as worth studying in their own right. Thus Freeden (1996, p. 7) seeks to 'reintegrate' the investigation of political ideologies 'into the mainstream of political theory'. He makes eclectic use of insights from Marxist analysis and modern social science in associating ideologies with 'social groups, not necessarily classes', and arguing that they 'perform a range of services, such as legitimation, integration, socialization, ordering, simplification, and action orientation, without which societies could not function adequately, if at all.' He sees ideologies as 'ubiquitous forms of political thinking' which are 'inevitably associated with power, though not invariably with the threatening or exploitative version of power'. But he also argues that 'ideologies are distinct thought-products that invite careful investigation in their own right' (1996, pp. 22–3), and goes on to treat them essentially as a specialist branch of political theory.

Studying ideology – the issue of bias

Vincent (1995, p. 20) observes 'We examine ideology as fellow sufferers, not as neutral observers.' The warning is apt. This is not a subject where one can expect objectivity. Those who write about ideologies in general have their own ideological convictions, which may be more or less apparent, however hard they seek to write dispassionately. Accounts of specific ideologies are even more likely to be partisan. Much of the literature on feminism or the Greens is written by committed supporters, and some is frankly propagandist, while modern accounts of racism and fascism are almost universally hostile. Accounts of the mainstream ideologies of conservatism, liberalism and socialism are more mixed. A few may be obviously and markedly critical (for example Honderich, 1990, on Conservatism), but even where they are clearly sympathetic overall, they will frequently reflect a particular interpretation or tendency.

Such obvious bias by both proponents and antagonists is scarcely surprising. Ideologies are action-oriented – paraphrasing Marx, they seek to change the world, not just interpret it. Those who are ideologically committed seek converts to their cause. Even academics who affect greater detachment inevitably have their own views which consciously or unconsciously influence the way they treat their subject. Moreover, as we have seen, the study of ideology itself inevitably reflects ideological preconceptions. There are very different views on the definition and nature of ideology, and the relationship of ideology to power and interests on the one hand and science and truth on the other.

All this suggests some problems for students, both in terms of interpreting what others have written on specific ideologies and ideology in general, and in terms of formulating and presenting their own views. The contested nature of the subject matter does not mean that in the study of ideologies 'anything goes', allowing a free rein to the ventilation of personal prejudices. As in any subject for academic study there is an obligation to standards of accuracy over detail and rigour in analysis. Views attributed to particular thinkers, politicians or parties require supporting evidence. The reasoning behind inferences and causal con-

nections should be explained. Above all, awkward facts which do not
fit a favoured interpretation should not be ignored. A particular standpoint or theory may ultimately be rejected, but in academic discourse
there is a presumed obligation to present it fairly and accurately first.

Political ideologies are the very stuff of controversy, which is why
many find them fascinating. But this means that no-one who comes to
the study of political ideologies can be free of preconceptions. It may
seem difficult to entirely separate academic enquiry from personal
political allegiance, yet commitment to a particular political position
should not preclude some reasonably dispassionate examination of its
development, supporting interests, core principles and problematic
areas. Equally, opposition to a particular ideology is not compromised
by an attempt to understand its appeal to others. There are advantages
to be derived from 'knowing your enemy'. Even ideologies such as
fascism or racism which may inspire repugnance still require some reasonably detached analysis to explain their apparent appeal to many,
both in the past and today.

A one-sided or inadequate view of an ideology may not reflect prior
prejudice, but simply weaknesses or bias in the source material. The
best safeguard against falling for a partial, narrow or eccentric interpretation of an ideology is to read widely but always critically. Contrasting
interpretations, including both hostile and sympathetic treatments
should be deliberately sought out. Such an approach will help to identify both points of agreement and controversy. In all reading a questioning, sceptical approach should be adopted. Nothing should be taken on
trust (including what is written here!). It is often useful to attempt to
discern the author's perspective. To know that a particular writer is a
Marxist or belongs to the New Right may assist in interpretation, and
also suggest critical questions.

Elements of ideologies

Although political ideologies may differ radically in terms of assumptions and practical implications, it is possible to identify some key elements which provide a basis for comparison. Three elements may be
broadly identified – an interpretation of existing social arrangements, a
vision of the future, and a strategy for realizing that future. While ideologies are essentially action-oriented and prescriptive, any prescription for political and social action must ultimately rest on some
assumptions, however crude, about the nature of existing society and

human behaviour. For those who are broadly happy with existing social arrangements, the vision of the future may closely resemble the present, and the strategy will be one of seeking to maintain the status quo. Those profoundly dissatisfied with the present will contemplate strategies for achieving radical change or revolution.

A view of existing social arrangements will commonly include some assumptions about human nature and individual motivation. Indeed such assumptions lie behind the ideas of most of the great political thinkers of the past. Plato, Machiavelli and Hobbes, for example, were all fairly pessimistic about the capacity of human beings to live together sociably and cooperatively, without a considerably element of coercion or brainwashing, while Aristotle, Rousseau and, in the last analysis, Marx, had a more optimistic view of human potential for fruitful cooperation. Among modern political ideologies, fascism makes some fairly cynical assumptions about the pliability of men and women, while socialism is essentially optimistic, and traditional conservatism rather pessimistic about human nature. Free-market liberalism, drawing heavily on classical economics, sees individuals as motivated by self-interest, but suggests that the net consequence of all pursuing their self-interest will be the greatest common good.

A linked consideration is the potential for changing human nature. Does vicious behaviour reflect the immutable nature of humanity, or is it the product of a particular environment, which might be changed? Anarchists, for example, believe that power corrupts. A society without hierarchies of authority, and without government in the sense of coercive power, would lead to more cooperative and civilised human behaviour. Socialists may argue that highly self-interested competitive behaviour is the product of the capitalist economic system rather than a universal human characteristic. They also suggest that substantial inequalities in human capacities and attainments are not innate, but can be reduced through enlarging opportunities.

Conservatives are usually rather more sceptical about the scope for improvements in human nature, although they may consider religious belief, or a stable family background as possible ameliorative factors. Some feminists would draw a major distinction between male and female natures, suggesting that men are naturally aggressive and competitive, and women caring and cooperative, although other feminists would suggest that this behaviour is largely culturally determined and that men could learn to be caring. The capacity for changing human behaviour is clearly important where prescriptions for the future require people to behave in different ways.

This highlights the question of the relationship of the individual to society. To Aristotle a proper human existence was inconceivable outside society; man was naturally a social and political animal. At the opposite extreme, some liberal thinkers have viewed society as an artificial construct, requiring a conscious and deliberate effort to bring it into being, and having no meaning apart from its constituent individual elements. Mrs Thatcher lies comfortably within this strand of liberal political tradition in her assertion that there is no such thing as society, only individuals and their families. By contrast, both traditional conservatism (or Toryism) and socialism have tended to view the individual as inseparable from society, with individuals, groups and whole classes bound inextricably to each other through ties of mutual dependence (although, of course, conservatives and socialists have sharply contrasting views on existing social relations under capitalism). So-called 'totalitarian' ideologies (such as fascism, Stalinism) involve, in theory at least, the total subjugation of the individual to the national whole.

Ideologies will commonly involve all kinds of other assumptions about the way society currently operates – the extent of equality within society, the organization of work and industrial relations, community relations, authority and power structures, and a host of further issues. Some of these assumptions may be substantially accurate, while others may be wildly inaccurate, but perceptions of how the world *is* inevitably colour perceptions of how it *should* be, so that description and prescription are closely interlinked.

Some people may be more fearful than desirous of change – for all sorts of reasons. They may be substantial beneficiaries of existing social arrangements. They may be persuaded, perhaps against what others would regard as their objective interests, that change is impossible, dangerous or undesirable. The essence of conservatism, as the term implies, is to avoid major change, and a radically different future is neither sought nor desired, although a degree of gradual reform may be countenanced. For conservatives the problem is rather how to maintain social stability, and avoid social unrest and revolution. The choice may often seem to lie between granting reforms to appease dissatisfied elements, or refusing any concessions for fear that these will only fuel demands for further change and create more instability in the long run. In general, conservatives are much more sceptical of the scope for deliberate social engineering than liberals or socialists, and more wary of the possible dangers of change. Some reactionaries, in the proper sense of the term, may seek a future which resembles a past, real or imaginary, which they regret.

Others may strive for a future which is nothing like the present or immediate past. The construction of utopias has been a favourite pastime of political thinkers since classical times. The problem with utopias, however, is how to achieve them. The proposed utopia may be far more appealing than existing society, but how does one progress from (a) to (b)? Ideologies thus generally involve some assumptions about social change, although this element can in practice be fairly weak. Marx was critical of some of his socialist predecessors for lacking any coherent theory of social change. They had a socialist vision of the future, but no realistic strategy for achieving it. A major debate among socialists since Marx's day has been over the prospects of the parliamentary road to socialism – whether socialism can be achieved solely or mainly through the ballot box and the election of governments with parliamentary majorities. Some socialists deny that this is possible, while parliamentary socialists tend to respond that the alternatives are even more problematic.

Classifying ideologies – left and right

One of the oldest ways of classifying ideologies involves locating them on the familiar left–right political spectrum. The terms derive from the seating positions in the National Assembly arising out of the 1789 French Revolution; the most revolutionary groups sat on the left and the more conservative or reactionary sat on the right. Since then the terms 'left' and 'right' over time have acquired common currency. In many legislatures, particularly where the chambers are semi-circular, seating arrangements still mirror those of the revolutionary National Assembly, but even in countries like the United Kingdom where they do not, politicians, parties and political programmes are freely classified according to the terminology of left and right.

A 'scale' suggests that the terms are essentially relative, and that is how they are employed. Indeed further sub-categories are often used, such as 'far (or hard) left', 'extreme right' or 'centre left', to describe the position occupied on the spectrum more precisely. Frequently it is suggested that a certain politician, party or trade union is more left or more right than another, and the terms are also commonly used to describe intra-party factions. This can be confusing. Thus a particular politician or group in the British Labour Party might be described as 'right-wing', strictly within the context of his party, while more generally he would be regarded as 'on the left'. Similarly, factions within the Conservative Party are often loosely termed left, right or centre to explain their ideological position relative to others within their party, while they all essentially belong to the right.

This emphasises the importance of context in interpretation. Yet if the classification is virtually universal, it is not unproblematic. What is the scale really about? A common interpretation is that the scale measures attitudes to change, with those seeking revolutionary change on the left, and those opposed to all change on the right, with cautious reformers somewhere in the middle (Figure 1.1). Thus socialists and communists are on the left, conservatives on the right and progressive liberals in the centre.

REVOLUTION	REFORM	REACTION

| FAR LEFT | MODERATE LEFT | FAR LEFT | MODERATE RIGHT | FAR RIGHT |

Figure 1.1   Left–right: revolution and reaction

Yet if revolutionaries succeed and become the new establishment, should they then be placed on the right? In practice, Lenin's Bolsheviks continued to be regarded as 'left' after they seized power and established a new social and political system in Russia. Similarly, there is a problem with the 'radical right', almost a contradiction in terms if 'right' means opposition to change. Margaret Thatcher instituted radical change in Britain, although she and her allies were generally considered further to the right than the rather more cautious 'One Nation' Conservatives whom they had effectively displaced.

Another way of interpreting the left–right scale is in terms of attitudes to authority – with those championing individual liberty on the left, and those emphasising discipline and order on the right. This also does not always accord with general usage. Thus anarchists and communists, both generally considered on the left or far left, tend to display radically different attitudes to authority, and there are similar differences between the 'libertarian' and 'authoritarian' right. By contrast, the concept of 'totalitarianism' developed by some western theorists in the post war period, implied that both communism and fascism, conventionally placed at opposite ends of the left–right scale, were essentially similar in subordinating individual liberty to state authority.

Perhaps rather more promising is a definition in terms of attitudes to state intervention in the economy, with 'left' associated with collectivism and 'right' with the free market (Figure 1.2). This definition is consistent with the description of communists and socialists as 'left' regardless of whether they constituted the establishment or the opposition, and also consistent with the common designation of free-market Conservatives like Thatcher or Redwood as more 'right-wing' than the 'interventionist' Michael Heseltine. Yet fascism, commonly placed on the far right, favoured protection and substantial state direction rather than the free market.

Left – Collectivism   **Right – *Laissez-Faire***

STATE DIRECTION STATE INTERVENTION STATE WELFARE FREE MARKET

Communists   Socialists New Liberals 'One Nation' Conservatives New Right

Figure 1.2   Left–right: collectivism and the free market

In view of the ambiguities and inconsistencies associated with the left–right scale, some have sought a revised classification, or a more elaborate two-dimensional model of political attitudes (Eysenck, 1957; Brittan, 1968; and see also the website http://www.political compass.org). However, it seems most unlikely that these alternative approaches will banish the long familiar language of left and right from political discourse. Thus a conventional left–right scale is adopted here, despite the problems.

Even so, this conventional left–right political spectrum (see Figure 1.3) is more readily applicable to some ideologies than others. In particular, there is a problem in locating nationalism, feminism and green thinking on a left–right continuum. They each cut across or render irrelevant the familiar distinctions based on economic intervention or social class interests. Nationalism in different times and places has been associated with ideas across the political spectrum from the left to the far right. Feminism is generally linked with the left, but there is some question over whether it should be. Although most green activists are also more commonly associated with the left, the familiar green slogan 'neither left nor right but forward' suggests they see themselves on another dimension altogether. Thus some would argue that 'left' and 'right' describe the old obsolete politics, while the women's movement and the green movement in common with other currents of thought such as postmodernism or communitarianism represent a new politics.

FAR LEFT   MODERATE LEFT   CENTRE MOD. RIGHT   FAR RIGHT

Communists Socialists Social Democrats Liberals   Conservatives Fascists

Figure 1.3   Left–right: conventional scale

Levels of ideology

Ideologies can be interpreted and analysed at a number of different levels – from sophisticated intellectual constructs down to inferences from political behaviour. While the traditional study of political theory has tended to focus on the writings of great thinkers and the relatively tiny political elite familiar with their ideas, the study of political ideologies is concerned with mass as well as elite ideas and behaviour. Ideologies may be systematically articulated, through for example the writings of major thinkers, or expressed more selectively and persuasively through political pamphlets of speeches, or they may be essentially latent, and unsophisticated, expressed if at all in shorthand slogans and symbols. The clenched fist may seem a long way removed from Marx's 'Das Kapital' but they are both aspects of one ideology.

Some 'great thinkers' studied within the political theory tradition have clearly made a significant contribution to particular political ideologies, for example Marx to socialism, Burke to conservatism or Mill to liberalism. Yet, often, writers who were not themselves profound or original thinkers did more to popularize particular doctrines. Harriet Martineau who wrote little fables embodying the principles of classical economics, Edward Baines the polemical editor of the *Leeds Mercury*, and Samuel Smiles the purveyor of Victorian homilies on self-help and other virtues were more widely read and understood than Ricardo or Nassau Senior, and in some ways can be considered more typical of *laissez-faire* liberalism.

At another level, the pronouncements and achievements of active politicians, whose ideas are insufficiently original or systematic for consideration in histories of political theory, may play a critical role in the development of ideologies and their subsequent interpretation. There are very few 'great texts' which provide much of a guide to an understanding of conservatism. Many interpretations of British conservatism place particular emphasis on the contribution of past politicians, especially Prime Ministers, such as Peel, Disraeli, Salisbury, Baldwin and, more recently, Mrs Thatcher. Some of these politicians did articulate their ideas with varying degrees of sophistication in articles, novels, speeches and manifestos, but the ideas of others must be substantially inferred from their behaviour and output. For while political ideologies, almost by definition, influence political behaviour, they can also sometimes appear as rationalizations of political behaviour, although few politicians would put it quite as bluntly as Herbert Morrison who declared that socialism was what the Labour government did.

Ideologies do not just inform the beliefs and behaviour of politicians, but of the masses. The popular version of an ideology may be less elaborate than that held by professional politicians and party activists but it will shape the attitudes people have to the great questions of the day, how people vote, or indeed whether they vote, and their readiness to indulge in other political activity, such as demonstrations, law-breaking or even, on occasion, revolution. Although there may be a difference in sophistication between the elite and mass versions of particular ideologies, they reflect a smilar outlook on life, and inter relate. Mrs Thatcher acknowledged the influence of the everyday maxims acquired during her upbringing in that celebrated grocer's shop in Grantham (Young, 1989, p. 5), but also acknowledged a debt to Adam Smith and Hayek (Thatcher, 1977), and it is difficult to assess which has made the more significant contribution to 'Thatcherism' although it is the everyday maxims, such as 'Stand on your own two feet', which have a greater resonance with the wider public. Newspaper headlines, slogans and graffiti, and non-verbal symbols, such as the British bulldog, or Britannia or photographic images may reinforce or express particular ideological approaches. Some political ideologies are indeed almost entirely lacking in sophisticated intellectual expression. The Nuremberg rallies and the slogans painted in Mussolini's Italy, 'Believe, Obey, Fight', 'Live dangerously', 'Better one day as a lion than a thousand years as a sheep', perhaps tell us more about the nature of fascism, and almost certainly had more influence on political behaviour than fascist theory.

Power, influence and indoctrination

Consideration of the ideological perspectives of the masses raises some awkward questions on the transmission of ideas – over, for example, the potential for deliberate indoctrination. There are some celebrated fictional accounts of thought control, and plenty of real-life illustrations of more or less successful attempts to mould opinion, by no means all of which are to be found in so-called totalitarian states. For example, the allied authorities in Germany after the Second World War embarked on a deliberate counter-indoctrination programme which employed many of the means of their Nazi predecessors – censorship of newspapers, burning of books, screening teachers for ideological soundness, and the like. Most attempts to influence people's minds on political issues are less extensive and systematic than this, but there is

still a certain amount of quite conscious manipulation, even in a supposed liberal democracy like Britain.

If deliberate manipulation of people's minds by the government or
the dominant element in society was regularly employed and always
successful, there would be no ideological conflict, just the universal
acceptance of one ideology. Plato wanted to eliminate conflict in this
way in his ideal state, and there have been celebrated recent fictional
examples, such as Orwell's *1984* and Huxley's *Brave New World*.
Real-life governments have found it rather more difficult to stifle all
dissent; however, at the very least it can be said that they have the
means at their disposal to influence opinion.

The role of the media in shaping opinion is another controversial area.
The narrow concentration of media ownership in the UK and the influence
of a handful of media tycoons rather undermines the comfortable liberal-
pluralist assumption that people are exposed to a wide range of sources
and views, enabling them to make up their own minds on political questions. Most national newspapers have long exhibited a marked political
bias, while the assumption of television and radio neutrality has been challenged from both left and right. Moreover, although the internet offers the
prospect perhaps of more open and pluralist political debate, it has hardly
yet engaged the masses. Media concentration and bias may not matter that
much if, as some academic research suggests, people use the media to
reinforce their own ideas, and filter out messages which do not match preconceived attitudes, but others argue that our thinking must be influenced,
if sometimes subliminally, by the constant repetition of media images and
associations. Thus not only our perceptions of particular politicians and
parties, but our images of women, our attitudes to minorities, and our
views on a whole range of issues from paedophiles to fuel protests, from
fox hunting to the European Union, are inevitably influenced and perhaps
even determined by the media, especially in the absence of any direct personal experience.

Too much emphasis can be placed on deliberate indoctrination by governments or on media propaganda. Far more significant, it might be
argued, is the largely unconscious process by which beliefs are transmit-
ted and sustained from the elite to the masses, and across generations.
Existing institutions, work practices, patterns of social organization, habits
and beliefs may generally be taken for granted. In some cases it may
require a considerable effort to even imagine alternatives. The weight of
tradition is always likely to be a major constraint on political thinking,
which will tend to justify the status quo and serve the interests of those
who benefit principally from the status quo. Thus the ideas of established

dominant groups will often be fairly generally accepted throughout society, without any deliberation action to ensure this. While the dominant ideology may not be all-pervasive, some of its core assumptions at least may gain wide acceptance among subordinate groups.

The battle of ideas, then, is inevitably fought with loaded dice. The failure of some political perspectives, such as radical feminism, or anarchism, or dark-green environmentalism, to gain a wider following may reflect inherent weaknesses in the ideology. Alternatively, it may be an indication of the overwhelming difficulties any radical perspective faces in combating the mass of routinely accepted assumptions bound up with the existing economic, social and political order. Yet it may not just be radical left-wing views which fail to secure a fair hearing; both neo-liberals and neo-conservatives have claimed that the post war progressive consensus effectively excluded their ideas from political debate until recently.

Ideology and pragmatism in British politics

An explicit assumption of this book is that political ideas are important, and indeed that 'all politics is ideological' (Seliger, 1976, p. 146). However, not everyone would agree that ideas have generally been important in British politics, or even indeed should be. Much has been made of British empiricism, involving a rejection of abstract reasoning. Although Mrs Thatcher showed a positive enthusiasm for ideology (see Chapter 9), this was markedly at variance with traditional British conservatism (as noted in Chapter 3). From Burke through Peel to Oakeshott (1962) and Minogue (1985) in the latter part of the twentieth century there has been a conservative distrust of abstract rational theory and doctrine and a positive aversion to 'ideology'. Yet an apparent British aversion to ideology is not just confined to conservatism, but can even be discerned in the British versions of liberalism and socialism. British liberalism, although more obviously influenced by theory than conservatism, has generally been flexible and pragmatic in execution. Even the British Labour Party was heavily constrained by the British empirical tradition and much less influenced by Marxist or any other theory than socialist or social democratic parties elsewhere.

Thus the 'running theme' of the political memoirs of John Cole, the former political editor of the BBC, is 'the contrasting styles of politics represented by Harold Wilson's belief in pragmatism and Margaret Thatcher's addiction to ideology'. Cole's own preferences for pragmatism are clear. The former Labour Prime Minister, Harold Wilson, is

Cole's unfashionable hero, while, he maintains, 'Lady Thatcher's "conviction politics" has transformed the tone of British public life, and not for the better' (Cole, 1995, pp. 1–2).

In this context, it is Mrs Thatcher's 'addiction to ideology' which seems somehow 'unBritish', and runs counter to the dominant pragmatic approach across political parties. Yet if 'ideology' clearly, for many, retains pejorative associations, 'pragmatism' is also, for some at least, a dirty word. Pragmatism 'all too easily slips into opportunism and is a synonym for short-term expediency' (Robertson, 1993, p. 394). Opportunism and short-term expediency were the charges critics often laid against Harold Wilson, who coined the phrase 'a week is a long time in politics', while the accusation of 'mindless empiricism' has been levelled against British politics in general. The relative neglect of 'grand theory' can be seen as an indictment of British intellectual life, while the absence of long-term vision is perceived as one of the limitations of British politics.

Ultimately, however, the dichotomy between ideology and pragmatism is a false one (Seliger, 1976, pp. 123–47). Indeed, John Cole (quoted above) goes on to argue that his preference for pragmatism 'is not an argument for value free politics ... Of course political leaders must project a vision of the Britain they would like to see, and how they hope to create it' (Cole, 1995, p. 2). Cole's 'vision' and 'hopes' are a major element of what others call 'ideology'. Politics can hardly be conducted without reference to values and principles (or ideology), but also inevitably requires flexibility and compromise (or pragmatism) in pursuit of ideological goals.

Moreover, 'pragmatism, with its dogmatic insistence on the impossibility of far-seeing deliberate reform, is itself a deliberate "ideological" standpoint on human nature' (Robertson, 1993, p. 394). Thus even those political thinkers such as Burke, Oakeshott and Minogue who apparently decry an ideological style of politics, themselves reflect ideological assumptions over, for example, human behaviour and motivation, the nature and distribution of property, and the scope and limitations of government. Indeed, for all their denunciation of 'reason', 'rationalism' and 'ideology', their writings were the product of a rational intellectual process, and were deliberately articulated as a persuasive interpretation of politics, with clear implications for political behaviour. Thus traditional conservatism was as 'ideological' as the Thatcherism which succeeded it.

The assumption here is that all politics implicitly or explicitly reflects ideological assumptions. Mrs Thatcher did not introduce ideology into the Conservative Party, still less into British politics generally. Similarly,

New Labour, for all its pragmatic emphasis on 'what works', is as ideological as old Labour. While ideologies may sometimes be inspired by utopian visions, they are all about influencing political attitudes and behaviour. They are not about pure ideas abstracted from reality but are 'action-oriented' and necessarily involve an interdependence between theory and practice, particularly when politicians obtain power and the chance to implement their ideas. Yet while policy is inevitably guided or constrained by ideological assumptions, practice, over time, is bound to modify initial theoretical expectations, reinforcing some and leading to the modification or discarding of others. Thus ideologies evolve as they are tested against reality. While 'Thatcherism' and, more recently, 'New Labour' emerged out of a conscious intellectual debate over ideas and values, as they developed they both embodied some rationalization of trial and error responses to specific problems and circumstances. They necessarily combine 'ideology' and 'pragmatism'.

Moderation and consensus in British politics

Yet if British politics is inevitably ideological, it is generally associated with continuity, moderation, and compromise. Since the violent upheavals of the seventeenth century there have been no revolutions, regime changes or sharp breaks in the development of the political system. Periodic crises which threatened political stability have been peacefully resolved, and strong opposition to the government of the day has seldom been translated into significant opposition to the whole system of government. Revolutionary parties and ideologies have rarely attracted a mass following, and communism and fascism have never secured more than fringe support. The Labour Party was never Marxist, and generally avoided the language of confrontation and class conflict. The Conservative Party would not have survived and thrived had it remained tied to narrow reactionary interests. In terms of the left–right ideological spectrum, British voters have been offered a constrained choice between the centre-left and the centre-right.

Indeed, it has often appeared that major British parties have been competing for the centre ground, and at times British politics has been more characterized by consensus (or agreement) than conflict. In war and periods of national emergency political leaders have been prepared to enter coalitions, or at least suspend normal party conflict. Yet at other times such as the 1950s and 1960s many have observed an absence of sharp ideological differences between the major parties.

While this 'post war consensus' appeared to break down in the 1970s and early 1980s, as the Conservatives under Margaret Thatcher moved to the right and the Labour Party increasingly appeared dominated by the left, some would argue that this was followed by a new Thatcherite consensus, while others would point to the more consensual style of John Major subsequently and Tony Blair's attempts to bring the Liberal Democrats and moderate Conservatives within his own 'big tent.' Extremism is of course a question of definition and perspective, but mainland British politics has rarely faced a significant internal challenge from those regarded as extremists (Ireland, of course, is another matter).

The British political tradition

Yet if British politics has rarely been characterized by violent or extreme conflict, it has involved significant disagreements or tensions. The dominant theme in some older influential interpretations of British politics (see for example Spencer, Dicey, Halevy) has been the tensions between libertarianism and collectivism, or between the free market and the state, and this has been reaffirmed in more recent accounts. Thus Beer's *Modern British Politics* (1982) documented the victory of Conservative and Labour collectivism over traditional liberal individualism. Barker (1978, p. 5) 'used attitudes to the modern state' as the main organizing principle behind his analysis of *Political Ideas in Modern Britain.* According to Greenleaf (1983, vol. 2, p. 5) 'the dialectic between the growing pressures of collectivism and the opposing libertarian tendency is the one supreme fact of our domestic political life as this has developed over the last century and a half.'

It is difficult to disagree that attitudes towards the state have been a massive theme in British politics, particularly for the mainstream ideologies of liberalism, conservatism and socialism. Nineteenth-century liberalism sought to uphold the liberty of the individual against the encroachment of the state, while the New Liberalism of the early twentieth century struggled to reconcile individual liberty with state-sponsored social reform (Chapter 2). Conservatives recurrently championed state protection of British agriculture and industry, and, subsequently, paternalist social reform (Chapter 3). The dominant British interpretation of socialism involved the growth of state intervention to provide public services (Chapter 4). Thus much of the internal debate within these mainstream ideologies as well as between them has been over the powers of the government and the freedom of the individual, and the boundary between public and private spheres, or state and civil society.

Yet important though the state/market debate is in the 'battle of ideas', it is a mistake to regard it as the only debate that matters in British politics. Even the mainstream ideologies are concerned with many issues which are only tangentially if at all connected with the state–market dichotomy, while for other political perspectives the issue of state economic intervention is secondary. Nationalism, for example, generally assumes that nations should constitute states, but is essentially concerned with the politics of identity and allegiance rather than economic arguments about the functions of the state (Chapter 5). Similarly, the politics of race and multiculturalism are more about issues of identity than economics, even if economic deprivation may be one of the factors which fuel racism (Chapter 6). Feminism, particularly in its radical form, asserts the primacy of gender relations over economic class conflict; the feminist slogan 'the personal is political' has redrawn the boundaries of politics, and transcends the old liberal distinction between the state and civil society (Chapter 7). Finally, Green ideas are about the relationship of humanity with its environment; the role of the state in this relationship is an important and controversial issue for Greens, but it is an essentially secondary question (Chapter 8).

Yet while the importance of these alternative perspectives should be emphasized, at the same time it is fairly clear that mainstream British politics over the last few decades has (rightly or wrongly) focused more than ever on the respective roles of the state and the market. Thus no apology is made for returning to the question in two contrasting later chapters which consider the transformation of the ideologies of their respective parties by Margaret Thatcher and Tony Blair. The rediscovery of the virtues of the free market by the New Right required the 'reining back of the state' (Chapter 9), while Tony Blair has articulated a 'third way' between centralized state provision and the free market (Chapter 10). Both projects remain acutely controversial. Much of the current debate in British politics is over the future of public services, their size and scope and how they should be financed and provided.

It did appear that this issue would remain at the centre of British politics for the foreseeable future, until the attack on the World Trade Centre on 11 September 2001 drove all other issues to the margins, at least for a period. Although it has become a truism that 'the world will never be the same again', normal politics has slowly returned, and with it the old arguments in Britain over the role of the state and the rather more recent arguments about the Private Finance Initiative and

Public–Private Partnerships. All the same, September 11th demonstrates once more how our transient political controversies can be overwhelmed by unforeseeable events. The book concludes with a brief survey of various possible futures for British politics (Chapter 11), but prophecy, now more than ever, is hazardous.

Further reading

Useful extended definitions of ideology and related concepts are provided in various specialist dictionaries such as those by Williams (1976), Bullock and Stallybrass (1977), Scruton (1983) and Bottomore (1991). These are handy reference works from which to begin an exploration of the numerous highly contested concepts discussed throughout this book, but the reader should be warned that the treatment of ideas even in such reference books reflects the different perspectives of authors.

Students may wish to sample some of the alternative surveys of modern ideologies, including Adams, (1993), Eccleshall *et al.* (1994), Vincent (1995), Heywood, 1997, Eatwell and Wright (1999). Most of these include brief introductory discussions on the nature of ideology which is usefully examined in a slim volume by McLellan (1995). Still the most useful and authoritative modern source is Seliger (1976). Freeden (1996) has contributed a thoughtful analysis of the relationship between ideology and political theory, which also includes his own analysis of the core components of mainstream ideologies, and a briefer discussion of feminism and green ideas.

The left–right scale has been criticized by Brittan (1968) among others. A more elaborate classification of political attitudes was advocated long ago by Eysenck (1957), and a similar two-dimensional approach has been used in a website (http://www.politicalcompass.org/) which offers a test to locate one's own ideological position, and also to further explanation and analysis, including estimates of the position of modern British politicians, and a linked reading list.

Modern British political ideas are summarized in Barker (1978, 1994) and Adams (1998). Beer (1982) provides one thought-provoking overall (but pre-Thatcherism) perspective, and Greenleaf (1983) another. The latter also explores the relationship between ideology and public policy – as do Fraser (1984), George and Wilding (1980), and Pearson and Williams (1984).

2

Liberalism

Introduction

Liberalism proclaims the freedom of the individual. It remains the mainstream political philosophy of the modern western world, despite the decline of political parties describing themselves as 'liberal' both in Britain and elsewhere. Most other political ideologies are defined in relation to liberalism, and it is the necessary starting point for any analysis of political doctrines today.

Liberalism has evolved over a long period and has varied considerably over time and space, which presents some problems for analysis. Although the term 'liberalism' was not employed until the early nineteenth century (Manning, 1976, p. 9; Gray, 1986, p. ix) its roots can be traced back much earlier, (Arblaster, 1984, p. 11). It drew its intellectual inspiration from the religious reformations of the sixteenth century, the seventeeth-century scientific revolution, and the eighteenth-century French or European enlightenment. It was, however, industrialization from the eighteenth century onwards which transformed economic and social relations and created new class interests with a commitment to a liberal political programme of reform.

In the first half of the nineteenth century, liberalism appeared a revolutionary creed on the European continent where absolutist or reactionary regimes generally prevailed. The cause of individual liberty was there inextricably bound up with national self-determination. Movements for national freedom or national unity were closely associated with demands for civil and political rights and for constitutional limits on government. By contrast, Britain's national integrity and independence seemed then unproblematic, while absolutism had been defeated and parliamentary sovereignty established from the seventeenth century. British liberalism certainly involved support for these goals abroad, but as they were already substantially achieved at home the liberal domestic programme necessarily concentrated on other objectives such as parliamentary reform, religious toleration and free trade.

A distinction is sometimes made today between economic and political liberalism. Modern neo-liberals see the free market as the quintessential liberal value. However, nineteenth-century continental liberalism was primarily a political creed, while even in Britain the centrality of free markets to liberalism has been exaggerated. Victorian liberalism stood for political reform at home and support for national and constitutional movements abroad. Its inspiration was derived more from religion (and specifically radical nonconformism) than classical economics. Moreover, from the late nineteenth century onwards, British liberalism explicitly repudiated *laissez-faire* and accepted the need for state intervention, particularly in the area of social welfare. This New Liberalism has been variously regarded as a natural and inevitable development out of the old liberalism (Hobhouse, 1911; Freeden, 1978, 1996), as an aberration (Arblaster, 1984, ch. 16) or even as a betrayal (Gray, 1984, pp. 32–3).

In twentieth-century Britain, liberal ideas conquered while their former political vehicle, the Liberal Party, suffered decline. Until the 1970s the dominant political and economic orthodoxy was essentially derived from the 'New Liberalism' which had flourished early in the century. Indeed, Keynes and Beveridge, the twin gurus of the post-Second World War political consensus, marked the culmination of New Liberal thinking. Moreover, when this consensus finally faced a challenge, that challenge came principally from an older free-market version of liberalism, or 'neo-liberalism'. The battle of ideas in the postwar era was arguably not so much between conservatism and socialism, nor even between right and left, but between the old and the new liberalism.

Today the term 'liberal' has distinctly different connotations in different parts of the world. It is not even easy to place it on the 'left–right' political spectrum. The modern British Liberal Democrats and their Liberal predecessors have long been regarded as centre or even left of centre, while in continental Europe liberalism is generally associated with the right. However, in the United States the term 'liberal' has become almost a term of abuse for radical-progressive and crypto-socialist ideas. Yet the 'liberal' or 'neo-liberal' label is also associated with advocates of the free market like Hayek and Friedman and their New Right disciples.

On some interpretations liberalism is the hegemonic ideology of the modern age. Almost all mainstream ideologies, even Marxism, may be regarded as 'variants of liberalism'. One problem with this view of liberalism as an all-embracing hegemonic ideology is that any clear identity, coherence and consistency is in danger of being lost. But whatever view is taken of liberalism today, the historical importance of liberalism cannot be denied; liberal values and ideas have been central to the development of the British political tradition. An analysis of liberalism is thus the central reference point for any examination of ideology in British politics.

This chapter begins by exploring key liberal values and underlying assumptions. It proceeds to examine various influences on the developing British liberalism, including the Whig and Radical traditions, classical economics and utilitarianism, religious non-conformism and the New Liberalism (Table 2.1). The chapter concludes with a discussion of the prospects for liberalism in the modern world, contrasting the revived free-market values of neo-liberalism with the progressive ideas associated with the Liberal Democrats.

Liberalism: underlying assumptions and values

While there are clearly major differences and tensions within the liberal tradition, it is possible to describe liberals or liberalism in terms which would command a wide element of agreement. Stuart Hall (1986, p. 34) suggests that liberals are 'open-minded, tolerant, rational, freedom-loving people, sceptical of the claims of tradition and established authority, but strongly committed to the values of liberty, competition and individual freedom.' Nineteenth-century British liberalism, according to Hall 'stood for individualism in politics, civil and political rights, parliamentary government, moderate reform, limited state intervention, and a private enterprise economy'. This is a description (by a non-liberal) which most liberals would endorse. Thus there is widespread agreement over key liberal ideas and values, even if there is not always equal agreement over their subsequent development and interpretation.

Individualism is the key liberal assumption. For the liberal, individual human beings, rather than nations, races or classes are the starting point for any theorizing about society, politics or economics. Society is seen as an aggregate of individuals, and social behaviour is explained in terms of some fairly basic assumptions about individual human psychology (Macpherson, 1962; Arblaster, 1984, chs. 2, 3). Indeed some thinkers within the liberal tradition saw society as an essentially artificial creation; they postulated a prior state of nature in which neither society nor government existed. Whether this state of nature

Table 2.1   The Whig–Liberal Tradition

Period	Description	Politicians and thinkers
17th century	**Puritanism and Parliamentarism**	
Late 17th century 18th century	**The Whig tradition** 'Glorious Revolution' Constitutional monarchy Government by consent Division of powers Religious toleration Oligarchy Mercantilism	John Locke Charles James Fox
Late 18th century Early 19th century	**Radicalism** Revolution Rationalism Rights of Man	Tom Paine
	Classical liberalism Individualism Free markets Utilitarianism Representative democracy	Adam Smith Thomas Malthus David Ricardo Jeremy Bentham James Mill
Mid 19th century Later 19th century	**Victorian Liberalism** Manchester liberalism Nonconformism Free trade Nationalism Municipal gospel	Richard Cobden John Bright William Gladstone John Stuart Mill Joseph Chamberlain
Late 19th century Early 20th century	**New Liberalism** Social reform State intervention Liberal imperialism National efficiency Constitutional reform	T.H. Green Leonard Hobhouse John Hobson Edward Grey Herbert Asquith David Lloyd George
1920s to 1970s	(Decline of Liberal Party progressive liberal consensus?)	J.M. Keynes William Beveridge
Late 20th century Early 21st century	**Liberal revival?** European Union Devolution	David Steel Paddy Ashdown Charles Kennedy

was perceived as a hypothetical model or historical fact, the implication was that society and government were purposefully created by individual humans in pursuit of their own self-interest. Liberals today still tend to see society as an aggregate of individuals; there can be no social interests beyond the interests of the individuals which constitute society. The individual is logically and morally prior to society.

Rationalism is another core liberal assumption. Individuals pursue their own self-interest rationally. No one else, not rulers, nor priests nor civil servants can determine the individual's own interest for them. Yet liberals have optimistically assumed that the general pursuit of rational self-interest will produce not only individual satisfaction but also social progress and the happiness of the greatest number.

Freedom is, however, the quintessential liberal value; liberals require that individuals should be free to pursue their own self-interest (Mill, 1859). This was originally interpreted in a predominantly negative sense. The individual should be as far as possible free from external constraints. In the early history of liberalism this freedom from constraint entailed firm limits to the power of government to interfere with individual liberty. An important application was the principle of toleration, particularly applied to religious belief and observance, and vigorously championed by Locke (1689, ed. Gough, 1966). It was to receive its most eloquent expression from John Stuart Mill (1859, ed. Warnock, 1962) who demanded full freedom of thought and expression. Subsequently, some liberals emphasized the freedom to enjoy certain benefits, a more positive conception of liberty which might entail extensive state intervention to enlarge freedom (Green, 1881; Hobhouse, 1911; Berlin, 1975). The conflict between these two contrasting negative and positive views of freedom, and their widely divergent practical implications, has been a major theme in the development of liberalism for over a century.

If liberalism has always involved a commitment to liberty, however defined, it has also involved some egalitarian assumptions. Thus liberals have stressed equality before the law, and equal civil and political rights, although there has not always been agreement over what these should entail in practice. Egalitarian considerations have also led many liberals to justify state provision of education and other services to create greater equality of opportunity. But a commitment to an equality of worth and opportunity has generally been accompanied by a liberal acceptance of considerable inequality of income and wealth. Indeed, liberals have regarded private property as crucial to freedom. Thus, critics allege, liberals in practice sacrifice equality to liberty (Arblaster, 1984, pp. 84–91).

Liberals themselves have argued that freedom entails the freedom to be unequal, but they have also denied that individual liberty is inconsistent with social justice. Although liberalism is based on the assumption of self-seeking individualism, it has never involved the cynical equation of might and right. Rather, liberals have embraced the language of justice and attempted to make it consistent with the pursuit of rational self-interest (Rawls, 1971). There is implicit in such arguments some fairly optimistic assumptions about human nature and the scope for reconciling individual and collective goals. It is here that liberalism parts company with traditional conservatism on the one hand, and socialism on the other. Conservatives have been more pessimistic about human nature and the unguided capacity of individuals to pursue their enlightened self-interest (see Chapter 3, below). Socialists, while sharing with liberals a more optimistic view of human nature, have not agreed that individual self-interest and social justice can be so easily reconciled (see Chapter 4, below).

The Whig tradition

Liberalism in Britain grew out of the Whig tradition. It is easier perhaps to distinguish liberalism from Whiggism than it is to distinguish conservatism from Toryism, but even so the Whig tradition slides naturally and imperceptibly into the liberal tradition, to the extent that it is not possible to mark precisely where the one ends and the other begins. Whigs originated in the seventeenth century as the party which opposed royal absolutism, and championed religious dissent. They supported the rights of parliament, and sought to place limits on royal power. John Locke (1632–1704) sought to ground this political programme in abstract principles. There were natural rights to life, liberty and property; government should rest on the consent of the governed, who were ultimately justified in rebellion if their rights were infringed. There should be constitutional limits on government, and a division between the executive and legislative powers (Locke, 1689, ed. Gough, 1966). These ideas came to be enshrined, albeit imperfectly, in the British constitution following the Glorious Revolution of 1688. They later helped to inspire or justify the American and French Revolutions.

Yet there were always contradictory tendencies in Whiggism. Behind fine sentiments there were material interests to advance and defend. The great Whig aristocrats and their allies among the merchants and bankers sought to preserve their own power, property and privileges from a perceived threat from the crown. The massive inequalities in income and wealth in eigteenth-century Britain were for them unproblematic (Arblaster, 1984, ch. 8). Locke spoke for their interests in defending rights to life, liberty and property.

Moreover the Whigs in general had no wish to spread power beyond the ranks of the propertied. Thus the constitution which they developed and defended was essentially oligarchic and conservative. Power was, furthermore, shamelessly exercised for the benefit of the wealthy, and prodigious fortunes were made out of war, the slave trade and India. Wealthy landowners enclosed land to enrich themselves at the expense of the rural poor in the name of agricultural progress. The game laws were ruthlessly enforced. Thus class interest lay behind Whig political principles.

Yet Whig principles were capable of a radical as well as a conservative interpretation. 'No taxation without representation', the slogan of the parliamentary opposition to the Stuarts, became the cry of the American rebels against George III, and many Whigs found it difficult to deny the justice of their case. The Declaration of Independence (1776) was based on classic Whig principles. The French Revolution was more divisive, but was initially welcomed by most leading Whigs. Despite the reaction which the subsequent course of the revolution provoked, the Whig leader Charles James Fox continued to defend its principles if not always its practice, and championed civil liberties in England until his death in 1806.

Their effective exclusion from power for most of the period from 1783 to 1830 permitted some reaffirmation and development of Whig principles. Free from the messy compromises of government, Fox's followers could proclaim their continued attachment to 'Peace, retrenchment and reform', with unsuccessful parliamentary reform bills introduced in 1797 and 1810 providing some precedent for the Great Reform Bill of 1832 (Watson, 1960, pp. 361–2, 450–1). The Foxite Whigs could also claim some credit for British abolition of the slave trade, while the traditional Whig demand for religious toleration was reaffirmed in their support for Catholic emancipation as well as Protestant dissent.

The defection of the 'Old Whigs' and the accommodation within the Foxite remnant of the party of a new generation of radicals with a strong commitment to reform, helped preserve or reestablish a politically progressive Whig tradition which ultimately merged into liberalism (Watson, 1960, pp. 436–7). The 1832 Reform Act can be seen as the culmination of that Whig tradition, but also underlines the cautious,

essentially conservative nature of Whiggism (Wright, 1970, pp. 31–6).
It was a strictly limited measure, involving a very modest extension of
the franchise to incorporate elements of the respectable propertied
middle classes, but even so it laid the foundation for Victorian liberalism by transforming the political geography of Britain. The new urban
centres gained at the expense of the shires, manufacture and commerce
at the expense of land. Whig aristocrats as well as Tory squires ultimately lost influence to the urban-based business and professional
middle classes, who were to provide the effective muscle behind
Victorian liberalism. Whiggism had developed in a pre-industrial, predominantly rural society in which land remained the overwhelming
source of wealth. It was an approach to politics which was increasingly
anachronistic in an industrial capitalist society, although Whigs
remained an important but diminishing element within the Liberal
coalition until the late nineteenth century.

Those who see liberalism almost exclusively in terms of free markets
and industrial capitalism neglect the Whig foundations of British liberalism. The Whig–Liberal tradition of thought is essentially a political
tradition, concerned with constitutional issues and questions of civil
liberties. Whiggism may have served economic interests but it was
never essentially an economic doctrine. It was about parliamentary sovereignty, government by consent, freedom of conscience and religious
observance, no taxation without representation, and a host of other
slogans (often imperfectly applied). It was not about free trade or free
markets. Whig foreign trade policy in the seventeenth and eighteenth
centuries remained mercantilist. It aimed to secure, through colonization, Navigation Acts, and war, as large a British share of world trade
as possible.

Radicals

Radicals seek fundamental reform. Alongside the Whig tradition, at
times interwoven with it, at times in opposition to it, there is a radical
tradition which has had a marked effect on both British liberalism and,
subsequently, socialism. Yet the term 'radical tradition', if it is to be
used at all, must be employed more loosely for the label 'radical' has
been employed to cover a wide range of politicians, thinkers and ideas,
and moreover has had different connotations for different periods. Yet
although the label is imprecise, the influence of radicalism on the nineteenth-century British Liberal Party, and British liberalism generally,
cannot be ignored. At the parliamentary level the boundary line

between Whigs and radicals was a shifting one. A succession of one-time dangerous radicals were subsequently absorbed into the Whig (and later Liberal) political establishment.

Tom Paine (1737–1809) was one major radical thinker who was never absorbed into that establishment. Although mainstream Whig politicians interpreted their proclaimed principles in ways which preserved their own power, property and privileges, Paine gave those same principles a far more radical interpretation. He argued that once ultimate sovereignty had been transferred from the monarchy to the people, once political equality had been accepted in theory, there was no logical case for restricting participation in the choice of a legislature. Paine himself championed full manhood suffrage (Paine, 1791–2, ed. Collinson, 1969). Although by turns reviled or neglected in Britain, his ideas were the logical outcome of Whig slogans. Indeed it can be argued that the only coherent way to counter such a revolutionary democratic ideology was by assailing its egalitarian and rationalistic assumptions, as Burke realized.

Paine has been claimed for both liberalism and socialism. Some argue 'his political theory was vintage liberalism', citing his uncompromising individualism, his sympathies for manufacturers, and his hostility to government (Foot and Kramnick, 1987, pp. 22–9). Ayer (1988, ch. 7), by contrast, talks of 'Paine's blueprint … for his Welfare State', and stresses his support for a highly redistributive graduated income tax. His writing enjoyed a wide circulation and later inspired the Chartists (Foot and Kramnick, 1987, p. 33) and other working-class movements. Yet Paine's ideas had more immediate impact in America and France than Britain, where his uncompromising republicanism, his total opposition to the hereditary principle, and his rejection of Christianity gave him a wild and dangerous reputation.

In the early nineteenth century some radicals like Cartwright or Hunt with a substantial popular following were distrusted or persecuted by the political establishment, while others such as Whitbread and Brougham constituted the progressive wing of the parliamentary Whig party. Also in touch with progressive Whig circles were the 'philosophical radicals' or utilitarians – Bentham and his followers (see below). More difficult to classify is William Cobbett, initially an arch-critic and later a champion of Paine. Yet Cobbett's radical populism harked back to a pre-industrial age, which was arguably true also of the so-called 'Tory radicals' such as Oastler and Shaftsbury. Very different was the radicalism of the Quaker manufacturer John Bright who belonged to the new generation of politicians who came to the fore after the 1832

Reform Act, and who in some ways personified the new age. However, Bright in turn lived long enough to be displaced by a new breed of radicals who took over the Liberal Party in the latter part of the century, by which time the term 'radicalism' was beginning to be associated with socialism.

Thus a variety of forms of radicalism influenced British politics in the nineteenth century. It was radical pressure which reinforced the Whig commitment to parliamentary reform in 1832 and subsequently. The association of radicalism with religious dissent in the second half of the nineteenth century imbued it with a strong moral character, and fuelled demands for non-denominational state education and disestablishment of the Church of England. Radicalism was also strongly associated with the 'municipal gospel' in local government. At the parliamentary level it was the fusion of Whigs and radicals with former Conservative Peelites which effectively created the British Liberal Party in 1859. While Whigs continued to predominate in Liberal Cabinets, radicals predominated at the increasingly important grass-roots level, particularly following the formation of the National Liberal Federation. Yet it was a relatively restrained, religiously inspired, and peculiarly British strand of radicalism which eventually prevailed rather than the fiercely rationalist, republican radicalism of Thomas Paine.

Classical economics and utilitarianism

If the moral inspiration of Victorian liberalism was derived from radical nonconformism, it drew intellectual sustenance from the ideas of the classical economists and the utilitarians. It was Adam Smith (1732–90), Malthus (1766–1834) and Ricardo (1772–1823) who virtually founded the modern study of economics, and established the importance of the market in the allocation and distribution of resources. Similarly, Jeremy Bentham's (1748–1832) 'principle of utility' was applied to a wide range of institutions and practices. Tradition and long usage were no justification in the face of Bentham's fiercely rationalist analysis. 'What use is it?' was his brutal question, cutting through the mystique in which constitutional and legal issues were generally surrounded. The 'only right and proper end of government', he declared, was 'the greatest happiness of the greatest number'.

The classical economists and the utilitarians had much in common. Both stemmed from a similar intellectual climate – the eighteenth-century enlightenment. Both shared the individualist and rationalist assumptions underpinning liberalism, and there were also clear connections between them. Bentham and his associates broadly accepted the *laissez-faire* implications of the economic theories of Smith, Ricardo and Malthus, while Smith's friend and colleague, the philosopher and historian David Hume (1711–76), had earlier laid the philosophical foundations for utilitarianism. Some thinkers, like Nassau Senior (1790–1864) and John Stuart Mill, had a foot in both camps.

Yet modern neo-liberals have identified a fundamental distinction between Benthamism and the ideas of Adam Smith, arguing that it is Smith and Hume, the great thinkers of the eighteenth-century Scottish Enlightenment who represent the true spirit of liberalism. Bentham and his followers, by contrast, are blamed for ideas which 'provided a warrant for much later illiberal interventionist policy' (Gray, 1986, p. 24; Barry, 1986, pp.19–21). It is not difficult to understand why neo-liberals opposed to state intervention should be critical of the utilitarians. Their 'greatest happiness principle' involved a potential breach with free-market economics. Bentham had been converted by his friend and associate James Mill to representative democracy, as only a government freely elected by the governed could be relied upon to promote the happiness of the greatest number (Dinwiddy, 1989). Yet democracy could involve electoral pressures for interference with free-market forces. Moreover, Bentham was an advocate of bureaucracy as well as democracy. He sought to redesign the whole system of British government from top to bottom on rationalist lines, involving the appointment of professionally qualified, salaried, public officials.

The contradictory implications of Benthamite thinking are evident in the utilitarian-influenced Poor Law Amendment Act of 1834. The Act's underlying assumptions were those of free-market economics. Incentives must be maintained. The able-bodied poor who sought relief must be prepared to enter a workhouse, where their condition would be 'less eligible' than that of the lowest independent labourer. Yet the New Poor Law also involved a comprehensive network of new administrative areas, a new hierarchy of administrative officials, and a novel form of central control and inspection that had rather different implications for the future. Bentham's formidable secretary, Edwin Chadwick (1800–90), a key figure in the development and the administration of the New Poor Law, was later converted from free-market orthodoxy to advocacy of state intervention, following his experiences in the public-health movement.

All this explains why modern neo-liberals have reservations about the utilitarians. Hayek (1975) is critical of Bentham's 'constructivist rationalism'. Gray (1986) similarly argues that because Bentham believed 'social institutions can be the object of successful rational redesign', his utilitarianism 'had an inherent tendency to spawn policies of interventionist social engineering'. For Norman Barry (1986), 'its central tenets stress artifice and design in the pursuit of collective ends'. All this is fair comment, yet the consequent refusal of neo-liberals to recognize Bentham as a liberal involves an artificial conception of liberalism which bears little relation to the British Whig/Liberal tradition, in which Bentham and his associates were directly and centrally involved, in terms of personal connections, ideas and practical influence on policy.

Although the major British classical economists – Smith, Malthus, Ricardo, Nassau Senior and, later, John Stuart Mill – contributed significantly to Victorian liberalism, their ideas were extensively vulgarized and oversimplified. While Adam Smith's 'invisible hand' provided a graphic and enduring vision of the beneficial operation of free-market forces, even Smith allowed for significant exceptions. It was popularizers such as Harriet Martineau, Edward Baines and Samuel Smiles who reduced the principles of classical economics to the simple injunctions of *'laissez-faire'* for governments and 'self-help' for individuals. Even so, *laissez-faire* was only one strand among many in Victorian liberalism, and public policy was never consistently informed by the principle. A series of interventionist Factory Acts, local and general Public Health Acts, and Acts to regulate the railways and banks were passed in the early Victorian period. Indeed, economic historians question whether there ever was an age of *laissez-faire*.

Victorian liberalism

A political ideology is not to be identified with the history of a political party, yet there is inevitably a strong connection between particular systems of ideas and their practical political expression. An account of British liberalism has perforce to pay some attention to the composition, support, and record of the British Liberal Party, especially during its heyday in the second half of the nineteenth century.

Although the term 'liberal' was applied in British politics from the early nineteenth century, the British Liberal Party only emerged in the 1850s from a party realignment involving Whigs, radicals and Peelite Conservatives. Gladstone (1809–98), who had started his political career as a Conservative follower of Peel, became the embodiment of Victorian liberalism, and was four times Prime Minister. He so dominated the party that he was substantially able to shape it in his own image. He was an Anglican landowner with no past reputation as a radical in a party which was becoming increasingly associated with manufacturing, dissent, and radical reform. Yet Gladstone was a politician who became more radical and populist with age. Furthermore and crucially, he was inspired by a Christian moral fervour which struck a receptive chord among his nonconformist followers. Gladstonian liberalism thus became something of a moral crusade (Vincent; 1966, Adelman, 1970, pp. 6–7).

This Gladstonian liberalism drew on several strands. Parliamentary reform was a theme derived from the Whig tradition, and the advocacy of Bright and later Gladstone himself turned it into a populist cause. Proposals for a fairly modest extension of the franchise soon developed into radical Liberal demands for full manhood suffrage. Nonconformism also loomed large. According to the religious census of 1851, almost half of the church-going population of the country was nonconformist, so that although the 1860s parliamentary party was 'still overwhelmingly Anglican', the Liberals were becoming 'the party of the Nonconformist conscience' (Vincent, 1966, p. 61–2). Nonconformist pressures spawned the Liberation Society, to disestablish the Church of England, and later the National Education League to campaign for a national, free and secular system of education. The League in turn provided the model for the National Liberal Federation in 1877 which established a national organization for the Liberal Party but tipped it decisively towards radical nonconformism. By the 1880s the parliamentary party as well as the party in the country was predominantly nonconformist (Adelman, 1970).

A similar attitude to foreign policy and Ireland helped unite Gladstone with the nonconformists. The importance of foreign affairs to British liberalism is often underestimated. It was support for liberal and nationalist movements on the continent, especially Italian unification, which helped create Palmerston's 1859 government and subsequently kept it together. It was Gladstone's campaign against the Bulgarian atrocities which brought him out of premature retirement and into close collaboration with the nonconformists. It was the religious fervour behind his mission to pacify Ireland which both split his party, but also strengthened the moral element in liberalism.

What has been called 'Manchester liberalism' was a significant but retrospectively exaggerated element of the Liberal Party after 1859. Free trade had certainly been clearly established as a liberal principle. Cobden and Bright, the leaders of that classic pressure group campaign, the Anti-Corn Law League, had seen their cause victorious in 1846. Repeal of the Corn Laws symbolically reflected the transfer of power from the landed to the manufacturing interest which both Cobden and Bright represented. Gladstone as Chancellor of the Exchequer in Palmerston's government built on their work by abolishing a whole range of duties, while Cobden himself negotiated the Anglo-French trade treaty of 1860.

Yet free trade did not entail *laissez-faire* in domestic policy. Cobden's opposition to Factory Acts in particular and government intervention in general seemed increasingly out of tune with the times. As for Bright, his 'theory of history and of politics did not derive from any abstract attachment to *laissez-faire* or political economy, or from any construction of his business interests' (Vincent, 1966, p. 168). Rather, it was a moral and religious fervour which informed his views on economics and foreign affairs, and a detestation of 'privilege' which led him to champion parliamentary reform.

Liberal practice entailed increased state intervention. Major reforms in education, the army, the law and civil service were accomplished by Gladstone's 1868–74 administration. Subsequently, the Third Reform Act in 1884 promised the triumph of radical demands for reform over Whig caution. Chamberlain's 'Unauthorized Programme' of 1885, and the 'Newcastle Programme' of 1891 marked a decisive shift towards radicalism in the British Liberal Party.

Behind the evolution of Liberal political practice there was a considerable development in political thinking, and not all Liberal thinkers were happy with the pace of change. Herbert Spencer (1820–1903) combined *laissez-faire* economics with evolutionary theories which emphasized the survival of the fittest. He opposed almost all forms of state intervention of the sort which Liberals of his day were increasingly advocating and introducing at both local and national level, and even argued for the privatization of the Royal Mint. Yet Spencer was out of step with his time. John Stuart Mill (1806–73), by contrast, was a key transitional figure in the evolution of liberalism.

In most respects Mill was a thorough individualist:

> The sole end for which mankind are warranted, individually or collectively, in interfering with the liberty of action of any of their number is self-protection... Over himself, over his own body and mind, the individual is sovereign. (Mill, 1859)

This sounds like a plea for minimal state intervention, and in some respects it was. Mill was eloquent in denouncing censorship and arguing for full liberty of thought and expression. It was his commitment to individuality which led him, despite his general advocacy of representative democracy, to fear the 'tyranny of the majority'. He worried about the intolerance of public opinion and the 'despotism of custom' which he saw as a greater threat to individuality than deliberate actions by governments. In other respects Mill allowed for considerable government intervention, despite his general espousal of the market in his *Principles of Political Economy* (1848). Indeed he has been described as 'a watershed thinker' in the development of liberalism from individualism to collectivism (Gray, 1986, p. 30; Greenleaf, 1983, p. 103).

Liberalism, capitalism and democracy

Liberalism as a political ideology has been closely associated with the rise of industrial capitalism; it was preeminently the creed of the bourgeoisie, the owners of industrial and financial capital. Its political objectives involved the enfranchisement of the new middle classes and the effective transfer of political power to the major manufacturing urban centres of industrialized Britain. Its economic theory could be seen as the rationalization of the interests of capital. Moreover, it was hardly coincidental that the British Liberal Party finally emerged in the 1850s when Britain's industrial and commercial dominance was unchallenged, the British bourgeoisie supremely self-confident, and the working classes as yet largely non-unionized and unenfranchised. The relative decline of British manufacturing and the rise of labour were part of the background to the subsequent decline of liberalism. Furthermore, even if one goes back further to the roots of liberalism, it has been argued that protestant dissent and more particularly puritanism embodied ideas favourable to the spirit of capitalist accumulation, while the political thought of Hobbes and more especially Locke involved a 'possessive individualism' which was highly compatible with the mercantile capitalism of the seventeenth century (Macpherson, 1962).

Even so, British liberalism cannot be simply derived from capitalism. The leading Whig parliamentarians, who retained a substantial presence in nineteenth-century Liberal governments despite their diminishing numbers, were large landowners. Many of the rank and file Liberal activists were not manufacturers but relatively small shopkeepers and tradesmen (Vincent, 1966). And even before their progressive enfranchisement, a substantial section of the working class had attached itself to the Liberal cause. Liberalism in practice involved a coalition of class interests. Some of the causes it embraced, such as temperance, religious disestablishment and Irish home rule were only tenuously, if at all, connected with the interests of capitalism. Leading British liberal thinkers such as John Stuart Mill, Ritchie, Hobhouse, Keynes and Beveridge gave only qualified support for capitalism.

The establishment of a capitalist economy was accompanied by the gradual establishment of a liberal democratic system in the United Kingdom, and this may not have been coincidental. Indeed some Marxists have argued that representative democracy affords the best shell for capitalism. If that is so, then it has hardly surprising that the party of the bourgeoisie should have been in the forefront of the parliamentary reform movement in Britain. Moreover, support for parliamentary reform in the mid-nineteenth century commonly stopped short of support for full representative democracy, and some critics have denied any reciprocal tie of dependence between liberalism and democracy. Arblaster (1984, p. 264) talks of the 'fear of democracy' and argues that 'middle-class liberals were fearful, not only for wealth and property, but also for the position and values of their class'. From a neo-liberal perspective, unlimited democracy 'cannot be liberal government since it respects no domain of independence or liberty as being immune to invasion by governmental authority' (Gray, 1986, p. 74).

Such verdicts involve a rather strained interpretation of the evolution of liberalism over the last two centuries. Democracy in the eighteenth century was a remote theoretical model, interpreted by educated Britons, if at all, through Thucydides, Plato and Aristotle. Representative democracy in the early nineteenth century was a largely untried system. In these circumstances it is not surprising that liberals were apprehensive about its possible consequences. Yet, as we have seen, Paine was a consistent advocate of manhood suffrage, James Mill converted Bentham to adult male suffrage, while John Stuart Mill argued for the extension of full political rights to women. Commentators have been quick to seize on any shortcomings in the commitment of these writers to democracy – the exclusion of women from James Mill's franchise, and his son's flirtation with plural voting. Yet in so doing they ignore the substance of their support for what was then a radical minority cause.

While many Whigs and Liberals in the early and mid-nineteenth century were more cautious than these thinkers, once the logic of the movement for parliamentary reform was accepted and British liberals became finally committed to the theory and practice of representative democracy, their conversion was wholehearted. Indeed, the arrival of 'government by the people' was seen by many liberals as a justification for abandoning former limitations to government intervention. Thus Chamberlain argued in 1885,

> I quite understand the reason for timidity in dealing with this question [poverty] so long as the government was merely the expression of the will of a prejudiced and limited few ... But now we have a Government of the people by the people... (Schultz, 1972, p. 59)

Herbert Samuel in 1902 argued that a reformed state could be entrusted with social reform. 'Now democracy has been substituted for aristocracy as the root principle of the constitution... the State today is held worthy to be the instrument of the community in many affairs for which the State of yesterday was clearly incompetent' (Schultz, 1972, p. 81). The acceptance of democracy marked a critical step towards the New Liberalism. There was an inexorable logic by which liberals progressed from parliamentary reform to representative democracy, to state intervention, and the apparent abandonment of some of the principles associated with earlier liberalism.

The New Liberalism

The 'New Liberalism' flourished in the late nineteenth and early twentieth centuries and involved state economic and social reform which marked a repudiation of *laissez-faire* liberalism. It has been the subject of intense controversy. To its advocates, the New Liberalism developed naturally out of the old, extending and refining familiar liberal principles and concepts. Others, including some Liberals at the time and modern neo-liberals have perceived the New Liberalism as the culmination of 'anti-liberal elements' which 'began to enter the liberal tradition itself from the mid-1840s in the work of John Stuart Mill' (Gray, 1986, p. 33). However, radical and socialist critics have dismissed the New Liberalism as a forlorn attempt to revive and update an outmoded ideology (Arblaster, 1984, ch. 16).

The origins of the New Liberalism have been variously attributed to the influence of Hegelian idealist philosophy (Pearson and Williams, 1984, p. 146), to a party project to win working-class support and head off the rising challenge from labour, and to the need to modernize the British economy and society and enable Britain to compete more effec-

tively in the world economy (Hay, 1983). Yet it also involved a rationalization of the substantial growth in government intervention which
had been taking place throughout the Victorian period, much of it
actively promoted by Liberals.

While Mill played an important transitional role in the evolution of
liberal thought, the key New Liberal thinkers were Green, Hobson and
Hobhouse. T. H. Green (1836–82) was an influential Oxford philosopher who derived his 'political obligations' from Kant and Hegel, and
served as a local councillor. Leonard Hobhouse (1864–1929) was a
philosopher and sociologist who wrote a seminal text on *Liberalism*
(1911, reprinted 1964). John Hobson was an economist who believed
that underconsumption was the cause of unemployment. They were
essentially engaged in an extensive project to redefine old liberal concepts and values in line with new political practice. Thus freedom, the
key liberal value, meant for Green 'a positive power or capacity of
doing or enjoying something worth doing or enjoying.' 'The ideal of
true freedom is the maximum of power for all members of human
society alike to make the best of themselves.' While individual liberty
remained the touchstone of liberalism, the New Liberalism, according
to Hobson involved 'a fuller realisation of individual liberty contained
in the provision of equal opportunities for self-development'
(Eccleshall, 1986, p. 204). Thus state intervention might be necessary
to remove obstacles to self-development. However,

> Liberals must ever insist that each enlargement of the authority and func-
> tions of the State must justify itself as an enlargement of personal liberty,
> interfering with individuals only in order to set free new and larger opportu-
> nities. (*Ibid.,* p. 206)

Some New Liberals advocated extensive programmes of state action.
Hobhouse justified interference with the market to secure 'the right to
work' and 'the right to a living wage'. There was, he argued, 'a defect
in the social system, a hitch in the economic machine'. Individual
workers could do nothing. 'The individual workman cannot put the
machine straight... He does not direct and regulate industry. He is not
responsible for its ups and downs, but he has to pay for them'
(Hobhouse, 1911, 1964 edition, pp. 83–4).

Liberal politicians were not always prepared to go as far as these
New Liberal ideologues, although Liberals at both local and national
level were increasingly interventionist. In local government, enthusiasm for civic improvements amounted to a 'municipal gospel'. Radical
Liberals saw city government as a test-bed for policies which could be

applied nationally. A key figure here was Joseph Chamberlain (1836–1914) who made his name as a radical Liberal mayor of Birmingham before making a successful transition to national politics. His campaign for the 'Unauthorized Programme' in 1885 drew extensively on his own local government experience. 'The experience of the great towns is very encouraging,' he urged.

> You have, in connection with the great municipal corporations, hospitals, schools, museums, free libraries, art galleries, baths, parks. All these things which a generation ago could only have been obtained by the well-to-do, are now, in many large towns, placed at the service of every citizen by the action of the municipalities. (Speech at Hull, 1885, Schultz, 1972, pp. 57–8)

Chamberlain explicitly rejected the principles of *laissez-faire*. The problem of poverty was, he said, one which 'some men would put aside by reference to the eternal laws of supply and demand, to the necessity of freedom and contract, and to the sanctity of every private right of property'. But, he observed, 'these phrases are the convenient cant of selfish wealth'. He went on to brush aside allegations that what he was advocating involved socialism:

> Of course it is Socialism. The Poor Law is Socialism. The Education Act is Socialism. The greater part of municipal work is Socialism, and every kindly act of legislation by which the community has sought to discharge its responsibilities and its obligations to the poor is Socialism, but is none the worse for that. (Schultz, 1972, pp. 58–9)

Chamberlain has rarely been claimed for New Liberalism because of his later split with Gladstone and alliance with the Conservatives. As a radical reformer with roots in local government, Chamberlain was only the most prominent of a whole new breed of Liberals who were coming to prominence in the party in the late nineteenth century. The radical, reforming approach of the 1885 Unauthorized Programme was echoed in the Liberal Party's 1891 Newcastle programme, although at national level there was little opportunity to implement the New Liberalism before the Liberal landslide victory of 1906.

Key figures in the 1906–14 Liberal Government were Asquith (1852–1928) and Lloyd George (1863–1945), although Winston Churchill (1874–1965), a recent convert from the Conservatives, also made a significant contribution. Welfare reforms included the provision of school meals and old-age pensions, and Lloyd George's introduction of national health and unemployment insurance in 1911. Lloyd George's controversial 1909 budget also involved some modest redis-

tribution of income and wealth through his land tax and progressive
income tax, while Churchill's labour exchanges indicated a readiness to
intervene in the operations of the labour market (Fraser, 1984, ch. 7).

How far was the New Liberalism stimulated by the 'rising challenge
of labour', about which Liberals were undoubtedly concerned? Some
hoped that social reforms would win votes; others feared they could be
an electoral liability. Later historians have disagreed over the electoral
appeal of state welfare. While welfare reforms were advocated by
leaders of the organized working class, they were not necessarily
popular with working-class voters, and might frighten the middle
classes. Rosebery, briefly Liberal Prime Minister after Gladstone, was
convinced that the radical Newcastle programme had cost the party
support (Bernstein, 1986, ch. 2). By contrast, Rosebery's Liberal
Imperialism could appeal to a chauvinistic working class while his own
more modest economic and social reform programme would promote
the 'National Efficiency' which progressive businessmen believed was
necessary to enable the British empire to compete successfully with the
rising political economies of Germany, the USA and Japan.

The decline of the Liberal Party – and the triumph of liberalism?

The New Liberalism ultimately failed to prevent the decline of the
Liberal Party. It is debatable how far this decline was inevitable
(Dangerfield, 1966; Clarke, 1971, ch. 15). However, the 1914–18 war
undermined Liberal internationalism, while the pressures towards collectivism and coercion associated with modern warfare created huge
strains for Liberal individualism, particularly on the symbolically
significant issue of conscription. After the war some of the causes with
which British liberalism had been identified, such as religious nonconformism, temperance and, above all, free trade, seemed less relevant.

Yet conversely it has been argued that 'the disintegration of the
Liberal Party signifies the triumph of liberalism... If liberalism is now
partly invisible, this is because so many of its assumptions and ideals
have infiltrated political practice and current awareness' (Eccleshall,
1986, p. 56). Indeed, the culmination of New Liberal thought can be
seen in the social welfare proposals of Beveridge and the economic
theory of Keynes which provided the basis of the post-Second World
War ideological consensus. Keynes and Beveridge were both large 'L'
as well as small 'l' liberals. The 1942 Beveridge Report was based on
the insurance principle, and, although far more comprehensive, was in

keeping with the spirit of the Lloyd George insurance scheme of 1911. Keynes' economic theory involved government intervention at the macro-level but allowed markets to operate freely at the micro-level. Neither Beveridge nor Keynes saw any need for an end to the private ownership of the means of production. It was precisely this kind of state intervention to promote employment and welfare provision which was favoured by earlier New Liberals like Green and Hobhouse (George and Wilding, 1980).

Other liberal ideas have long been put into practice and absorbed into British political culture. Thus a number of legislative changes in the 1960s, including divorce, homosexual and abortion law reform, and some relaxation of censorship, were compatible with the principles of individual liberty proclaimed by Mill in 1859. Subsequent legislation on equal pay, equal opportunities, and race and sex discrimination in the 1970s is also thoroughly consistent with liberal ideology. Thus a progressive 'liberal' orthodoxy was established, supported by both leading Labour and Conservative politicians as well as the much diminished Liberal Party. (Although the continuing widespread prevalence of sexist, racist and homophobic views suggests also significant resistance to this orthodoxy.)

Yet this apparent triumph of the economic and social ideas of the New Liberalism has been considerably complicated by the revival, from the 1970s onwards, of an older form of liberalism, the free-market liberalism associated with classical economics. As a consequence, the term 'liberal' today can only be invested with more precision by qualifying it with some modifying adjective or prefix. There are progressive or social liberals who are enthusiastic about penal reform, civil liberties, the protection of the rights of minorities, freedom of expression and open government, and who are generally unashamed interventionists in the economic sphere. There are also neo-liberals, market liberals or economic liberals, such as Hayek and Friedman, who favour free-market ideas and are generally regarded as on the right of the political spectrum. These thinkers influenced the New Right and the brand of Conservatism associated with Mrs Thatcher (and are discussed further in Chapter 9).

The ideas of modern Liberals and Liberal Democrats

A modest revival in Liberal Party fortunes began in the 1960s and accelerated in the mid-1970s and was given renewed impetus by the alliance with the Social Democratic Party (SDP), launched by Labour defectors in 1981. The two parties eventually merged to form the

Liberal Democrats who, by the beginning of the twenty-first century were involved in coalition in the devolved governments of Scotland and Wales, had a substantial role in English local government, and, after the 2001 election, had 52 MPs at Westminster. This revival in party political fortunes has been accompanied by some renewal in interest in associated political ideas.

The policies of the Liberals and Liberal Democrats have involved a continuation of the New Liberal tradition – welfare capitalism with a strong emphasis on individual rights. Distinctive Liberal policies included early advocacy of UK entry into the EEC, devolution, incomes policies, partnership in industry, electoral reform (as part of a package of constitutional reform), and a focus on the community (Tivey and Wright, 1989, pp. 83–6). This last element has been closely linked with Liberal successes in local government.

Whether the postwar British Liberal Party really did much to extend or develop liberalism may be doubted, however. The party was fertile in policy proposals, without producing any startling new ideas or major thinkers. Neither its electoral successes nor its failures seem to have owed much to liberal ideology. The crucial decisions with which its leadership was faced were tactical rather than ideological – whether to accept Heath's offer of a coalition in 1974, whether to support the Labour government after 1977, how to handle the SDP breakaway from Labour after 1981, and how soon and how fast to promote a merger with the SDP. All these decisions had ideological implications, but they were not ideologically driven.

In fact there was rather more intellectual ferment among the modern Liberal Party's uneasy allies, the SDP, and their post-merger remnants (Owen, 1981; Williams, 1981; Marquand, 1988). It could be argued that the dividing line between New Liberalism and Fabian socialism or labourism was always thin. Hobhouse talked of 'liberal socialism' in 1911, while Hobson made the transition to Labour following the First World War. It has perhaps grown thinner still as a consequence of revisionist tendencies on the right of the Labour Party in the 1950s, and the SDP breakaway in the 1980s. In this context the Liberal/SDP Alliance and subsequent merger can be seen as the practical expression of an ideological convergence which was already well underway (Behrens, 1989). Thus social democrats like David Marquand could be claimed for liberalism (although Marquand eventually rejoined Labour in 1995). Yet ultimately the Liberals effectively swallowed the SDP rather than the other way around, and the modern Liberal Democrats are the clear lineal descendants of the old Liberal Party.

Paradoxically, as the fortunes of the party have risen, Liberal Democrat ideas have become less distinctive. This is hardly their fault. For most of the post-Second World War period Liberals adopted an intermediate position between the two major parties. Briefly, in the early 1980s, the Liberals and their allies could offer a distinctive middle way between Thatcherism and left-wing socialism. Since then Labour in particular has reoccupied the centre ground it had previously vacated, leaving the Liberal Democrats with little ideological space and few distinctive ideas and policies. On the management of the economy, constitutional reform, Europe, defence and foreign policy the differences between the two parties are more of degree than kind. Under the leadership of Ashdown, coalition with Labour appeared logical and for a time likely. Blair seemed keen to heal the divisions on the centre-left which had left Conservatism dominant for most of the twentieth century. Coalitions in local government and devolved government provide some continuing impetus, but the sheer scale of Labour's victory in 1997 and resistance within both parties has weakened the Blair–Ashdown project. Under Ashdown's successor, Charles Kennedy, the Liberal Democrats have pursued a more independent and critical line, without yet returning to the old policy of equidistance between the major parties.

Attempts have been made to articulate a distinctive Liberal Democrat philosophy in these unpromising political circumstances (Wallace, 1997; Russell, 1999; Ballard, 2000), but the terminology of 'cooperation' 'working with others' and 'partnership politics' which they employ are shared by New Labour and progressive Conservatives. Moreover, the higher political profile of the Liberal Democrats has drawn attention to the considerable diversity of views within its ranks. Thus the Party contains 'free market Liberals, social liberals, conservatives with a social conscience and dissatisfied ex-Labour voters, greens, anarchists...'. This may demonstrate tolerance and inclusiveness as Ballard (2000) claims, but hardly ideological coherence. The real problem seems to be that there is no longer much distinctive ideological ground for the Liberal Democrats to occupy, but that underlines the widespread acceptance of liberal ideas across mainstream British parties.

Further reading

Eccleshall (1986) provides a good reader on liberalism, with a useful introduction – see also his own account of liberalism in Eccleshall *et al.* (1994). An earlier reader by Shultz (1972) is particularly useful on the New Liberalism. 'Variants of Liberalism' are briefly but cogently discussed from a Marxist perspective by Stuart Hall in Donald and Hall (eds, 1986). Gray (1986) provides a provocative neo-liberal interpretation of liberalism, while Arblaster (1984) offers a critical socialist perspective. Greenleaf (1983) and Freeden (1996) advance contrasting views of the British liberal tradition. The New Liberalism is explored from different angles by Freeden (1978), Clarke (1971) and Hay (1983).

Among liberal texts, John Stuart Mill's *On Liberty* (1859) provides the classic defence of free speech and toleration, and much of his other writing is at least worth dipping into (many modern editions). Hobhouse's *Liberalism* (1911, 1964) was written at the height of the New Liberalism. Wallace (1997), Russell (1999) and Ballard (2000) explore modern Liberal Democrat ideas.

3

Conservatism

Introduction: traditional and contemporary Conservatism

There are ambiguities and tensions in all mainstream political ideologies and conservatism is no exception. This is hardly surprising. In British politics the term 'conservatism' dates back to the 1830s and the roots of the philosophy much further – through the 'Toryism' established from the late seventeenth century, and arguably further back. It would be surprising had Toryism/conservatism not evolved and changed considerably in response to altered circumstances. Moreover, terms commonly associated with conservatism are 'pragmatism' and 'flexibility'.

Conservatism is often held to indicate not an elaborate system of thought, but rather an attitude of mind; not the application of some predetermined blueprint, but a commonsense approach to immediate practical problems. The Conservative Party has been characterized as a pragmatic rather than an ideological party. Conservative theory is rather thin, and there is an absence of key texts and authoritative ideas. Indeed, ideological inspiration has commonly come from outside Tory or Conservative ranks – from the Whig, Edmund Burke, from the radical Liberal Unionist Joseph Chamberlain, from Keynes, and more recently from classical liberalism and neo-liberalism. Often conservative ideas have to be inferred from the performance of the Conservative Party.

The party has also been notably flexible in adapting policies to altered circumstances, which explains much of its enduring success in holding on to power and its capacity to bounce back from occasional disaster (for example in 1832, 1906, 1945). Such flexibility hardly suggests much consistency in conservatism over its long history. Yet, according to the editor of one anthology, 'An impressive feature of all these expressions of Conservative beliefs is the consistency of outlook which runs from Halifax and Burke to Churchill and Lord Hugh Cecil' (Buck, 1975, p. 26).

Yet some observers, including some Conservatives, note a sharp shift in direction more recently. Here the date of Buck's anthology, 1975 (cited above), is perhaps significant, for this was the year when Margaret Thatcher became leader and brought a change of style and direction to the party. She was a conviction rather than a consensus politician, and her approach appeared ideological rather than pragmatic. She was inspired by thinkers many of whom were not associated with mainstream British conservatism. Her governments from 1979 no longer reflected the assumptions which guided previous postwar governments, Conservative and Labour. A former Conservative Cabinet Minister, Ian Gilmour (1977, 1992, 1997), claims 'Thatcherism' marked a decisive break from the mainstream conservative tradition.

Many Conservatives would profoundly disagree. An early admirer, T. E. Utley, described Mrs Thatcher as 'an instinctive and wholly English Conservative' (Cowling, 1978; p. 50). Indeed, the breach with the past can be exaggerated, or interpreted as a pragmatic shift to meet new domestic and global conditions, a shift which was quite consistent with traditional conservative flexibility. Even so, while important elements of continuity are acknowledged, the New Right, Thatcherism and contemporary conservatism are here treated in a separate chapter. It has become difficult for anyone who came to maturity after 1975 to interpret conservatism except through assumptions about the party acquired since then. In particular, it is commonly imagined that the Conservative Party was always the champion of free-market forces and individualism: far from it, as (hopefully) will become clear. This chapter will therefore concentrate on traditional conservatism, and a later chapter will explore the New Right and modern conservatism.

The Tory tradition

Just as British liberalism emerged out of the Whig tradition, British conservatism grew out of the Tory tradition. This creates some additional complications in the case of conservatism, for while the term 'Whig' has dropped out of modern political discourse, 'Tory' is still a familiar synonym for 'Conservative'. Here we are essentially concerned with the Tory foundations of modern British conservatism. Historically Toryism, like Whiggism, dates from the seventeeth century, whereas conservatism derives from Sir Robert Peel's modernization of his party, and more specifically from the 1834 Tamworth manifesto. Strictly, the label 'Conservative' should not be used before then, but just as the term 'liberalism' is often extended backwards in time to include earlier thinkers who would not have used or even known the word, so the conservative tradition is frequently and not unreasonably taken to encompass thinkers and ideas which seem to provide the foundations for the subsequent development of conservative ideology. In this context the rather unhistorical use of the term 'Conservative' rather than 'Tory' is useful in claiming for conservatism individuals like Edmund Burke, who was actually a Whig politician in his lifetime and could not be described as a Tory. Thus conservatism can be projected backwards before 1834 in a sense which distinguishes it from Toryism. Some writers would also project the term 'Tory' forwards after 1834, to denote the older, traditional ideas and interests within the conservative tradition, but this has never involved a clear-cut distinction with conservatism, rather a difference in emphasis. In common parlance a 'Tory' is simply a conservative, (Table 3.1).

The labels 'Whig' and 'Tory' were admittedly lacking in precision and variable over time, but some reasonably valid generalizations can be made. While the Whigs wished to limit royal authority, the Tories supported the monarchy. While the Whigs upheld the right to religious dissent, the Tories were the party of the Church of England. Most important of all perhaps, the Whigs, although led by aristocratic landowners, were associated with developing commercial and manufacturing interests, while the Tories were the party of the landed gentry. Behind these interests the Tories stood for traditional authority and hierarchy in society, although such ideas were less systematically articulated than their Whig counterparts. These Tory values and interests were largely carried forward into conservatism.

Conservatism: reaction and gradualism

Conservatism at its simplest suggests 'conserving', keeping things as they are, with a sceptical attitude to change summed up in the well-known aphorism, 'If it aint broke, don't fix it.' Michael Oakeshott, an influential twentieth-century conservative thinker, has written eloquently on what he calls the 'conservative disposition' and more particularly on the conservative attitude to change and innovation. 'To be conservative', he suggests, 'is to prefer the known to the unknown, to prefer the tried to the untried, fact to mystery, the actual to the possible, the limited to the unbounded...'. Because the conservative enjoys the present he is generally averse to change:

Table 3.1   The Tory–Conservative tradition

Period	Description	Politicians and thinkers
Late 17th century	**Toryism** Monarchy, Church of England, landed interest	
18th century	Jacobitism tradition, limitations of reason	Bolingbroke (Burke) (Hume)
Early 19th century	**Reactionary Toryism** Fear of revolution, repression agricultural protection, romanticism	Liverpool Castlereagh (Coleridge)
1820s	**Liberal Toryism** 'Liberal' foreign policy, reform, Catholic emancipation	Canning Robinson Huskisson
1830s, 1840s	**Peelite Conservatism** Pragmatism, gradualism, acceptance of parliamentary reform, repeal of Corn Laws	Peel
1860s, 1870s	**Disraeli Conservatism** 'One nation', paternalism, patriotism and imperialism, 'Tory democracy'	Disraeli R. Churchill
Mid-1880s to 1930s	**Unionism** Preservation of Union with Ireland, imperial preference, protection, social reform	Salisbury J. Chamberlain Balfour Baldwin
1940s to 1960s	**Postwar One-Nation Conservatism** Keynesianism, mixed economy, welfare state, conciliation of trade unions, end of empire, planning	W. Churchill Butler Macmillan Macleod
1970s, 1980s	**'Thatcherism'** Free market, competition, privatisation, 'traditional Conservative values' strong state, national sovereignty	Thatcher Joseph (Hayek) (Friedman)
1990s	Post Thatcherism	Major, Hague Duncan Smith

Innovation entails certain loss and possible gain, therefore, the onus
of proof ... rests with the would-be innovator... The man of conservative temperament believes that a known good is not lightly to be
surrendered for an unknown better. (Oakeshott, 1962, p. 168ff)

Yet conservatives can hardly just maintain the existing state of affairs, for
this would involve resisting change until it occurs and then defending the
newly-established status quo, even perhaps conserving a revolution. In
practice they may be 'reactionary' not only in the sense of reacting against
change while it is taking place, but sometimes in seeking to restore the
past or 'put back the clock'. Indeed, Tories and conservatives have often
been pejoratively described as reactionaries by their political opponents.
However, the British right has rarely been reactionary in the sense of
seeking the restoration of some previous constitutional order or regime,
although in the eighteenth century the Tory cause was for a time tainted
with, and divided by, Jacobitism (support for the rival claim to the British
throne by the Old and Young Pretender).

Yet British Tories and Conservatives might be described as reactionary in the more literal sense of reacting against the changes proposed or made by their opponents, as must any group of people whose
interests are essentially bound up with the status quo. Thus, in the seventeenth century Tories were reacting against the Puritan assault on the
authority of the Church in general and bishops in particular, against the
limits the parliamentary opposition to the Stuarts wished to place on
royal authority, and against new sources of income and wealth which
appeared to threaten their interests.

Eighteenth-century Toryism and nineteenth-century conservatism
can be seen more generally as a reaction against the major upheavals
and developments in the western world over that period. Here there is a
clear contrast with liberalism. Liberalism was a product of the eigth-
eenth-century Enlightenment, the American and French revolutions,
and, most important of all, industrial capitalism. Toryism and subsequently conservatism involved a reaction against all these. It was suspi-
cious of the claims made for reason by writers of the Enlightenment,
and with the threat this presented to traditional secular and spiritual
authority. It was hostile to the language of equal rights expressed by the
American rebels and French revolutionaries, and particularly horrified
by the claims and conduct of the latter. It was fearful of many of the
changes resulting from industrialization, and the ideas associated with
it. Many Tory squires felt threatened by the new wealth and its growing
political weight.

However, the British Conservative Party has seldom been purely reactionary in the sense of resisting all progress. Indeed one of the reasons why the Conservative Party maintained itself as the leading party of government in Britain while equivalent political movements elsewhere generally became marginalized was because of its readiness to adapt and change. Thus British conservatives have sometimes fiercely resisted change, but have subsequently accepted it. Alternatively, they have become convinced of the need for change and promoted it themselves.

Yet conservatives have generally preferred cautious and gradual reforms which grow out of the past and are consistent with tradition. Edmund Burke (1729–97) perhaps best expresses this conservative attitude to reform. Burke has come to be regarded as one of the founding fathers of British conservatism, although he continued to call himself a Whig to his death. Like all Whigs he celebrated the 'Glorious Revolution' of 1688. Like many Whigs he also supported the Americans in their war of independence, and was a leading critic of George III's party. It was the French Revolution which split Burke from his former Whig friends, who were, at least initially, broadly sympathetic to developments in France from 1789. Burke was horrified almost from the start. In his *Reflections on the Revolution in France* (1790, ed. Hill, 1975) he was careful to distinguish what he regarded as the essentially conservative ideas behind the English 'revolution' of 1688 from the more radical ideas behind the French revolution. 'All the reformations we have hitherto made have proceeded upon the principle of reference to antiquity', Burke argued. 'The very idea of the fabrication of a new government is enough to fill us with disgust and horror.' Reform should grow organically out of the past and should be based on 'precedent, authority and example' rather than abstract reason (*ibid.* p. 296).

Sir Robert Peel, the founder of the modern Conservative Party, might be considered the best exemplar of its attitude to organic change and reform. On three major issues – Catholic Emancipation, Parliamentary Reform, and Corn Law Repeal – he long resisted change, but finally conceded it. He helped Wellington carry Catholic Emancipation in 1829 once he became convinced it was necessary. He opposed parliamentary reform, but once the 1832 Act was passed, recognized that the clock could not be put back in the 1834 Tamworth Manifesto, which articulated his own gradualist approach to reform (Buck, 1975, pp. 56–8). Finally, after years of defending the Corn Laws which protected British agriculture, he became convinced that their repeal was necessary, and carried it through with Whig support against the majority of his own party in 1846 (speech reproduced in Eccleshall, 1990, pp. 100–2).

A preference for gradual reform and organic change, rather than reaction on the one hand or radical change on the other, has often been seen as almost a defining characteristic of British conservatism – although there are some significant exceptions, including Disraeli, Joseph Chamberlain (if indeed he properly belongs to conservatism at all) and Mrs Thatcher who all might be regarded as 'radicals'. The more typical 'gradualist' line is represented by the 'trimmer' Halifax from the seventeenth century, Burke and the younger Pitt from the eighteenth century, Sir Robert Peel and Lord Salisbury from the nineteenth century and Stanley Baldwin (who campaigned under the slogan 'Safety First'), Rab Butler and William Whitelaw from the twentieth.

Reason and tradition

Conservatives often combine their preference for limited change with a suspicion of the pure reason behind schemes for radical reform. Thus Burke challenged head on the prevailing rationalist assumptions of his time, the eighteenth-century 'Age of Enlightenment' or 'Age of Reason' as it has been described. 'In this enlightened age I am bold enough to confess that we are generally men of untaught feelings.' He goes on to confess,

> We are afraid to put men to live and trade each on his private stock of reason, because we suspect that the stock in each man is small, and that the individuals would do better to avail themselves of the general bank and capital of nations and of ages. (Hill, 1975, p. 354).

Burke denies that men in practice act particularly rationally, and furthermore suggests that most men would be better advised to rely on unreflective habits and instincts rather than on 'naked reason'.

Burke clearly has a conception of human nature which is far removed from the dispassionate rational calculator assumed by Jeremy Bentham, and it is Bentham's utilitarianism (see Chapter 2) which is the explicit target of the nineteenth-century Conservative politician and thinker Benjamin Disraeli:

> In this country since the peace [i.e. since 1815] there has been an attempt to advocate a reconstruction of society on a purely rational basis. The principle of utility has been powerfully developed...There

has been an attempt to reconstruct society on a basis of material motives and calculations. It has failed ... How limited is human reason, the profoundest of enquirers are most conscious. (Disraeli's *Coningsby*, Everyman edition, 1911, pp. 199–200)

Disraeli, however, does not draw the same cautious conclusions from the limitations of human reason as Burke. Oakeshott from the twentieth-century is perhaps more generally characteristic of the conservative criticism of the rationalist approach to politics and the conservative attitude to reform. 'The Rationalist', says Oakeshott, 'stands for independence of mind on all occasions, for thought free from obligation to any authority save the authority of "reason"'. He is 'the enemy of authority, of prejudice, of the merely traditional, customary or habitual'. This approach applied to politics means that 'to the Rationalist nothing is of value merely because it exists...familiarity has no worth'. This means that he regards patching up and repair as a waste of time. 'He always prefers the invention of a new device to making use of a current and well-tried expedient' (Oakeshott, 1962, pp. 1–36). Oakeshott goes on to argue that the conservative prefers innovations which appear to grow out of the present, which are in response to some specific defect. 'Consequently, he will find small and slow changes more tolerable than large and sudden; and he will value highly every appearance of continuity' (Oakeshott, 1962, p. 170).

Human imperfection

Some commentators would suggest that conservatism not only involves at least considerable reservations about individual intellectual capacities and the potential for rational conduct, but also implies some fairly pessimistic assumptions about human nature and human potential for individual improvement or social progress. It is a 'philosophy of imperfection' (O'Sullivan, 1976; Quinton, 1978). Compared with liberalism or socialism, less reliance is placed on the reason or the inherent goodness of man, and there is accordingly less optimism about the prospects for improving society. Quintin Hogg has commented that 'man is an imperfect creature with a streak of evil as well as good in his inmost nature' (Hogg, 1947, p. 11). Norman St John Stevas (1982) has noted that belief in the perfectability of man is a liberal or socialist error – conservatives have on the contrary a consciousness of original sin, although, Stevas goes on to point out, not everyone would give the point a theological formulation.

There is indeed a compatibility between conservative ideology and some expressions of religious belief. The inherent weakness and wickedness of man has been proclaimed by Christian thinkers down the ages; man is incapable of redeeming himself through his own efforts. Therefore, ideologies such as liberalism, socialism, and most especially anarchism, which present an optimistic picture of human nature and human potentiality, are at odds with mainstream orthodox Christian faith, which suggests that Christ's intercession is necessary for human salvation. And, just as human beings are too inherently flawed to achieve everlasting salvation through their own unaided efforts, so these same weaknesses prevent spontaneous cooperative social endeavour, and require authority and strong government to keep men in order.

Anthony Quinton (1978), while acknowledging the strength of this religious tradition, has attempted to detach conservative doctrine from 'what is often alleged to be an essential dependence on religious foundations'. He distinguishes between a religious and secular tradition of conservative thought. One tradition, he argues, 'derives its conservative politics to some extent from religious premises, in particular from the moral imperfection of human nature'. Quinton associates Hooker, Clarendon, Johnson, Burke, Coleridge and Newman with this tradition. But Quinton also argues there is a 'secular tradition of conservative thinking' initiated by Halifax, Bolingbroke and Hume, and kept alive more recently by Oakeshott. This emphasizes the 'radical intellectual imperfection of the human individual' as well as a 'parallel belief in the moral imperfection of mankind'. But Quinton considers that the latter, although sometimes derived from 'the Christian dogma of original sin', is also shared by many 'secular and even atheistic thinkers, for example Hobbes, Hume and Freud' (Quinton, 1978, pp. 9–16).

It is perhaps unfortunate from Quinton's point of view that he is unable to claim Hobbes for this conservative secular tradition, for it was indeed Thomas Hobbes (1588–1679) who painted one of the most celebrated and gloomy pictures of human nature in the raw. Without a common power to keep men in order there would be a continuous war of every man against every man, and life would be 'solitary, poor, nasty, brutish and short'. It was this nightmare vision which required strong government, for Hobbes a government with absolute powers. But although Hobbes' general pessimism about human nature has been widely shared by conservative thinkers, he has been rarely claimed for British conservatism. Quinton disqualifies him on three counts – his absolutism, his rationalism, and his individualism (Quinton, 1978, p. 30).

Without Hobbes, Quinton's conservative secular tradition seems relatively insubstantial compared with what must be considered the mainstream Christian tradition. Many conservatives have quite explicitly associated their political principles with their Christian faith. Indeed, although all mainstream British political creeds derive some inspiration from Christianity, Anglicanism in particular is highly compatible with conservatism. Not only do they share the same pessimistic assumptions about human nature, they also both involve an acceptance of authority and hierarchy, which might seem a logical corollary of human moral and intellectual deficiencies.

Authority, leadership, and Tory democracy

If individual human beings are not rational calculators, and if furthermore the general benevolence of most men and women is at least a doubtful question, then certain implications may be considered to follow. In particular, democracy appears a hazardous enterprise. Indeed, for much of the nineteenth-century conservatives viewed democracy with abhorrence. Peel opposed the first Reform Bill, objecting that 'all its tendencies are, to substitute for a mixed form of government, a pure unmitigated democracy' (quoted in Wright, 1970, p. 119). Salisbury in 1860, reacting to demands for a further extension of the franchise, in similar vein referred to 'the struggle between the English constitution on the one hand, and the democratic forces which are now labouring to subvert it'. He argued that 'Wherever democracy has prevailed, the power of the State has been used in some form or other to plunder the well-to-do classes for the benefit of the poor' (Buck, 1975, p. 104).

Conservatives only moved to a qualified acceptance of democracy when it became clear that it was compatible with maintenance of the existing social order and the defence of property. Thus Disraeli perceived that the working classes could be won for conservatism, and persuaded his party to 'dish the Whigs' by promoting the 1867 Reform Bill (McKenzie and Silver, 1968). His judgement proved defective in the short run, for Gladstone's Liberals gained an emphatic victory in the ensuing 1868 election, but was vindicated in the longer run as the Conservatives managed to win and subsequently hold a substantial minority of the working-class vote. Disraeli had earlier toyed with the idea of an alliance between the working classes and the aristocracy against the industrial bourgeoisie. Behind this rather fanciful notion there was a realization that there was no harmony of interest between industrial workers and their liberal bosses. It was perhaps no accident that Lancashire, the home of Manchester liberalism in the mid-nineteenth century, later established a strong tradition of working-class conservatism.

Acceptance of democracy did not mean any real dilution of the characteristically conservative endorsement of authority, hierarchy and the mixed constitution. Beer argues that 'Authoritative leadership is a permanent social necessity for the Tory'. He goes on to suggest that 'parliamentary government and the mass suffrage have been grafted onto and adapted to' a Tory view of the Constitution in which all the initiative comes from government. 'Tory democracy gives the voters power. But it is the power of control, not initiation, exercised under government by consent, not by delegation' (Beer, 1982, pp. 94–8). This is very similar to the version of democracy later endorsed by Joseph Schumpeter (1943), in which all the initiative comes from leaders rather than the masses. Democracy thus involves a constrained competition for the people's vote rather than popular participation in government.

Coupled with all this is the Tory view of an organic society composed of unequal but mutually dependent classes, in which a relatively small number have the attributes, experience and leisure to be qualified to govern. The mass of the people, in this view, are willing to defer to the judgement and experience of this governing class. Bagehot (himself a Liberal) suggested that the 'deference' of the English people was one of the main supports of the English constitution. Lord Randolph Churchill, who coined the term 'Tory democracy', believed it was possible to secure popular support for existing institutions. Conservatives assume a common national interest which transcends individual or class interests, that all to some degree share the benefits of an ordered society and system of government, that the poorest can be made to appreciate the sanctity of property and existing social arrangements.

To critics of conservatism this is a transparent confidence trick which serves to conceal from subordinate classes their own interests in sweeping reform or revolution. The Tory perspective can thus be summed up in the familiar couplet, 'God bless the squire and his relations, And keep us in our proper stations.' Conservatives would tend to respond that inequality is both natural and inevitable. To preach equality and social justice is to stir up envy, hatred, and unhappiness, for the passions aroused can never be satisfied. Moreover, the conservative would argue, everyone, ultimately, has an interest in the sanctity of property.

The defence of property

Conservatives have generally been unequivocal in their defence of property (Nisbet, 1986, p. 55 ff), an attitude which contrasts strongly not only with that of socialists, but also liberals whose approach to the subject has been ambivalent. Starting from libertarian and egalitarian assumptions, a faith in reason and a distrust of traditional social arrangements, liberals have felt a need to produce elaborate justifications for property, based for example on natural rights, labour or utility. Sometimes this has led them to justify some forms of property, but not others – there have been particular problems with land and inherited wealth. Conservatives have generally devoted less time and space to the justification of private property, for the simple reason that the issue for them is unproblematic. Existing property rights are part of traditional social arrangements endorsed by conservatives. Inequality in property reflects profound inequalities in abilities and energies. The conservative would allow that the existing distribution of property does not necessarily accord with desert, but would deny that an ideal social justice is obtainable. Attempts to justify interference with existing property rights in pursuit of social justice threatens the whole institution of private property. The most the conservative is generally prepared to concede is that the possession of property entails obligations and responsibilities.

Thus Conservatives have wholeheartedly defended private property, and justified its extremely unequal distribution. Burke argued that 'the characteristic essence of property, formed out of the combined principles of its acquisition and conservation, is to be unequal'. Great concentrations of property 'form a natural rampart about the lesser properties in all their gradations'. Inherited property is also strongly defended: 'The power of perpetuating our property in our families is one of the most valuable and interesting circumstances belonging to it, and that which tends the most to the perpetuation of society itself' (Hill, 1975, pp. 316–17).

Modern Conservatives have been as committed to the defence of property. Oakeshott associates the possession of private property with freedom, and goes on to suggest that private ownership of the means of production, essentially capitalism, is also necessary for liberty:

> The freedom which separates a man from slavery is nothing but a freedom to choose and to move among autonomous, independent

organizations, firms, purchasers of labour, and this implies private property in resources other than personal capacity. (Oakeshott, 1962, p. 46)

Scruton (1980, p. 99) talks of 'man's absolute and ineradicable need of private property'. This, he says, 'represents the common intuition of every labouring person'. Against the classical liberal or the modern neo-liberal, Scruton is prepared to justify state regulation of private property and market forces, but at the same time he strongly attacks deliberate state intervention to achieve the redistribution of property through progressive taxation, wealth and inheritance taxes (Scruton, 1980, p. 108).

The problem with property for conservatives has been more one of strategy rather than of principle – how to persuade the majority with little or no property to accept its existing distribution. Conservatism was initially associated with a particular form of property – land – and indeed there still lingers among some conservatives a distrust of other forms of wealth (Nisbet, 1986, p. 63). Towards the end of the nineteenth century the British Conservative Party became the party not just of landed property but of property in general, as the manufacturing interest increasingly deserted the Liberals, alienated by radicalism and Irish Home Rule. Yet a wider base of popular support was required for electoral survival.

Various strategies were employed in practice, including social reform and imperialism, but there has also been, particularly recently, a deliberate attempt to widen and extend property ownership. It was Eden who used the phrase 'property owning democracy', and postwar Conservative governments have sought to promote home ownership and, more recently, wider share ownership. Earlier, Conservatives at both central and local level had supported public housing, and had been content to encourage home ownership through tax relief. More recently the party has encouraged and subsequently compelled the sale of council houses, and actively discouraged further council-house building. The result has been to turn owner occupation into the majority form of housing tenure. Some tax concessions, but more notably the privatization of major nationalized industries on favourable terms for small investors, enabled Mrs Thatcher to claim that there were now more share-owners than trade unionists. Thus the ownership of property, both in the tangible sense of bricks and mortar and in the more symbolic participation in capitalism, has been significantly extended, although its extremely uneven distribution persists.

Paternalism and social reform

Until recently the defence of private property has not for most conservatives entailed an unqualified defence also of the free market.
Indeed it might appear that 'self-help' and *'laissez-faire'* were inappropriate injunctions for the many people who, according to conservative views of human nature and intellectual capacity, were generally
incapable of perceiving and pursuing their own rational self-interest.
On the contrary, it seemed clear to many Tories that such people
needed help and guidance, and sometimes also firm control. The
authority of the state was thus required to provide a framework of
order and discipline, but also support for those unable or incapable of
helping themselves. Moreover, others who were fortunately placed in
terms of natural endowments or wealth had an obligation to provide
that help, guidance and control. Society was more than a mere aggregate of individuals. It was rather an organic whole, necessarily
involving ties of mutual dependence which in turn suggested social
duties and responsibilities as well as individual rights. This was the
basis for what has been termed 'Tory paternalism'.

Disraeli is the Conservative preeminently associated with paternalism. In his novel *Sybil* there is a strong attack not only on the 1832
Reform Act, but also, and more importantly, on the whole system of
capitalist values which Disraeli associated with industrialization:

> If a spirit of rapacious covetousness, desecrating all the humanities
> of life, has been the besetting sin of England for the last century and
> a half, since the passing of the Reform Act the altar of Mammon has
> blazed with triple worship. To acquire, to accumulate, to plunder
> each other by virtue of philosophic phrases, to propose an Utopia to
> consist only of WEALTH and TOIL, this has been the breathless
> business of enfranchised England for the last twelve years. (Disrael's
> *Sybil*, 1980 edition, p. 56)

Here Disraeli is assaulting all the ideas and slogans associated with the
Whig/Liberal tradition of thought, but particularly those of *laissez-faire*
economics. Behind such wholesale condemnations of new values and
interests lay a nostalgia for a vanished past which perhaps only existed
in Disraeli's romantic imagination – an ordered society of mutual
dependence, where privilege entailed obligations to those less fortunate
and where social divisions and class conflict did not exist. For Disraeli
liked to think that somehow social conflict could be healed. In another

off-quoted passage from *Sybil* (p. 96) he talks of the Victorian England of his day in terms of 'two nations' of the rich and the poor,

> between whom there is no intercourse and no sympathy; who are as ignorant of each other's habits, thoughts and feelings, as if they were dwellers in different zones, or inhabitants of different planets; who are formed by different breeding, are fed by different food, are ordered by different manners, and are not governed by the same laws.

Disraeli was thus fully aware of the depth of social divisions in the England of his day but, like later conservatives who adopted the 'One Nation' slogan, hoped that somehow they could be transcended and one nation made of two. The Conservative Party has always claimed to stand above class and for the nation as a whole. For political opponents, particularly for socialists, this is a transparent 'con trick' – a capitalist society necessarily involves class conflict, and conservatives mask this social reality in their own interests (Honderich, 1990, chs 6,7). Disraeli himself revealed an element of class interest in his concern for social reform when he observed 'the palace is not safe, when the cottage is not happy' (quoted in Beer 1982, p. 267). Even so, Conservative politicians have had little difficulty in convincing themselves of the idea of a conservatism standing for the nation and against sectional interests, and it has had a potent appeal.

It should be noted, however, that this paternalism did not then necessarily imply state action. Disraeli's biographer has claimed, 'He had a genuine hatred of centralization, bureaucracy and every manifestation of the Benthamite state' (Blake, 1966, p. 282). For Disraeli the state was almost the last rather than the first resort. He was well aware that for numbers of the poor 'self-help' was a futile injunction, but anticipated that the help they required should be forthcoming from the traditional aristocracy, from the church, and from voluntary activity of all kinds. In *Sybil* his targets were the uncaring landowners who neglected their tenants and the new capitalists who exploited their workforce, and these are contrasted with examples of philanthropic aristocrats and caring industrialists. In his political speeches he took much the same line. At Shrewsbury in 1843 he blamed current political evils on the development of property divorced from duty. Much of this of course runs directly counter to the notion of rational self-interest and self-help, but hardly suggests that Disraeli saw the state as the principal vehicle for the alleviation of social distress.

Arguably he became more committed to state action subsequently. In his 1872 speech to the National Union he described the 'elevation of the condition of the people' as the third great object of the Tory party, although the speech was longer on rhetoric than specifics. While much has been made of Disraeli's commitment to social reform both before and after he became Prime Minister (Beer, 1965, ch. 9), historians have exposed the myth that there was any clear consistent programme of social reform behind his administration's legislative record (Smith, 1967, p. 202). Disraeli's modern biographer, Lord Blake, apparently anxious to reestablish his subject's reputation in a Thatcherite era, has observed, 'His policies have been much misinterpreted, not least by those who unplausibly regard him as an ancestor of the welfare state – a sort of arch wet' (*Guardian*, 4 October 1982).

The commitment to social reform of Disraeli's immediate successors is also questionable. Randolph Churchill's enthusiasm for Tory democracy and reform involved more rhetoric than reality, but his early resignation in any case removed any prospect that Salisbury's government would pursue 'the social question'. Even the adhesion of the radical Liberal Unionist, Joseph Chamberlain, made little difference to what has been described as a period of 'Conservative inertia' (Beer 1982, p. 271). Indeed, by 1894 Chamberlain had so far moderated his earlier radicalism to complain that 'the resolutions of the TUC... amount to universal confiscation in order to create a Collectivist State' (quoted in Adelman, 1970, p. 107).

Protection and Tory collectivism

In so far as some Conservatives wished to interfere with market forces, it was less in the interests of social reform than economic protection and industrial reorganization. In the early nineteenth century the Tories were the party of protection, particularly the protection of agriculture through the Corn Laws. After the party split over Repeal in 1846 the bulk of the party remained protectionist until reluctantly persuaded that the cause was no longer practical politics. Later in the nineteenth century the demand for 'fair trade' as opposed to 'free trade' was articulated. In 1903 Joseph Chamberlain turned the issue into a veritable crusade with his demand for imperial protection. It was this issue on which Baldwin's 1923 government was defeated at the polls, and it was the Conservative protectionists whose views eventually prevailed in the National governments of the 1930s. Neville Chamberlain as Chancellor of the Exchequer was to boast that his Import Duties Bill provided the government with 'a lever as has never been possessed before by any government for inducing or, if you like, forcing industry to set its house in order' (Beer, 1982, p. 293). It was only after the Second World War that the Conservative Party dropped its enthusiasm for protection.

Protection necessarily involves state action of a sort, but the term 'collectivism' implies rather more state intervention. For modern Conservatives collectivism has acquired strong negative connotations, becoming closely associated with socialism, but it was not always so. Thus Gilmour (1978, p. 36) carefully describes Neville Chamberlain's state-interventionist policies to rationalize industry in the 1930s as 'collectivist... rather than socialist'. Yet Chamberlain's Tory collectivism involved managed capitalism rather than socialism.

It was the conservatism of the period after the Second World War which can be most plausibly associated with collectivism. Macmillan had once provocatively declared that Toryism had always been a kind of paternal socialism and he preached an interventionist 'Middle Way' between *laissez-faire* capitalism and socialist state planning. The wartime Tory Reform Group urged the acceptance of social reform and, more specifically, the state welfare recommendations of the Beveridge Report which was declared the 'very essence of Toryism' (Beer 1982, p. 307). In opposition from 1945–51, the commitment to social reform was firmed up. Butler, the architect of the 1944 Education Act, declared in 1947 'We are not frightened at the use of the State. A good Tory has never in history been afraid of the use of the State.' This sweeping verdict was endorsed by Anthony Eden. 'We are not the political children of the laissez faire school. We opposed them decade after decade' (Beer, 1982, p. 271).

The rhetoric of these modern-day heirs of Disraeli was rather more matched by reality than that of the Victorian politician. The Welfare State established by the coalition and Labour governments was maintained and even in certain respects enhanced. A policy of compromise and accommodation was applied to the trade unions and industrial relations. Most remarkably, perhaps, after the initial denationalization of steel and road haulage, other state-owned industries were maintained. Overall, the role of government continued to expand, and public expenditure continued to rise. Indeed, Prime Minister Harold Macmillan accepted the resignation of his entire Treasury team in 1958 rather than the cuts in spending which they demanded. The commitment to full employment policies was maintained, through orthodox Keynesian demand-management policies, by successive Tory chancellors. When such policies did not succeed in correcting such deep-seated problems as low growth, balance of payments deficits and weak sterling, Macmillan's government moved towards more intervention rather than free-market solutions. The National Economic Development Council signalled a new interest in long-term economic planning, and the National Incomes Commission institutionalized the new Conservative concern with incomes policy. This was perhaps the highwater mark of Tory collectivism.

As with liberal critics of the New Liberalism, there are some Conservatives who would regard this whole approach as a monstrous aberration, a departure from true conservatism. A few who participated in these governments, most notably Lord Joseph (1976), have since recanted and declared they only discovered true conservatism subsequently. Others such as Sir Ian Gilmour (1978) have continued to claim that Butler and Macmillan represent the mainstream Tory tradition, and that it is the free-market neo-liberal nostrums of the New Right which are heretical.

There are indeed some interpretations of conservatism, particularly Beer's (1982), which have seen the postwar One-Nation Conservatism as the culmination of a Tory collectivist tradition, but this has always involved a rather selective interpretation of Conservative history. Beer emphasizes some periods and some individuals, and ignores others. Salisbury, who presided over Conservative Party fortunes longer than Disraeli, and who has some claims to be considered an important conservative thinker, is not even mentioned by Beer, who dismisses his period of dominance as a period of 'Conservative inertia'. Alternatively, Greenleaf (1973, 1983) suggests a lasting tension within conservatism between its 'libertarian' and 'collectivist' strands. However, Freeden (1996, ch. 9) has characterized this 'dual British conservative tradition' as 'a chimera'. The contradictions were more apparent than real and partly reflected a rhetorical conservative response to the contrasting challenges of liberalism and socialism.

Arguably, both the libertarian and collectivist strands of conservatism require a strong state and an emphasis on leadership and authority which would be anathema to many liberals and socialists (Gamble, 1988). The need for leadership has been a perennial Tory theme, from Bolingbroke in the eighteenth century, through Carlyle and Disraeli in the nineteenth century, to Churchill and Mrs Thatcher in the twentieth century. Respect for authority is a key message in the thought of Burke and Salisbury.

Patriotism and imperialism

The strong state was a requirement in foreign policy even more than domestic policy. Reverence for the authority of the state chimed in easily with Conservative nationalism and imperialism, yet until the later nineteenth century Conservatism had no monopoly of patriotic sentiment. Indeed, nationalism was closely associated with liberalism, and the Whig-Liberal Prime Minister Palmerston had been notably successful in exploiting patriotic feeling in his own and his party's interest. Later, however, Disraeli's assiduous promotion of imperialism and the national interest contrasted with Gladstone's internationalism, and associated the Conservative Party with patriotism. This proved a highly successful electoral strategy, particularly with the newly enfranchised working classes. Beer (1982, p. 272) argues imperialism's 'mighty appeal to the voter' effectively made Tory social reform redundant in the late nineteenth century.

McKenzie and Silver (1968) document Conservative party literature addressed to the electorate which exploited nationalist and imperialist sentiment from the 1880s to the 1960s. Liberals, radicals and socialists were constantly accused of being unpatriotic and undermining English and imperial interests. Thus the Liberal government in 1895 was accused of being

> a weak, vacillating, craven Ministry... which dares not defend British interests effectively, and which will submit to be kicked and kicked and kicked until at last the spirit of the English people is aroused in its majesty. (McKenzie and Silver, p. 53)

In 1900 the radicals were associated with 'a Small England, a Shrunken England, a Degraded England, a Submissive England' (*ibid.,* p. 56). By 1910 socialists were associated with radicals in a Conservative pamphlet which claimed 'If you fight for radical socialism you fight for a divided nation ... a divided Kingdom – the union sold! a British Isle no more, Ireland breeds treason at the Empire's core' (*ibid.,* pp. 63–4). In 1924 the Labour Government was accused of putting 'the foreigner first' and preferring 'the Bolsheviks' to 'our own people' (*ibid.,* p. 65) and in 1951 it was argued 'Socialists sneered and still sneer at what they call "Imperialism" ...The Conservative Party, by long tradition and settled belief, is the Party of the Empire' (*ibid.,* p. 68).

While such language is not found in more erudite statements of party philosophy, it could be argued that it is perhaps a better guide to the popular appeal and interpretation of conservatism. Of course nationalist sentiment is by no means confined to the Conservative Party; the musical halls, the press, and later the electronic media have helped created a popular nationalist culture which has also coloured British Liberalism and Labourism (Schwarz in Donald and Hall, 1986, p. 177). But it was the Conservative Party which most successfully exploited the patriotic theme, reinforcing claims to stand above narrow class interests and for the nation as a whole. 'Being Conservative is only another way of being British' claimed Quintin Hogg (McKenzie and Silver, 1968, p. 18).

Baldwin and Churchill in their different ways were particularly skilful in associating themselves and their party with British values and interests. The more internationalist climate in the post-Second World War era, coupled with the decline in the British empire and British power, for a time made patriotic rhetoric appear somewhat outmoded. Under Macmillan and then Heath the Conservatives pursued entry into the European Community, and appeared to have converted their party to the European ideal. However, Enoch Powell's English nationalism, expressed in his opposition to black immigration, the EEC and concessions to the opposition in Ulster, although scorned by the establishment and rejected by Heath, showed that chauvinism still had popular appeal, not least from elements of the working class. This was further demonstrated by Mrs Thatcher. While the Falklands has been the most dramatic illustration of this renewed Conservative nationalism, the emphatic assertion of British interests has been a consistent theme in defence and foreign policy since 1979. This serves as a reminder that Mrs Thatcher's brand of conservatism involved significant elements of continuity with the past. However, in other respects Thatcherism or the New Right seemed to involve a break with the Conservative tradition, and this will be discussed in a subsequent chapter (see Chapter 9).

Further reading

The most reliable introduction to British conservative thinking is the anthology, with introduction and notes, by Eccleshall (1990). Other anthologies include those edited by Buck (1975) and Kirk (1982). O'Sullivan (1976) and Nisbet (1986) both offer interesting interpretations of conservatism in an international context. Scruton (1980) provides a provocative and idiosyncratic account from his own neo-conservative perspective and Honderich (1991) a sledgehammer demolition. Contrasting analyses of Tory/conservative thought are contained in Beer (1982), Greenleaf (1973, 1983) and Freeden (1996). Blake's one-volume history of the Conservative Party (1997) also gives a valuable insight into conservative thought at different periods. On specific periods, Quinton (1978) is useful on the seventeenth and eighteenth century foundations of conservative thinking, while Barnes in Seldon and Ball (1994) discusses twentieth century conservative ideas.

Classic conservative texts include Burke's *Reflections on the Revolution in France* (various editions, for example Hill, 1975) and Oakeshott's elegant collection of essays *Rationalism in Politics*. An insight into Disraeli's ideas can be gathered from his novels *Sybil* and *Coningsby*, although a more balanced account of the contribution of the mature Disraeli to conservativism might be derived from his biography by Blake (1966).

4

Socialism and Labourism

Introduction

Socialism, like liberalism, was a product of the modern world – of the rise of science, industrialization and associated political upheavals. Socialism thus shared with liberalism a post-Enlightenment rationalism, and optimism over progress. It adopted much of the liberal political programme, most notably for a reform and extension of the franchise, and the establishment of civil rights and embodied many liberal values.

Yet socialism also involved a reaction against, and a radical alternative to, liberal capitalism. In terms of class interests, socialism can be seen as the political ideology of the new urban working class, effectively created by industrialization, just as conservatism was, initially, the ideology of the landed interest and liberalism the ideology of the bourgeoisie. While conservatism involved a defence of traditional social arrangements, and liberalism provided a justification and support for an ongoing industrial transformation, socialism developed as a radical or revolutionary ideology requiring a fundamental transformation of existing society and its underlying assumptions and values.

Thus socialists sought a radical overhaul of existing property relations and a massive redistribution of income and wealth in favour of the working classes. This was linked with a rejection of the free-market values and competition lauded by liberals in favour of planning and cooperation. Most socialists instinctively felt that it should be possible to improve on the unplanned outcome of market forces under capitalism, its periodic booms and slumps, and associated unemployment and misery.

Further generalization is difficult as socialism has many variants, and the British experience of socialism is particularly distinctive. While in many other countries variants of socialism are represented in contending political parties – Communists, anarchists, socialists, social democrats – in Britain there has never been a significant left-wing or socialist rival to the Labour Party. Yet Labour's socialist credentials are contested. Some critics deny that Labour has ever been a socialist party, and employ instead the term 'labourism' to describe the party's ideology (Miliband, 1972; Saville, 1988).

This chapter necessarily focuses on socialism in Britain, with sections exploring the specific experience of the British working class, the relative weakness of Marxism, the importance of trade unionism, and the contrasting contributions of ethical socialists and Fabians to the development of Labour thought. Labour thinking inevitably involved some rationalization of Labour practice, and so reference is also made to the experience of Labour governments and the predominance of parliamentarism and centralized state socialism over alternatives such as guild socialism or local socialism. Yet although British socialism or labourism is distinctive and contested, it has necessarily been subject to wider influences, and needs first to be placed in the context of the development of socialism generally.

Socialist values

Socialism adopted the French Revolutionary principles, 'liberty, equality, fraternity'. 'Equality' is the defining socialist value, contrasting with the conservative emphasis on hierarchy, leadership and natural inequality, and the more limited liberal commitment to formal legal and political equality rather than economic and social equality. Socialism involved from the beginning a critique of existing inequality under capitalism and a programme for redistribution and equalization of income, wealth and power. Yet socialists has not always agreed over the meaning of equality. For a few it means the total abolition of personal private property: for others it is only the private ownership of the means of production which needs to be replaced by common or public ownership. Revisionist socialists, often described as social democrats, claim the promotion of equality no longer requires wholesale public ownership; they argue that progressive taxation coupled with state welfare benefits will lead to a more egalitarian society.

While both advocates and critics acknowledge that socialism is about equality, the importance attached to liberty is rather more contestable (Freeden, 1996, ch. 12). Conservatives and liberals have often accused socialists of sacrificing liberty to equality. Socialists have generally maintained that equality is a condition of liberty. Equality does not mean uniformity, but rather frees individuals to develop their full and different potentials. The socialist commitment to liberty has also been strongly reemphasized by modern British Labour Party politicians (Hattersley, 1987). Socialists, like some New Liberals, tend to see freedom in a positive rather than a negative sense – freedom *to* enjoy something which is valued, rather than freedom *from* restraint and coercion. 'Liberty implies the ability to act, not merely to resist' (Tawney 1964, p. 165). Critics argue that socialism inevitably involves loss of liberty. Neo-liberals like Hayek identify freedom with the market order. Any state intervention or planning, even of the milder kind associated with moderate parliamentary socialism, restricts freedom. By contrast, socialists have generally argued that the freedom celebrated by classical liberals and neo-liberals is fairly meaningless in the context of severe economic and social deprivation. Socialists see human behaviour as largely socially determined, the product of its environment, an assumption which cuts across a basic tenet of classical liberalism that individuals know and pursue their own interests. Thus freedom in a capitalist society is largely illusory for the majority.

Behind the notion of fraternity or the 'brotherhood of man' lies an affirmation of the inherent worth of all humanity, regardless of class, nation, colour, creed or gender (despite the sexist terminology which leads some socialists to prefer allied concepts such as 'solidarity', 'community' or 'fellowship'). 'Fraternity' focuses specifically on the interrelations between human beings and on the value and importance of social interaction and community. There is an implicit assumption that human beings have the capacity to live peacefully and cooperatively with each other. This conception of humans as essentially social and potentially selfless contrasts markedly with both conservative notions of a fatal flaw or evil streak in human nature and the competitive, self-seeking individualism which underpins liberalism. It is upon these optimistic assumptions that the feasibility of socialism essentially depends. Conservatives regard the socialist view of human nature as naive and unrealistic, invalidated by the abundant evidence of man's inhumanity to man. Liberals assume a need for individual rewards and incentives. Most socialists would reply that violent, competitive and acquisitive behaviour is socially determined – it is learned rather than natural. A socialist society would foster different values and behaviour.

Evolutionary and revolutionary socialism

Socialists differ considerably over the means to achieve socialism. A fundamental distinction can be drawn between those favouring an evolutionary, gradualist route to socialism, relying on rational or moral persuasion, and those who, enthusiastically or reluctantly, endorse revolution. Evolutionary socialism has always been the dominant strain in Britain, although ideas and analysis have sometimes been borrowed and adapted from the alternative revolutionary tradition.

Revolutionary socialism was inspired by the French revolution, which provided a precedent for further attempts to secure the transformation of society through insurrection. But many socialists rejected the revolutionary route to socialism. The French Revolution had disappointed many early enthusiasts for it had 'destroyed its own children', and culminated in dictatorship. Thus it was not an example to be followed but a failure and a warning. By contrast, some early socialists (particularly in Britain) hoped to build socialism peacefully, from the bottom up, sometimes through ambitious attempts to establish small-scale model socialist communities, but more usually through practical experiments in mutual aid and self-help for working people, such as consumer and producer cooperatives, friendly societies and trade unions, as well as through education. Yet attempts to build socialism from the bottom up substantially ignored the problem of power. Such initiatives could not, in isolation, produce that fundamental transformation of society and redistribution of income and wealth which socialists sought. Marx and Engels thus attacked this form of socialism as 'utopian', as there was no realistic strategy for its achievement.

Marx's own brand of revolutionary socialism was based on an analysis of underlying trends in the historical evolution of societies. Key elements in this historical evolution were social classes, defined in terms of their relations with the means of production. In a capitalist society the crucial division was between the owners of capital, and the industrial proletariat who owned only their own labour. The dynamics of capitalism required the exploitation of the proletariat by the capitalists in pursuit of profit. This fundamental conflict of interest could not be resolved, and indeed it was bound to be intensified as competition between capitalists inevitably increased the exploitation and misery of the workforce. For Marx, a successful working-class revolution would be the inevitable consequence of the intensification of class conflict in a capitalist society. Marx's revolutionary socialism provided the inspiration for the Russian revolution, and numerous other revolutions since, although neither the background circumstances nor the actual course of these revolutions have closely reflected Marx's analysis. Lenin, in particular, provided his own gloss on Marx, extending the notion of a temporary dictatorship of the proletariat, and developing the concept of democratic centralism to establish an authoritarian, highly centralized state socialism.

Meanwhile an alternative evolutionary, parliamentary route to social-ism seemed increasingly plausible with the extension of the franchise to the working-class in Britain and other liberal capitalist countries from the second half of the nineteenth century onwards. The parliamentary route involved the formation of new working class socialist parties, competition for votes and parliamentary seats, and ultimately the capture of the apparatus of the state through a parliamentary majority. Thus power could be won, and socialism established, through peaceful and democratic struggle. Indeed, for many, socialism seemed the natural corollary of democracy. Political equality would lead in-exorably to social equality.

But although socialist parties were to enjoy considerable electoral success in western Europe, progress towards socialism has been, for many, disappointing. Sometimes this has been ascribed to betrayal by the parliamentary leadership – a familiar complaint on the left. Indeed, there are, arguably, endemic pressures towards accommodation and compromise within the parliamentary system (Michels, 1962). Compromises with socialist objectives were necessary to win votes and were thus an inescapable consequence of the electoral strategy. It was too readily assumed, both by early socialists and some of their oppo-nents, that political democracy would lead rapidly to a major redistribu-tion of income and wealth in favour of the masses. The extent to which the values of liberal capitalism were embedded in society as a whole was insufficiently appreciated, and the task of converting the working class to fundamentally different values in a hostile climate was corre-spondingly underestimated (Coates, 1980). Some would further argue that parliamentary socialism inevitably involves a 'top-down', elitist or paternalist approach, producing a centralized state socialism which is the antithesis of the participative, cooperative socialist ideal.

Attitudes to the state have varied markedly among socialists. While anarchists would totally reject the authority of the centralized state, others such as the British Fabian socialist, Sidney Webb, have identified the expansion of the state with socialism. Marxists argue that the exist-ing state apparatus in a capitalist society inevitably reflects a narrow class interest and involves coercion, and thus must be replaced by new institutions. But while Marx suggested that the state would 'wither away' after the revolution, this was not the experience in Communist political systems. Western parliamentary socialists, while abhorring the Leninist state, have still tended to see socialism in terms of centralized state economic planning and state welfare provision. More decentral-ized, participative forms of socialism have been less evident.

Socialists in Britain and elsewhere have also disagreed over the relative merits of parliamentary and extra-parliamentary (particularly industrial) action as a means to achieve social and political change. While British trade unionism was predominantly legalistic, respectable and limited to immediate practical objectives concerned with pay and conditions, industrial muscle could also be employed to achieve wider economic and political ends. Syndicalists (inspired by the French thinker Georges Sorel) rejected parliamentarism in favour of such industrial action. Workers should use their power to seize control of industry. In theory this could be non-violent. Disciplined strikes would immobilize the country and lead to a peaceful revolution. In practice such industrial action was often associated with violence. Moreover, syndicalism involved a clear class-conflict view of politics, and thus belongs more properly in the revolutionary rather than the evolutionary strand of socialism.

Radically different strategies for achieving socialism mask underlying differences over the analysis of existing society. While Marxists assume a fundamental and irreconcilable conflict of interest between capital and labour in a capitalist society, British Labour Party socialists have more often avoided the language of class conflict. Free enterprise or *laissez-faire* capitalism is condemned as immoral and inefficient, with the implicit assumption that socialism is ultimately in the general or national interest rather than a class interest. It follows that even dominant interests in existing society may be persuaded of the benefits of socialism, a notion which to the Marxist is simply naive.

Working-class politics in nineteenth-century Britain

If socialism reflects the interests of the industrial working class, Britain should have afforded a suitable environment for its rapid development. As the first industrializing nation, Britain was the first country in which something like a modern industrial working class emerged. Previously there were labouring classes, but not a working class conscious of its identity and collective interest. Industrialization involved a new concentration of workers, both in workplaces and in fast-growing urban settlements. This facilitated the communication of ideas and organization, and made the working class a factor in politics which could no longer be ignored.

There was certainly plenty of evidence of discontent among the labouring classes in Britain in the early stages of industrialization

(Thompson, 1980). Some tradesmen and artisans showed revolutionary sympathies in the late eighteenth century. The Luddite riots of 1811–13 involved an understandable reaction against the impact of mechanization on the employment and living standards of skilled workers. There were mass meetings and demonstrations, such as that broken up at Spa Field Manchester in 1819 by cavalry, and early attempts to form trade unions. There were also revolutionary plots, culminating in the 1822 Cato Street conspiracy. Subsequently Chartism emerged in the 1830s as a broad-based working-class movement with radical political objectives, including the vote for all adult males, but involving a variety of ideas and strategies, Whether all this working-class political activity posed a real danger to the existing social order is debatable, although the political establishment feared intensifying class conflict and revolution.

Working-class radicalism did not necessarily involve socialism, but socialist ideas were advanced in the first half of the nineteenth century. Thus William Thompson (1775–1833) and Thomas Hodgskin (1783–1869) derived socialist conclusions from Ricardo's labour theory of value. The most influential early British socialist was, however, Robert Owen (1771–1858). Owen had demonstrated at his model factory and worker's houses at New Lanark, Scotland, that it was possible to make money by enlightened capitalism, and at his more ambitious American model community, New Harmony, that it was equally possible to lose a fortune. But even in his early years he was more than just an enlightened philanthropist. His work at New Lanark reflected a conviction (characteristic of socialism) that people are moulded, for good or ill, by their environment. Such a view contradicted the conventional religious notion of personal moral responsibility, and indeed Owen's irreligion soon lost him the respectful attention he had briefly enjoyed in parliamentary circles. But as his influence with the political establishment declined, his reputation among the radical working class grew, and Owen was strongly associated with an ambitious spread of trade unions in the 1830s and the establishment of the co-operative movement in the 1840s (Owen, ed. Claeys, 1991).

Owen's legacy was considerable and controversial. Marx and Engels attacked him in the *Communist Manifesto* as a utopian socialist, along with Saint-Simon (1760–1825) and Fourier (1772–1837). The charge reflects Owens' involvement in model socialist utopias and his failure to develop a plausible strategy to achieve socialism. Owen eschewed revolution, while his support for trade unionism and the co-operative movement could be comfortably accommodated within Victorian working-class self-help. Yet Owen thoroughly immersed himself in working-class politics and causes, and Engels later delivered another more generous verdict: 'Every social movement, every real advance in England on behalf of the workers links itself to the name of Robert Owen' (Marx and Engels, 1962, vol. 2, p. 127).

From the 1850s both socialism and working-class militancy, following the collapse of Chartism, made little headway, and British working-class leaders largely accepted the gradualist reformist parliamentary culture. Political and social reforms seemingly confirmed the existing system's capacity for change. Religious and other cleavages which cut across class divisions helped blunt social conflict. The benefits of early industrialization and imperialism improved living standards among elements of the working class, particularly from the mid-nineteenth century onwards, when skilled craftsmen organized themselves into effective unions, creating an 'aristocracy of labour' (Gray, 1981). All this reduced hostility to the economic system, to the extent that accommodation within capitalism rather than its wholesale transformation was increasingly sought by leaders of the organized labour movement, many of whom saw no reason to go beyond radical liberalism in their political demands (Pelling, 1965, p. 6).

Thus in marked contrast with developments in France and Germany, socialist ideas were only weakly articulated in Britain in the period after 1848, and there was virtually no organized socialist activity before the 1880s (Pelling, 1965, pp. 13–15), by which time socialist ideas and socialist parties were already established with a mass following in several other European countries. Even after distinct socialist organizations emerged in Britain from the 1880s onwards, the influence of radical liberal thinking remained strong. Bentham, Mill, Hobhouse, Hobson, and later Keynes and Beveridge, all arguably had a bigger influence on the character and development of British socialist thought than many thinkers with more authentic socialist credentials. British socialism thus substantially grew out of radical liberalism, and has long continued to bear the marks of its origins.

Marxism and the British labour movement

The failure of British workers to develop a stronger class consciousness and a revolutionary programme was sadly noted by two celebrated foreign observers of British politics. Marx and Engels spent the bulk of their working lives in England, studied conditions in England extensively and involved themselves in British working-class politics. Moreover, Britain, as the most advanced capitalist country in their day, might appear the prime candidate for a Marxist-style socialist revolution. Despite all this, Marxist ideas have had less influence in Britain than in Germany, France, Italy, Russia, China and many other countries where the ground for their reception might seem less fertile.

Indeed, although the British authorities kept a watchful eye on the socialist agitator in their midst, they concluded he was not particularly dangerous. Grant Duff, a Liberal MP who arranged a meeting with Marx at the suggestion of Queen Victoria's eldest daughter, enjoyed three hours civilized conversation with him and concluded, 'It will not be Marx who, whether he wishes it or not, will turn the world upside down' (McLellan, 1976, p. 445). Yet this prediction would have been less wide of the mark if applied exclusively to Britain. The relatively weak influence of Marxist ideas in Britain can be largely attributed to factors already explored – political stability and a tradition of gradualism, a blurred and fluid class system, the existence in Owenism of a distinct native strand of socialism, the relative prosperity of sections of the working class, the extension of the franchise and the reforms apparently secured through parliamentarism, the acceptance of trade unionism by the political establishment, and the consequent movement of labour leaders towards accommodation within the existing economic and political system.

Marx's theories were familiar in British socialist circles, although not always fully understood or appreciated. William Morris (1834–96), while enjoying the historical parts of *Capital* confessed that he 'suffered agonies of confusion of the brain over reading the pure economics of that great work' (Morris, ed. Briggs, 1962, p. 34). George Bernard Shaw (1856–1950) tried to convert his fellow Fabians to Marxist economics, but was soon persuaded to repudiate Marx in favour of more orthodox theories (Foote, 1985, p. 25). In general, early British socialism was eclectic, and Marx was only one influence among many.

Hyndman's Social Democratic Federation (SDF) was the leading British Marxist organization in the late nineteenth and early twentieth centuries. H. M. Hyndman (1842–1921) was a former Tory imperialist who managed to upset his mentors, Marx and Engels, and quarrel with most other leading socialists of his day (Pelling, 1965, pp. 18–32; Pierson, 1973, pp. 60–75; Callaghan, 1990, ch 2). He was particularly scathing about the theory and practice of trade unionism. While the SDF helped form the Labour Representation Committee (LRC) in 1900, it left within a year and was subsequently transformed into the British Socialist Party, which in turn combined with others to form the Communist Party of Great Britain in 1920 following the Bolshevik revolution of 1917 which renewed interest in Marxist ideas both inside and outside the Labour Party (Callaghan, 1990, ch. 7).

The subsequent refusal of the Labour Party to allow Communist Party affiliation emphasized the split between revolutionary and evolutionary socialism, in Britain as elsewhere. The hardening division between western parliamentary socialism (represented by the Second International) and soviet style communism (represented by the Third International) rendered Marxist analysis suspect in Labour circles. Communists, following the changing line from Moscow, variously sought to penetrate Labour ('entryism'), to form broad left alliances ('popular front') and to denounce other socialists as 'social fascists'. Meanwhile, the electoral progress of the Labour Party in the 1920s apparently confirmed the faith of the leadership in parliamentarism and constitutionalism.

Later, the economic crisis and collapse of the Labour government in 1931 led some British socialists like Strachey (1901–63) to question gradualism and embrace Marxism, and rendered the alternative Soviet model of socialism more attractive (ironically at the height of the Stalinist terror), even to the arch gradualists, Sidney and Beatrice Webb. Marxism and Russian-style communism remained intellectually fashionable throughout the 1930s, but its influence on the leadership of the Labour Party and the bulk of the working class remained marginal (Pimlott, 1977). After 1945, the Cold War and growing economic prosperity in the west again rendered Marxist analysis suspect or seemingly irrelevant. Thus Strachey repudiated his earlier Marxist views (Foote, 1985, p. 210).

Yet Marxism continued to be fashionable in left-wing academic circles, and was articulated by a number of fringe left groups. In the 1980s sophisticated Marxist analysis had some impact on thinking within the Labour Party (especially through the journal *Marxism Today*), and at another level there were some highly publicized attempts at infiltration of constituency parties and trade unions by the Militant Tendency, and its more fundamentalist Marxism. Even so, the real influence of Marxist ideas on the Labour Party remained relatively weak (Coates 1980, p. 163).

Trade unionism and labourism

The failure of revolutionary socialism to have much impact in Britain might be ascribed in part to the strength and character of British trade unionism. Trade unionism and socialism share a concern to advance

the interests of the working class; they place a similar emphasis on collective values, but otherwise do not necessarily coincide on ultimate
objectives or strategy. Trade unions exist to promote the interests of
their members, largely in terms of pay and conditions, through collective bargaining, backed by sanctions, including ultimately the withdrawal of labour. They do not necessarily seek, as socialists do, a
fundamental transformation of the economic and social system. Indeed,
free collective bargaining implies some accommodation within a capitalist system. Moreover, immediate interests in the workplace are not
identical with the collective interests of the working class as a whole,
including those outside the paid labour force – children, the old, the
sick, disabled, unemployed, and unwaged women.

The craft unions for skilled workers which developed in Britain from
the mid-ninereenth century onwards were moderate in their methods
and objectives. The gains they secured from the existing economic
system rendered them less susceptible to the attractions of radical
socialism. Socialist ideas were more prevalent among the leaders of
semi-skilled and unskilled workers, who became effectively organized
for industrial purposes later in the century (Callaghan, 1990, ch 4).
Even so, the bulk of trade unionists seemed indifferent or hostile to
socialism and many retained strong links with radical liberalism. Thus
trade unionism did not necessary imply socialism, nor even separate
labour parliamentary representation. Until the late nineteenth and early
twentieth centuries many trade unionists preferred to concentrate on the
immediate issues of wages and conditions, avoiding wider political
activity. In so far as they sought political influence, they were content
with the two established political parties which, from self-interest, were
increasingly sensitive to labour pressure.

Yet, ultimately, the Labour Party 'emerged from the bowels of the
trade union movement' (Ernest Bevin). Several factors caused a change
in outlook, including the reluctance of the established parties to endorse
working-class candidates, some bitter industrial disputes in the early
1890s and, most significantly, growing anxieties about the legal position of trade unions, following a series of disquieting court cases culminating in a judgement in 1901 that trade unions were liable for damages
caused by industrial action (Pelling, 1965, pp. 200–13). Thus some
unions joined with three socialist societies to establish the Labour
Representation Committee in 1900, and affiliations soon tripled following the 1901 'Taff Vale' judgement. Subsequently, the commitment of
the trade union movement to what was soon renamed the Labour Party
was never in serious doubt.

Yet that commitment remained initially (and arguably always essentially) to labour representation rather than socialism, although there were already some reciprocal ties between trade unionism and socialism. Socialists had given encouragement and support to the New Unionism from the 1880s, while many trade union activists were themselves socialists. Moreover, those unions who joined the LRC were plainly prepared to enter an alliance with established socialist organizations. But there were considerable mutual suspicions. Hyndman's general hostility to the limitations of trade unions soon led to the SDF's withdrawal from the LRC, while the Fabians were patronizing and disparaging about both the unions and the working classes (Adelman, 1986, p. 10). It is scarcely surprising that some trade unionists were in turn critical of middle-class intellectual socialists whose commitment to trade unionism and the labour movement seemed at best doubtful.

Yet the 'contentious alliance' (Minkin, 1992) between the trade unions and the Labour Party survived and thrived. While there was always some latent potential for ideological conflict between the two wings of the labour movement, this was minimized by the general compatibility between British trade unionism and the mainstream British interpretation of socialism. Both were essentially moderate, reformist and gradualist. Both were content to work legally within the existing state apparatus.

Indeed, one perhaps surprising consequence of the major role of trade unions in the British Labour Party was to establish the primacy of parliamentary rather than industrial action as the strategy for the achievement of socialism. Once the Trades Union Congress (TUC) decided to back parliamentary representation, it committed the trade union movement wholeheartedly to parliamentarism. There were of course trade union leaders who were attracted to anarcho-syndicalist ideas and industrial action to achieve political objectives both before and after the First World War, but these were a minority within the trade union and labour movement. When a General Strike did occur in Britain 1926, the moderate, non-revolutionary character of both wings of the labour movement was clearly demonstrated. The unions showed an impressive collective solidarity in obedience to the strike call, but neither the TUC General Council nor the Labour parliamentary leadership was remotely interested in the strike as a political weapon. Instead the purely industrial character of the dispute was emphasized. The outcome confirmed to both the Labour parliamentary and trade unionist leadership the futility of industrial action for political purposes, and reinforced parliamentarism (Miliband, 1972, p. 151).

Indeed, after the failure of the General Strike in 1926 the trade unions became more committed than ever to the Labour Party. Yet although the unions supplied the bulk of the Labour Party's finance, the majority of places on its National Executive Committee and through their affiliated membership the overwhelming majority of votes at the Labour Party Conference, this power was seldom used to embarrass the Parliamentary leadership at least until the 1960s, despite Conservative claims that the party was effectively controlled by the unions (McKenzie, 1963).

However, trade union attitudes and values strongly coloured the Labour Party's ideology, which arguably remained essentially 'labourist' rather than socialist (Miliband, 1972, p. 61; Saville, 1988). The term 'labourism' implies an ideology which articulates the felt interests of labour, or the working class, involving the protection of free collective bargaining, improvements in living standards and welfare benefits, such as cheap public housing and free health care, but accommodation with, rather than a fundamental challenge to, the dominant economic, social and political order.

Ethical socialism

If Labour began essentially as a trade union party, it always contained socialists, and from 1918 at least was apparently committed to socialist objectives. Yet the extent and nature of the Labour Party's socialism has been contentious since its origins. In marked contrast with some continental socialist parties which began as revolutionary and became reformist over time, Labour began as a trade unionist reformist party which moved tentatively towards socialism. However, it was always unlikely that its brand of socialism would owe much to Marx; instead it involved a blend of the ethical socialism particularly associated with the Independent Labour Party (ILP) and the gradualist and social scientific outlook of the Fabians.

Ethical socialism was sometimes inspired by religion. There has been a significant strand of Christian socialism within Britain, from Kingsley (1819–75) and Maurice (1805–72) in the nineteenth century, through Tawney (1880–1962) and Cripps (1889–1952) in the early and mid-twentieth century, to John Smith and Tony Blair. Some of these Christian socialists were Anglicans and others Roman Catholics, but there were particularly strong links between nonconformism, especially Methodism, and the British labour movement.

For others, socialism was almost a religion itself. Religious language and imagery pervaded much turn-of-the-century socialist propaganda, particularly the Independent Labour Party founded by Keir Hardie in 1893, and one of the three socialist organizations which in 1900 joined with the trade unions to form the Labour Representation Committee. Hardie (1856–1915), Labour's first leader, contrasted the 'glorious Gospel of Socialism' with 'the gospel of selfishness'. John Glasier referred to the 'Religion of Socialism' and the 'sacrament of socialism' (Foote, 1985, p. 34). Such language came easily to working people brought up in an atmosphere of Christian evangelism in nonconformist chapels, and served the same function of conversion to the faith, whether Christian or socialist (Greenleaf, 1983, Vol p. II, 414; Callaghan, 1990, p. 67).

A strong moral element has been evident in British labourist and socialist ideology down to the present day. Socialists were consciously articulating a new morality involving unselfish, cooperative behaviour, which challenged the self-interested individualist assumptions behind classical economics and *laissez-faire* liberalism. This ethical approach emphasized the 'brotherhood of man'. Hardie, and after him most British socialists, explicitly rejected the Marxist doctrine of the class war. The influential Christian socialist, R. H. Tawney, pinned his hopes on education and the development of a new social consciousness.

Yet there was an intellectual fuzziness at the core of this ethical socialism. A thorough-going Marxist analysis was implicitly rejected, but there was little in the way of a convincing alternative theoretical foundation for socialism. Ethical socialism was long on commitment and evangelical fervour, but short on economic and social analysis. Foote's verdict (1985, p. 37) is brutal; 'It was basically a withdrawal from the world, and as such, it was impossible to translate into the practical politics of government.' While the ethical socialist vision could win converts, and thus help win power, it offered little guidance in using power. Visions of the socialist millennium were little help in coping with the pressing problems of the present.

Fabian socialism

The Fabians were in many respects the antithesis of the ILP. If the imagery and rhetoric of the ILP was moralistic and quasi-religious, the Fabians prided themselves on their rational and scientific approach to economic and social issues (Greenleaf, 1983, Vol II, p. 392). While the

ILP recruited working-class activists and aspired to become a mass party, the Fabians began as a small group of middle-class intellectuals, with ambivalent attitudes towards working-class politics. The Fabian Society, founded in 1884, was named after a Roman General who defeated Hannibal by patient delaying tactics (effectively refusing to fight him), and it adopted the emblem of the tortoise on its early publications. Both name and emblem were symbolic of a commitment to gradualist, non-revolutionary socialism. Beyond that there was no party line, and the early Fabians contained a diversity of ideas and a rare array of intellectual talent, including two authors who were to establish a world reputation, Shaw and Wells, a celebrated children's writer, Edith Nesbit, an important if neglected social scientist, Graham Wallas, the neo-Malthusian, Annie Besant and the psychologist, Havelock Ellis. It was, however, Beatrice and Sidney Webb who were to become most closely identified with Fabian socialism (Greenleaf, 1983, Vol. II, p. 381).

Some would deny that the Fabians were socialist, although Sidney Webb (1859–1947) helped draft Clause IV of the Labour Party's constitution in 1918, with its commitment to the common ownership of the means of production, distribution and exchange. Critics of the Fabians have focused on their gradualist parliamentarian strategy for achieving socialism rather than their objectives. The Webbs believed, like Marx, in the inevitable triumph of socialism, but whereas Marx saw this as the result of class conflict and revolution, the Webbs viewed it as the irresistible end-product of the steady growth of state intervention in society, the 'inevitability of gradualness'. Lovingly, Sidney Webb chronicled all the activities once 'abandoned to private enterprise', now controlled or regulated by the state. While many continental socialists saw the existing state apparatus as the enemy, Webb assumed the advance of the state was synonymous with the advance of socialism.

The Webbs believed the trend towards collectivism was irreversible, because state provision was manifestly more efficient than private provision. Good government was essentially a matter of applying the appropriate expertise, based on scientific research and professional training (Greenleaf, 1983, Vol. II, p. 397 ff.). The Webbs themselves were indefatigable researchers; they saw their socialism as essentially dispassionate, rational and scientific. It was also paternalist and elitist. The Fabians were imbued with middle-class attitudes, and despite their early involvement in the Labour Party, initially had little faith in trade unions or the working class. Socialism was to be applied from the top down for the benefit of the working class, rather than won by pressure from below. Their vision of socialism involved scientific administration by disinterested, properly qualified civil servants, and owed more to the British utilitarian tradition than to continental socialism. It was to be achieved by rational persuasion – the Webbs hoped their ideas would permeate society, including the current political establishment, and before the First World War they pressed their recommendations on leading Liberal and Conservative politicians.

This rational, scientific and paternalist socialism was very different from the evangelical and populist socialism of the ILP. Even so, the ideas of the ethical and Fabian socialists were not incompatible. Both had their roots in strands of liberalism – the Fabians in utilitarianism, the ILP in nonconformist radicalism. Both wished to transcend the radical liberal tradition and the labourism associated with trade union-ism. Yet both at the same time rejected the class war, and Marxism. Both were parliamentarist, and, despite the millennial rhetoric employed by the ethical socialists, essentially gradualist. Their role within the Labour Party was, until 1918 at least, complementary rather than competitive. The ILP was the recruiting agent, trying to win the working-class for socialism, the Fabians were more an intellectual think-tank, carrying out policy-oriented research.

After 1918, and the establishment of a national organization for the Labour Party, with individual membership, the ILP lost its distinctive role in recruitment and effectively became a party within a party. With the influx of the 'Red Clydesiders' in the 1920s they also became more revo-lutionary, at least in terms of rhetoric. The resulting tension between a reformist parliamentary leadership and an increasingly critical and radical left ILP ultimately led to disaffiliation from the Labour Party in 1932. Its influence was subsequently marginal. By contrast, the Fabian Society, eclectic and undoctrinaire, has continued to provide a forum for ideas and a research capacity for the Labour Party until the present day.

State socialism and alternatives to state socialism

The ideology of the Labour Party was the product then of four main influences – radical liberalism, trade unionism, Fabianism and ethical socialism (associated initially largely with the ILP). In terms of sheer numbers, organizational strength and financial support, trade unionism was by far the most significant of these contributory elements. Yet, on wider political issues the trade union wing of the labour movement was generally content to defer to the leadership of the parliamentary party, and at this level other influences predominated. Thus the dominant figures in Labour's early history, Keir Hardie its first leader, Ramsay MacDonald its first Prime Minister, and Philip Snowden its first Chancellor of the Exchequer, all came up via the ILP, although Hardie and MacDonald had also been members of the Fabians, whose influence reached a peak after 1918 when Sidney Webb helped to write the new party constitution and joined the Labour governments of 1924 and 1929–31. Nor should the influence of radical liberalism be underestimated. MacDonald's early links with Liberals through the 'Rainbow Circle' were reinforced by his association with anti-war Liberals after 1914, many of whom subsequently joined Labour. Significantly, ex-Liberals figured prominently in MacDonald's governments Figure 4.1).

Socialists disagree as much over means as ends, and the British Labour Party has attracted perhaps more criticism over its strategy than its values. The circumstances in which the Labour Party was founded involved a clear commitment to electoralism and parliamentarism. In contrast with Marxism, syndicalism and anarchism, Labour assumed that the state was benign (Barker, 1978, p. 48), and accepted without question most of the apparatus of the British state. Socialism was to be

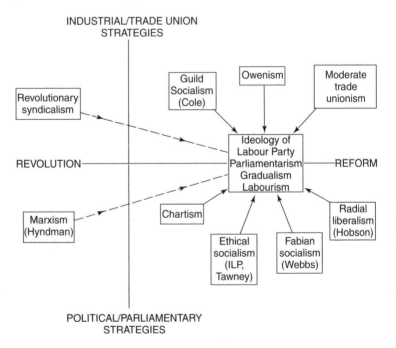

Figure 4.1   Influences on the ideology of the Labour Party

achieved by acquiring, through the ballot box, control of Westminster and Whitehall, winning and using the power of the state. This implied a centralized state socialism, imposed from the top downwards.

Alternatives to this centralized state socialist model were advanced. The roots of early British socialism lay in grassroots working-class self-help. The socialism of Robert Owen and, later, William Morris, was bound up with the life and work of ordinary people, not with the state. The co-operative movement, in which Owen had played a leading part, was an effective practical demonstration of what could be achieved by mutual action. Socialists were also actively involved in local government from the late nineteenth century onwards, pursuing socialism at the grassroots or municipal level. Subsequently, both the co-operative ideal and municipal socialism became absorbed within the labour movement and effectively subordinated to the mainstream goal of securing a parliamentary majority and control of central government. When some Labour councils tried to pursue radical socialist municipal policies, notably at Poplar in the 1920s, 'Poplarism' was outlawed by the courts and effectively disowned by the Labour leadership (Branson, 1979).

Anarcho-syndicalism was a more potent threat to mainstream Labour ideology in the years before the First World War. Anarchists were fundamentally opposed to the state; and syndicalists favoured direct action, including strikes and sit-ins, not just to improve wages and conditions but to secure workers' control of industry. This militant industrial strategy at the level of the workplace was in marked contrast to Labour's state socialism and parliamentarism. Ramsay MacDonald was particularly determined to counter this dangerous heresy, which he identified with the extreme libertarianism of Herbert Spencer rather than socialism (MacDonald, 1911, pp. 123–4).

Revolutionary syndicalism proved rather more influential in France, Italy, Spain, and even the United States than Britain, yet watered-down syndicalist ideas were one strand in a peculiarly British doctrine which flourished particularly in the 1920s – Guild Socialism. Other elements included participative democracy and a rather romantic revulsion against industrial mass production, derived from Ruskin and Morris and the arts and craft movement. Its grassroots emphasis appealed to those who favoured a socialism built from the bottom up, yet Guild Socialism as articulated by it ablest proponent, G. D. H. Cole (1889–1959), involved a compromise with, rather than an alternative to, Fabian collectivism. Cole, unlike the revolutionary syndicalists, rejected neither the state nor parliamentarism. Parliamentary democracy needed to be supplemented with industrial democracy rather than

replaced by it. Thus Cole opposed the syndicalist notion of a revolutionary general strike.

Labour in power? MacDonaldism

One reason why these rival socialist currents of thought ultimately made
little headway after the First World War was because Labour's rapid
advance seemed to confirm the wisdom of the Westminster-centred
electoral strategy. Labour overtook the Liberals in 1922 to become the
second largest party in Parliament, and the official opposition.
Unexpectedly, they soon exchanged opposition for office. In 1924 and
again from 1929–31, MacDonald headed minority Labour governments.
It was questionable how far office involved real power; Labour was constrained by the lack of a parliamentary majority, and this alone ruled
out radical socialist reforms. Yet there were few signs of radical inten-
tions. MacDonald and his colleagues were keen to reassure the political
establishment of their moderation, and they were firmly committed to a
gradualist, one step at a time approach. Their socialism remained an
article of faith, but it was a distant aspiration. For the present they had to
operate the existing capitalist system by traditional methods.

It was Labour's misfortune to be in office from 1929 when the whole
western economic system was in a deepening crisis which failed to
respond to orthodox solutions. From a Labour perspective the crisis was a
crisis of capitalism. Theoretically the remedy was socialism, but there was
no electoral mandate and no parliamentary majority for socialism. Distant
visions of a socialist millennium appeared irrelevant to the urgency of the
immediate situation for which Labour had no remedy. Thus the government was helpless in the face of rising unemployment, and finally broke
up in 1931 in disagreement over the spending cuts demanded by business
and financial interests (Skidelsky, 1967; Marquand, 1977). MacDonald
agreed to stay on as Prime Minister to head a (largely Conservative)
National government, and parted company with his party which was
decimated at the ensuing general election.

For some socialists, 1931 confirmed Communist criticism of Labour
and parliamentarism and led to a revival of interest in the Soviet route
to socialism, ironically at a time when the Stalinist tyranny was at its
worst, culminating in purges and show trials. Others, like the majority
of the ILP, rejected both communism and Labour's gradualist parliamentarism, seeking an alternative 'revolutionary' route to socialism
which was never too well-defined (Brockway, 1977). Yet such defec-

tions ultimately had little impact on the Labour movement, for whom MacDonald and his associates were convenient scapegoats. Thus MacDonald's treachery only demonstrated to his embittered former supporters that he had never really been a socialist. In truth MacDonald's ideas were only too typical of the socialism of the Labour Party, which combined the cautious rational pragmatism of the Fabians and the millennial socialism of the early ILP. The Labour split in 1931 was not essentially ideological. Purged of MacDonald, the new party leadership remained committed to his version of socialism and his gradualist parliamentary strategy – 'MacDonaldism without MacDonald' as Miliband (1972) described it.

Labour in power – the Attlee government

The Second World War and Labour's role in the coalition government from 1940–45 helped to revive the party's fortunes and interest in socialist ideas. The war involved state planning of output, partly presided over by Labour politicians, while alliance with the Soviet Union also rendered central planning more fashionable. Moreover, war both accustomed people to high levels of state activity and state spending and taught them to look to the state to meet peacetime needs. Thus hopes for postwar reconstruction and social reform assumed a large measure of state direction and control. All this was highly consistent with the ideas of the Labour Party, which was well-placed to realize public hopes and expectations after 1945, when it won a landslide parliamentary majority.

Both at the time and for a generation afterwards it was the record of the 1945–51 Attlee government which seemed to embody what the Labour Party meant by socialism – both what it was and what it was not. Labour's continuing commitment to a reformist parliamentary strategy rather than the alternative Soviet approach was clear from its foreign policy, in which it showed strong support for NATO and the American alliance in the developing Cold War with the communist world. The Attlee government's domestic policy involved the establishment of a welfare state, nationalization of key industries to promote a mixed economy, Keynesian economic planning, and the promotion of industrial harmony through partnership with the trade unions. These policies provided the basis of a new political consensus which was to last into the 1970s and essentially involved not the replacement of the capitalist economy by a socialist planned economy, but a modification of capitalism and a qualified acceptance of it.

This was most obviously true of the adoption of Keynesian economic theories, which became a key ingredient of the Labour Party's postwar thought, although Labour politicians such as Bevin and Dalton and a younger generation of Labour thinkers headed by Evan Durbin, Douglas Jay and Gaitskell had advocated the ideas of Keynes rather earlier (Foote, 1986). Acceptance of Keynesian economic theory was thoroughly consistent with Labour's gradualist state socialism. Keynes himself was a committed Liberal, never a socialist. Although critical of many aspects of capitalism, he was in the last resort and essentially a defender of the capitalist system. Keynesian macro-economic planning involved governments attempting to influence aggregate demand through fiscal and monetary policy, and removed the necessity for government intervention at the micro level to determine the output of particular industries. Keynesianism appealed to Labour as it involved planning of a sort. Moreover, for a long time it successfully delivered full employment, a goal which had eluded interwar governments. Yet Keynesian planning was effectively a substitute for, rather than a step towards, full socialist planning as it had previously been understood.

The establishment of a welfare state providing a system of social security 'from the cradle to the grave' drew on socialist values, although it built on reforms achieved by Liberals and Conservatives and on proposals developed under the wartime coalition government. The new system of national insurance derived from the 1942 report of William Beveridge, a lifelong Liberal whose commitment to individual responsibility was embodied in the insurance principle. However, Aneurin Bevan's National Health Service, funded largely from taxation and initially free to all users, was rather more socialist in inspiration.

The further incorporation of trade unions into the political establishment was facilitated by a Labour government with strong organizational links with the trade union movement. Yet this was a process which had been begun as early as the First World War (Middlemas, 1979), and had been promoted by Churchill's coalition government. Whether the arrival of trade union leaders like Ernie Bevin into the heart of government heralded a socialist revolution is, however, to be doubted. It involved rather the high point of a trade unionist or labourist ideology. The trade union movement acquired power and influence on the tacit understanding that this would be exercised moderately, in the national interest. Thus trade unions cooperated in wage restraint policies, as they were to do again in the 1960s and 1970s.

The Labour government's nationalization policies derived more obviously from socialist inspiration, and specifically from Clause IV of the

Party's constitution. Even so, pragmatic rather than ideological arguments were advanced for the nationalization of specific industries,
while the government made clear that its nationalization programme
was limited to the 'commanding heights' of the economy – mainly fuel
and transport. Finally, under the guidance of Herbert Morrison, nationalization took the form of wholly state-owned public corporations, run by
appointed managers rather than the workers. Although a significant
section of industry was now publicly owned, implying a 'mixed' rather
than a capitalist economy, critics argued it involved 'state capitalism'
rather than socialism.

Yet the Attlee government retained substantial public support, demon-
strating that Labour's version of socialism was compatible with parliamentary democracy. The achievement was also fairly durable, lasting
substantially for a generation. Labour's values were effectively incorpo-
rated into a cross-party consensus, variously described but sometimes
called social democratic. Even so, the Attlee government's very success
left an awkward legacy for the Labour Party. From the perspective of the
leadership, Labour's programme was essentially completed by the
1945–51 government. It was not the first instalment of a socialist transformation of Britain's economy and society, but the culmination of that
mixture of radical liberalism, trade unionism and Fabianism which was
the essence of British socialism. Attlee, Bevin and Morrison had fulfilled
their strictly limited socialist revolution, leaving their successors with little
more to do than defend that achievement. A problem which only became
apparent later was the extent to which it depended on its least socialist
element, Keynesian economic theory. The apparent breakdown of
Keynesian analysis and prescription in the 1970s not only challenged
much of Labour's case for government economic intervention and a
mixed economy, but also undermined the viability of the welfare state.

Revisionism, fundamentalism and pragmatism

Theoretical justification for Labour's policies lagged somewhat behind
practice. Although several Labour politicians and thinkers such as
Morrison, Dalton and, from a younger generation, Evan Durbin and
Douglas Jay contributed to the evolution of Labour ideas in the 1930s
and 1940s (Foote, 1986, ch. 9), it was only after Labour was once more
in opposition from 1951 that a comprehensive attempt was made to
update the party's ideology to bring it more in line with what a Labour
government had actually tried to do.

The most significant contribution to this reappraisal was Tony Crosland's *The Future of Socialism* (1956), which sharpened, although it did not inaugurate, a developing ideological schism within the Labour Party between social democracy and a more fundamentalist socialism. The schism effectively began with Nye Bevan's resignation from the Attlee government in 1951 over the introduction of health service charges. It developed into a personalized division between the supporters of Bevan and those of his arch rival of the right, Hugh Gaitskell, which survived the deaths of both the leading protagonists to become a long-running and deep-seated struggle between left and right factions for the soul of the party from the 1960s through to the 1980s.

Crosland thought he was redefining rather than abandoning socialism. 'Revisionism' is a term widely employed, especially by Marxists, to describe efforts to moderate or water down socialism. Crosland (1956, p. 2) was certainly dismissive of Marxism. 'In my view Marx has little to offer the contemporary socialist either in respect of practical policy, or of the correct analysis of our society, or even of the right conceptual tools or framework.' Yet Crosland was 'revising' a party ideology which had never been Marxist, and only moderately socialist. He argued that capitalism in its old nineteenth century sense no longer existed. It had been transformed out of all recognition by progressive taxation, welfare reforms and state enterprise, but above all by the divorce of ownership from effective control of industry. Thus ownership of the means of production was no longer critical. What was required was professional management, coupled with effective influence and control in the public interest. This was compatible with various forms of ownership – Crosland's own preference was for a pluralistic diversity of forms, a genuinely mixed economy. Yet socialism was essentially not about nationalization but the pursuit of equality, through universal social benefits, progressive taxation and the redistribution of the product of economic growth.

Although this revisionist socialism substantially reflected Labour's record in office, it was less compatible with the party's explicit Clause IV commitment to common ownership. Modernizers believed that this commitment to nationalization alienated voters, so following a third successive election defeat in 1959 the party leader, Hugh Gaitskell, campaigned to drop Clause IV, and even canvassed a change of the party name (Jenkins, 1991). Gaitskell's attempt to change the party failed yet his old supporters continued to act as a faction within the party through to the 1980s when some of them broke away to form the SDP. Retrospectively it could be said that they always stood for social democracy rather than socialism within the Labour Party, although Crosland for one continued to proclaim his socialism until his death in 1977.

The left initially fought an essentially defensive battle which did not involve any elaborate ideological reformulation, although it subsequently gained some inspiration from a variety of sources, including the academic Marxist New Left and various radical social movements – most notably the peace movement and the women's movement. In the 1970s the left renewed its attempt to commit the party, in line with Clause IV, to an extensive further programme of nationalization including the banking and building industries, and the encouragement of workers' co-operatives.

The most bitter conflicts between the Labour left and right were not, however, ostensibly over rival interpretations of socialism, but over party organization, and over defence and foreign policy issues. Disputes over party organization reflected different interpretations of internal party democracy, but ultimately were about power to control the party agenda and leadership. Bitter divisions over nuclear disarmament in part stemmed from a strong moralistic and quasi-pacifist tradition which Labour inherited from the Liberals, although behind the issue of the bomb were also differences over the western alliance which reflected contrasting assumptions about the objectives of the superpowers, the USA and the USSR. Yet the most bitter issue dividing left and right in the 1970s and early 1980s was the European Community. It was not initially so, when supporters and opponents of EC membership could be found on both wings of the party. Subsequently Europe became the crucial test of allegiance, with the social democratic right championing membership and the socialist left demanding withdrawal.

Between the left and right were those who sought balance and compromise in the interests of party unity. As a 'broad church', the Labour movement has always contained a range of interests and tendencies, including social reformers, both moderate and militant trade unionists, and various kinds of socialists. Moreover, Labour could only achieve power in Britain's parliamentary system if it could retain the commitment of both its socialist left and reformist right. Arguably, the preservation of some ambiguity over ultimate values and objectives was necessary to keep different factions happy. Thus Labour leaders Wilson, Callaghan and Foot all tried to preserve a pragmatic balance between left and right.

Critics argued that Harold Wilson, in his 1964–70 and 1974–76 Labour governments, was more concerned with day-to-day party management and presentation than longer-term socialist objectives.

Wilson's death in 1995 assisted a more positive reappraisal, already underway, of the achievements of his governments, which secured a significant expansion in educational opportunities and presided over modest progress towards a more equal and tolerant society (Pimlott, 1992). Even so they did little to advance or further define British socialism, but involved an increasingly desperate defence of the 'social democratic consensus' established by the Attlee government which, by the 1970s, was under threat. Keynesian economic management no longer appeared effective. Industrial compromise had broken down and the union alliance had become an electoral liability. The nationalized industries and the whole concept of a mixed economy was under ideological assault. Even the welfare state appeared to be failing in important respects and to be under threat, with taxpayers increasingly unwilling to meet its escalating costs.

Callaghan, Wilson's successor, embodied both the strengths and limitations of labourism. He had earlier frustrated Wilson's attempt to reform industrial relations, and as Prime Minister he pursued to breaking point Labour's 'contentious alliance' with the trade unions until incomes policy finally fell apart in the 'Winter of Discontent'. Neither in his earlier spell as Chancellor of the Exchequer (which culminated in devaluation in 1967) nor as Prime Minister was he largely responsible for the economic problems over which he presided, yet he had no convincing answers to those problems either, and further contributed to the reputation for economic mismanagement which dogged his party. Indeed, with Labour in apparently terminal disarray after electoral defeat in 1979, it long appeared that Callaghan would be his party's last Prime Minister.

Socialism inside and outside the Labour Party

Both Marxist and revisionist critics suggest that Labour's ideology was always 'labourist' rather than socialist or even social democratic. Marxist socialists coined the term to describe and criticize the cautious reformism and parliamentarism of the Labour Party (Miliband, 1972; Saville, 1988). Social democrats on the right of the party employed the same term to describe the class politics associated with the trade-union link. While the Marxist left assumed a class-conflict model and the need to replace capitalism by socialism, the social democrat right, by contrast, sought to reform rather than abolish capitalism To them, labourism stood for an outdated class politics which they hoped to transcend (Foote, 1986, pp. 230–2; Marquand, 1999).

Socialists who despaired of the prospects for socialism through the Labour Party generally discovered that those prospects were hopeless outside it; thus a succession of left-wing parties have failed to make any headway in Britain. The Communist Party, founded in 1920, has never secured the election of more than two MPs, and none since 1950. The Independent Labour Party found it could not survive outside Labour after it disaffiliated in 1932. Common Wealth failed to outlast the unusual war-time circumstances which assisted its establishment in 1942. More recently, the Socialist Workers Party, Scargill's Socialist Labour Party and the Socialist Alliance have had little impact. Yet those social democrats who despaired of reforming Labour also, ultimately, found it no easier to build a viable progressive alternative to Labour.

Although Labour managed to see off potential rivals on the left, it still faced the most serious crisis of its history in the 1980s. This was not just an electoral crisis or a membership crisis but an ideological crisis (Whiteley, 1983). The ideological crisis in part reflected the continuing internal battle for the party's soul but this was soon dwarfed by wider shifts in political thinking nationally and globally. For most of the twentieth century, Labour, whether in government or opposition, had seen the ideological tide flowing it its direction – towards increased welfare provision and planning. After 1979 the collectivist tide was receding and Labour had to adjust to altered circumstances. 'Thatcherism' was to change the Labour Party almost as much as it changed the Conservative Party. Worldwide, the prospects for socialism of any kind seemed more problematic, particularly following the collapse of the Soviet Union. These shocks compelled some ideological reassessment. The transition to 'New Labour' is discussed separately, in Chapter 10.

Further reading

Crick's (1987) useful, if idiosyncratic, introduction to socialism includes short extracts from British texts, while Wright (1983) has introduced and edited a one-volume reader. Two commentaries on the development of British socialist thought can be recommended, Foote (1986) and Callaghan (1990). Sassoon (1997) provides a stimulating overview of the history of the West European left which helps to place British socialism in context.

From the massive literature on specific aspects and periods the following are worth a mention (in rough order of subject matter): Thompson's (1980) classic but controversial account of the rise of the

English working class in the early nineteenth century, Pierson (1973) on Marxism and British socialism, Pelling (1965) on the early history of the Labour Party, Miliband (1972) on parliamentary socialism, Saville (1988) on labourism, and Minkin (1992) on the labour–trade union link. Morgan (1992) contains insights into Labour politicians, and among specialized biographies Marquand (1977) on MacDonald, Pimlott (1992) on Wilson and Morgan (1997) on Callaghan are particularly useful.

5

Nationalism

Introduction

Nationalism is theoretically thin, and its ideological credentials have been questioned. Yet if ideologies are 'action-oriented', nationalism has demonstrably influenced political behaviour over the last two centuries, more so perhaps than supposedly 'mainstream' ideologies. Men and women have been prepared to die for their nation, and to kill for it. Today the nation state and nationalism face contrasting pressures towards globalization on the one hand, and devolution of power downwards to regions and local communities on the other. Yet nationalism continues to confound predictions of its impending demise, retaining and even increasing its appeal in advanced industrial or post-industrial countries, in former communist states, and in the developing world.

Britain's status as a mature nation state long seemed uncontroversial. The nationalist principle was something to be applied to others: to Greece, Italy, Hungary, Rumania or Poland. Although British governments were increasingly forced to confront Irish nationalism and, subsequently, nationalist movements in Britain's overseas empire, nationalism within Britain itself remained largely unproblematic, until around the 1960s and 1970s. Then the demise of empire accompanied by 'coloured' immigration into Britain, the resurgence of Irish nationalism in Northern Ireland coupled with the growing strength of Scottish and Welsh nationalism and the issue of Britain's relations with Europe all combined to raise issues of national identity and the future of the British or UK state. The programme of devolution implemented from 1997 and the revived controversy over the European Union are in large part the product of these pressures, but raise further issues of allegiance, power and sovereignty which are fundamental to the future politics and government of these islands and their relationship with their neighbours. Nationalist ideas, in some shape or form, are now of paramount importance for political institutions and behaviour in Britain, as they have long been elsewhere.

What is nationalism?

Nationalism presupposes the existence of nations, but it is not easy to define a nation. It is essentially a community of people, bound together by some characteristic such as a common language, religion, culture or ethnicity. Yet, in the last resort there are no satisfactory objective criteria – a nation exists where a people feel they constitute a nation. Nations exist in the minds of their members. They are 'imagined communities' (B. Anderson, 1991).

The concern here is with nationalism as a political doctrine. Some writers distinguish between political and cultural nationalism. The celebrated early German nationalist, Herder, was concerned with German language and culture, not political formations. Yet where the nation is regarded as the natural focus for pride and loyalty this almost inevitably has wider political implications, involving demands for some autonomy and, more usually, full independence as a sovereign state. Thus Ernest Gellner (1983) succinctly defines nationalism as 'a political principle which holds that the political and the national unit should be congruent.' In other words, nations should form states, and states should consist of nations. This is commonly taken to mean an independent sovereign state, with a monopoly of coercive powers within its own borders, and free from external interference. However, nationalist sentiment may sometimes perhaps be satisfied with a form of devolved government which falls short of sovereign independence.

Nationalism is an ideology which can have a general application. The Italian nationalist Mazzini argued that the world (or at least Europe) was divided naturally into nations, which should each form states, and coexist in international peace and harmony. The American President Woodrow Wilson likewise hoped that applying the principle of national self-determination would end the wars caused by aggressive competing dynastic empires and inaugurate a new era of world peace.

Yet most nationalists have been less concerned, if at all, with nationalism as a general principle, and have concentrated almost exclusively on the rights and qualities of a particular nation. Indeed, for Breuilly (1993, p. 2) a basic assertion of nationalism is that the interests and values of the nation take priority over all other interests and values. The implication is that loyalty to one's nation should override all over interests and loyalties – to self, family, tribe, class or religion. Success in competition with other nations, in the military, economic or even the sporting arena may provide gratifying confirmation of the particular merit or virtue of the nation, strengthening national loyalty and pride.

When and why nationalism developed

Nationalists commonly maintain that nations are ancient, their origins lost in prehistory, and that nationalist demands developed naturally as peoples became conscious of their national identities and their right to self-determination. Academics generally perceive nations as of comparatively recent origin. According to Greenfeld (1992, p. 14), 'The original modern idea of the nation emerged in sixteenth century England, which was the first nation in the world' and, she adds, 'the only one for about two hundred years.' Others would discern national consciousness developing early elsewhere (Smith, 1991; Kellas, 1991). However, most accounts of the ideology of nationalism see it originating in the late eighteenth or early nineteenth century (Hobsbawm, 1990; Gellner, 1991; Breuilly, 1993; Alter 1994).

Kedourie (1993, p. 1) bluntly declares 'nationalism was a doctrine invented in Europe at the beginning of the nineteenth century'. The French revolution was the catalyst. The revolutionaries denied the conventional assumption that states were the property of their ruling dynasty, and claimed instead that supreme power or sovereignty was derived from the people, the French nation. Such a principle could be applied to governments generally. The French revolution directly encouraged Italian and Polish nationalism and helped stimulate German, Spanish and Russian nationalism, both in imitation of, and in reaction against, French nationalism.

Some critics would argue that nationalism spread through elite manipulation rather than through growing popular consciousness of national identities. Kedourie (from the right) blamed the subversive propaganda of liberal intellectuals, while alternatively some socialists argued that dominant classes fomented nationalist ideas to divert the workers (who 'had no country') from their common economic interests and class loyalty. There is something in the insinuation of elite manipulation. Particular nationalist causes involved much reinterpretation and sometimes invention of history, and the creation of new national myths and symbols. Moreover, new nation states were commonly forged by a relatively small intellectual elite, and a mass national consciousness fostered subsequently. Gellner (1983, p. 55) tartly observes, 'It is nationalism which engenders nations, and not the other way around.' Thus the Italian nationalist d'Azeglio (1792–1886) declared 'We have made Italy; now we must make Italians' (Hobsbawm, 1991, p. 111).

Yet the importance of nationalist ideas and propaganda may be exaggerated. Gellner (1983, p. 125) explicitly criticizes Kedourie for treating nationalism 'as a contingent, avoidable aberration, accidentally spawned by European thinkers'. Eric Hobsbawm, working within a broadly Marxist theoretical framework, makes a similar point. It is not ideas, like nationalism, which change history; instead, new ideas are articulated in response to historical change. Nationalism was the consequence of industrial modernization, which required the breakdown of traditional and local restraints on trade, a mass, fluid and mobile society, and the development of a national economy. It also required, as previous agrarian societies had not, mass education and mass literacy involving in turn a standardization of language, officially recognized and taught, in place of the essentially local or regional dialects and cultures which predominated earlier. Indeed, nationalism has been attributed to a revolution in the technology of communication (Deutsch, 1966), an argument supported by Gellner (1983, p. 127): 'It is the media themselves, the importance of abstract, centralized, standardized, one to many communication, which itself automatically engenders the core idea of nationalism.'

Compatible with the linking of nationalism with industrial modernization is a quasi-sociological/psychological explanation which points to the needs of individuals in a modern atomized mass society to find some identity or allegiance to which they can attach themselves, following the breakdown of traditional ties and communities under modern industrial capitalism. Thus nationalism is the consequence, not the cause (as Kedourie implies) of the breakdown of other allegiances.

One implication of identifying the rise of nationalism with a particular phase of historical development is that another phase might see its decline or extinction. Indeed, just as nationalism has been identified with modern industrial society, so it has been suggested that it is incompatible with post-modern, post-industrial global economy and society. This may eventually prove to be the case, but there are few signs as yet of nationalism's imminent demise. Its continuing appeal in changed circumstances suggests it may answers some psychological need in modern humanity.

Varieties of nationalism

For two centuries the simple core principle of nationalism has been that nations should form states. Even so, the ideas with which nationalism has been associated have changed quite considerably. Indeed nationalism has a chameleon quality, taking colour from its ideological context. Thus while most other political ideologies can be readily placed on the conventional left–right political spectrum, nationalism has been promiscuously associated with ideas across the spectrum. Accordingly, Freeden (1996, p. 7; 1998) suggests that nationalism is not a distinctive ideology but a component of other ideologies. Here it is argued that nationalism is a distinctive ideology in so far as it prioritizes the nation over other interests and values, although it is acknowledged that it can take a wide variety of forms.

It began as a revolutionary doctrine, posing a profound threat to the prevailing social and political order in Europe in the early nineteenth century. The idea that political authority should derive from the nation was particularly damaging to foreign dynasties, or those who ruled over multi-national states. Nationalism threatened Russian rule in Poland and Finland, Austrian rule in north Italy, Hungary, Czech Bohemia and elsewhere. Much of this rule was associated with absolutism and reaction and thus opposed by liberals who sought individual political freedoms and constitutional reform. Thus liberalism and nationalism in the early nineteenth century were closely linked. Individual self-determination appeared to go hand in hand with national self-determination. Popular sovereignty entailed both the extension of political rights and the creation of states by national communities.

A distinction is sometimes drawn between unification nationalism and separation nationalism. Where a nation was divided into several independent states (for example nineteenth century Italy and Germany), nationalists sought unification to form a single nation state. Where a nation was part of a multi-national state (for example the Hapsburg empire) nationalists sought separation. Application of the principle of self-determination thus depended on circumstance.

Yet early liberal nationalists tended to assume limits to the establishment of independent nation states. States had to be economically, politically and militarily viable, which implied a certain minimum threshold size and defensible frontiers, as well as a developed national consciousness. Very small states seemed inconsistent with economic modernization and cultural progress. Mazzini envisaged a Europe divided into no more than 12 nation states (of which Ireland was not one). John Stuart Mill's support for the nationalist principle in general did not extend to Bretons and Basques, who, he argued, benefited by being brought within 'the current of ideas and feelings of a highly civilised and cultivated people – to be a member of the French nationality.' Progress involved the extinction of the Breton nation. Almost parenthetically, Mill suggested that the same was true of Scottish Highlanders or the Welsh, with reference to Britain (Mill, 1861, 1972 edition, p. 395).

This 'threshold principle', as it has been termed, was subsequently largely abandoned (Hobsbawm, 1990, 1994) and self-determination was applied to some relatively small and poor nations, most notably in the Balkans, leading to the derogatory expression 'Balkanization' to describe the proliferation of small, potentially unstable states. Yet there was never any clear criteria to determine limits to the process. Thus the American President Woodrow Wilson was confronted with demands for self-determination from peoples of whom he had never previously heard in his attempts to apply the principle to Europe at the end of the First World War.

A more intractable problem was the inter-settlement of peoples and the continued existence of national minorities within new nation states. The application of self-determination is necessarily an untidy affair at best, with undesired consequences for the resulting minorities. The national principle often proved inimical to the individual rights which liberals championed. Thus the creation of new nation states could involve the denial of minority rights and sometimes expulsions, forced transfers of population, and even extermination, or 'ethnic cleansing'. To the disillusion of some early liberal nationalists, rival national interests within and between states subsequently appeared a spur to conflict and war rather than international cooperation and peace.

But if some liberals became disenchanted with nationalism, some conservatives increasingly found it useful as a political creed which could be harnessed in the interests of the existing social order. While in the early nineteenth century the concept of the nation was invoked against the state, once nation and state were conflated, an official state-sponsored nationalism could be utilized against radicals and socialists preaching class conflict and revolution. Patriotism appeared to transcend class loyalties. Moreover, in the increasingly important struggle for working class votes, nationalism proved a cheaper and more effective alternative to social reform (see for example Beer, 1982, p. 272).

Much of the nationalism of the late nineteenth century and early twentieth centuries was also more assertive and aggressive than the earlier essentially liberal nationalism of Mazzini and others. Instead of proclaiming the universal rights to self-determination of all national communities, it involved advancing the claims of particular nations, often at the expense of other national interests. Behind it there were more competitive assumptions, bound up with Darwinian notions of the survival of the fittest in international relations. Strong nations could and indeed should flourish at the expense of their weaker adversaries. Economic, diplomatic and military success could be attributed to the superior virtues of the nation. To the dismay of those liberals and socialists who championed international brotherhood, the mass of workers in all western European countries demonstrated the overriding strength of their national allegiances in 1914.

The nationalism of western European countries was also closely bound up with colonialism and imperialism. The rights to self-determination proclaimed for peoples in Europe were rarely applied to peoples in Africa and Asia. They were 'lesser breeds without the law', incapable of self-government. Indeed, such comforting assumptions of cultural and racial superiority enabled Europeans to see imperialism as an idealistic crusade – a 'white-man's burden' to bring good government, religion and civilisation to 'primitive peoples'. The easy acquisition of colonial empires (secured with modern weaponry) confirmed for Europeans the superiority of the white man in general, and their own nation in particular (see Chapter 6).

Both assertive nationalism and imperialism were closely (although not exclusively) associated with the right and conservatism. The concept of national community fitted comfortably with an organic theory of state and society, advanced by some conservative thinkers in opposition to the atomized individualism of liberalism. Although nationalism is a product of the modern world it derives much of its appeal from the past. Thus the history of the emerging nation is portrayed in terms of key defining moments, of brave struggles by national heroes, of potent historical myths and symbols. Even ruling dynasties of foreign descent could, through the rediscovery or invention of appropriate traditions or ceremonies, hope to identify themselves with the national spirit. In Britain, coronations, jubilees and other more routine ceremonial occasions such as the trooping of the colour or the state opening of parliament, helped to promote a nationalist sentiment steeped in tradition, even if some of that tradition was of relatively recent origin (Cannadine, in Donald and Hall, 1986).

However, if nationalism could become associated with such (real or imagined) traditional values, in some countries such as Japan and Turkey it was aggressively employed as an instrument of modernization by a ruling order determined to overcome traditional practices and loyalties which were seen as an obstacle to progress. Here a state-sponsored nationalism deliberately rejected traditional culture and dress, encouraging alien western ways as part of a process of national regeneration. This confirms further the chameleon character of the ideology.

Both the traditional and modernizing implications of nationalism were present in fascism, which was perhaps the most extreme manifestation of the ideology, employing racist ideas to establish the superiority of specific national communities over others. German nationalism from the late eighteenth century was based particularly on German language and culture, but some German nationalists went on to claim that the German volk were a distinctive race which could be marked off from Slavs, or Latins or Jews. (Fascism and racism are explored in more detail in Chapter 6).

Although nationalism became closely associated with the right and particularly the far right in Europe in the late nineteenth and the first half of the twentieth century, there were also nationalist movements which were supported by socialists, particularly those which involved resistance against colonialism and imperialism. At first sight, socialism and nationalism appear incompatible. Socialism essentially involved a reaction against, and an alternative to, capitalism. For a socialist the fundamental divisions in human society were economic class divisions, and the common interests of the working class transcended national boundaries. Socialism, in theory at least, proclaimed the universal brotherhood of man.

Yet socialists had to provide some explanation for nationalism and imperialism. Lenin neatly linked the phenomenon of imperialism with another problem for Marxists – improved living standards for the working classes in advanced capitalist countries, which ran counter to predictions of increasing proletarian misery which would ultimately provoke revolution. For Lenin, imperialism enabled advanced capitalism to postpone the collapse predicted by Marx. Exploitation of peoples and resources in other continents allowed western capitalist states to avoid intensifying the exploitation of their own working class, who instead would reap some of the rewards of imperialism.

Yet for Marxists, and indeed most socialists, imperialism involved exploitation which should be opposed and resisted. Thus they supported anti-colonial movements, which, in demanding freedom and independence from the colonial power, inevitably borrowed the terminology and ideas of European nationalism, using against them their own slogans of freedom, equality and self-determination. They often also employed the language of socialism which could be readily applied to their own situation. Their leaders, largely western-educated, imbibed western socialist teaching, particularly Marxism, although some of them also discerned a distinctive form of socialism in their own native cultures. Thus socialism and anti-colonial nationalism became closely linked.

The extent to which socialism and nationalism are ultimately compatible remains contentious. If nationalism requires an overriding loyalty to the nation (Breuilly, 1992, p. 2) this presents problems for socialists. As Hobsbawm (1989, p. 125) tartly observes 'any Marxists who are not, at least in theory, prepared to see the "interests" of their own country or people subordinated to wider interests, had best reconsider their ideological loyalties'. Yet other socialists and Marxists have seen no incompatibility between their nationalist and socialist convictions (Nairn, 1981, 2000). The argument partly depends on the definition of nationalism, and the extent to which nationalism is, or is not, exclusive.

Anti-colonial nationalism clearly involved separation from the colonial state, and separatist nationalism has generally predominated over unification nationalism in the modern world (Table 5.1). The break-up of the Soviet Union provided a further stimulus to separatist nationalism in Eastern Europe, while even some of the mature nation states of Western Europe such as Spain, France and Italy have faced significant separatist movements. Some, but not all, of these reflect economic inequality or 'uneven development' within the state, and the reaction of a relatively deprived 'periphery' against a more prosperous 'core'. It is sometimes described as 'peripheral nationalism'.

Regarding contemporary expressions of nationalism a distinction is sometimes drawn between civic nationalism and ethnic nationalism. Civic nationalism is related to liberal nationalism; it is inclusive rather than exclusive in the sense that 'all permanent residents fully enjoy the human rights conferred by citizenship, irrespective of ethnic criteria'. It is also compatible with other identities and loyalties, both within and outside the nation. Ethnic nationalism by contrast relates the nation to a specific ethnic group (which might be based on race, tribe, language or culture). Thus it excludes from the nation residents who lack the appropriate ethnic qualification. Ethnic nationalism commonly also requires an overriding loyalty to the nation which subordinates or excludes other identities and loyalties. In its more extreme manifestations it is chauvinist, xenophobic, ethnocentric and racist (Griffin in Eatwell and Wright, 1999, pp. 154–5).

Nations and states in Britain

If nationalism requires that nations should form independent states and states should consist of nations, there is an immediate difficulty in applying the ideology to Britain, where the very identity of state and

Table 5.1   Varieties of nationalism

Type of nationalism	Associated ideas	Countries	Politicians/thinkers
Revolutionary nationalism	Popular sovereignty, national sovereignty	Revolutionary France and client states	Rousseau, Abbe Sieyes
Cultural nationalism	Language and culture	Germany early 19th century, Wales 19th century	Herder
Liberal nationalism	National self-determination, constitutionalism, minority rights, Threshhold principle, Europe of nations, Free trade	Unification nationalism: German. Italy Separation nationalism: Greece, Belgium, Hungary, Poland	Mazzini John Stuart Mill
Conservative nationalism	Patriotism, social integration, national unity fatherland, imperialism, social Darwinism, economic protection, autarky	Bismarck's Germany, Czarist Russia, Late 19th century Britain and France	Bismarck List Disraeli Joseph Chamberlain Renan
Modernization nationalism	Modernity, industrialization, westernization, breach with tradition	Japan from 19th century Turkey in 20th century	Kemal Attaturk

Table 5.1 Varieties of nationalism *cont.*

Type of nationalism	Associated ideas	Countries	Politicians/thinkers
Fascist and Nazi nationalism	Fascist totalitarian state, New Roman empire Germany: 'blood and soil', 'Ein Volk, ein Reich, ein Fuhrer', (Master) race, racial purity, racial persecution, extermination of minorities	Fascist Italy, Nazi Germany, Rumania, etc. Vichy France? Japan to 1945? S. America: Peronism?	Houston Chamberlain, Hitler, Mussolini Mosley
Anti-colonial nationalism	Colonial freedom, socialist nationalism? Imperialism as the higher stage of capitalism	India Southeast Asia Africa continent	Lenin, Stalin Gandhi Mandela
Modern separation nationalism	Language, culture, national identity, federalism, internationalism	Scotland, Wales, Baltic states, Basques, former Yugoslavia	Hugh MacDiarmid Tom Nairn

nation is clouded in ambiguity. The state is officially the United Kingdom of Great Britain and Northern Ireland, but is often referred to as the UK, Great Britain or simply Britain while part of the state, England, is commonly confused with the whole. It is sometimes suggested that this political unit constitutes a nation state, implying a single 'British' nationality. Yet the historian Norman Davies (1999, p. 870) categorically maintains, 'The United Kingdom is not, and never has been, a nation-state.' More commonly, the United Kingdom is reckoned to include four nations, English, Scots, Welsh and Irish. Some of those living within the United Kingdom claim a dual national allegiance – British and Irish, or British and Scots, while others arbitrarily describe themselves as English or British depending on mood or circumstances. There are also members of ethnic minorities who are full citizens of the United Kingdom, but whose national identity and allegiance is doubtful in the eyes of others, and sometimes perhaps to themselves.

Many of these difficulties surrounding national identity are derived from the history of the British Isles and its changing political units (Davies, 1999). England was politically united from the tenth century, with strong links with Scandinavia until the Norman conquest, and then with France until the fifteenth century. From the sixteenth century, under the Tudors, an English national consciousness developed (Greenfeld, 1992). Wales was politically subject to the English crown from the thirteenth century and Wales was formally united with England in 1536 in the reign of Henry VIII. The Welsh themselves had little say in the process of absorption under English rule. They retained their own language and culture, but this seemed under threat by the nineteenth century. Ireland was more erratically controlled by the English monarchy from the twelfth century, but unlike Britain remained obstinately Catholic, apart from Ulster which was forcibly settled by Scottish Protestants from the seventeenth century. In 1801 it was politically united with England under an Act of Union.

It was rather different with Scotland which existed for several centuries as an independent state with its own crown, parliament and legal system, although it had a troubled relationship with its powerful southern neighbour, and might like Wales have been brought under English rule from the reign of Edward I had not the exploits of William Wallace and Robert the Bruce preserved Scottish independence, eloquently asserted in the Declaration of Arbroath of 1320, for another three centuries. While Scottish nationalists have derived powerful inspiration from these early indications of a separate national consciousness, it is not clear how far it extended beyond a tiny elite. Moreover, Scotland was internally divided almost throughout its history, with clan rivalry in the highlands and conflicts between rival noble families in the lowlands on top of old ethnic and linguistic divisions. To these divisions was added religious conflict in the sixteenth century, when John Knox converted most of Scotland to Protestantism and transformed Scotland's external relations from the 'auld alliance' with France against England to a common Anglo-Scottish interest in resisting Catholic France and Spain. The succession of James VI of Scotland to the English throne in 1603 ensured that Scottish and English interests remained closely entangled throughout the seventeenth century. The combination of Scottish presbyterianism and English puritanism effectively destroyed the government of Charles I, while Scottish and English interests were involved in both the restoration of the Stuarts in 1660 and the 'Glorious Revolution' of 1688.

The Union with Scotland in 1707 created a British state, symbolized by the figure of Britannia on coins, and celebrated in Thomas Arne's patriotic anthem, 'Rule Britannia'. Although Scottish nationalists have generally regarded the Act of Union of 1707 as a craven betrayal of Scottish interests by the old Scottish Parliament (see for example Nairn, 2000, pp. 93–9), many educated Scots willingly acquiesced in their new designation as North British and the incorporation of the Cross of St Andrew into the Union Jack. Advocates of the Union in Scotland saw positive benefits in terms of peace, security for the Scottish religion, a degree of political freedom, and, most of all, trade. Subsequently, although not necessarily as a consequence of Union, Scotland enjoyed a flowering of economic, intellectual and cultural life in the eighteenth century.

Nationalism in nineteenth-century Britain

Thus nationalism in its early nineteenth-century liberal form as a political doctrine asserting the right to national self-determination appeared to have little relevance to Britain. Britain was already a nation state which did not need to be freed from foreign rule or united. Nationalism was a principle to be applied to others. British politicians and intellectuals gave enthusiastic support to a whole range of nationalist causes abroad – notably Greek, Belgian, Hungarian, Polish and Italian nationalism. There was in the nineteenth century no significant movement for Scottish or Welsh independence. Ireland of course was a very different matter, although Britain's rulers continued to regard Ireland as an integral part of the Union until Gladstone became converted to Irish Home Rule in 1886.

Nationalism in its later nineteenth-century version as a political doctrine asserting the primacy of national loyalties over other loyalties, and glorying in the superiority of one's own nation over other nations was deliberated stimulated in Britain – by the revival or invention of ritual, through the arts and popular culture (particularly the music hall) and through education. British nationalism and imperialism became key ingredients of Conservatism from the late nineteenth century, but were also enthusiastically endorsed by large sections of the Liberal and Labour Parties. British colonial acquisitions, and British victories in wars, provided convincing confirmation of national superiority.

All this implies a conscious attempt by the rulers of the British state to secure the full political integration of its once separate elements. Indeed, the new officially sponsored British identity never succeeded in obliterating older national loyalties. Ireland in particular obstinately maintained a distinctive Irish national identity, which was intensified rather than destroyed by the Act of Union of 1801. A sense of Scottish nationhood also persisted. The writer Sir Walter Scott helped to invent a powerful romantic tartan culture, which was enthusiastically adopted by the British royal family and did much for the tourist trade, but had little to do with any incipient Scottish nationalism. Indeed, Britain's ruling class came to appreciate that a 'state-fostered cult of a depoliticized Scottish identity' was a more reliable tactic for securing Scotland's allegiance than cultural integration (Crick, 1991, p. 91). Significantly, also, the most numerous participants in the British state maintained an attachment to 'England' which was proudly or sentimentally celebrated by poets from Blake to Tennyson and Rupert Brooke.

Scottish and Welsh nationalism

While Irish nationalism was clearly a significant political factor throughout the nineteenth century, and led ultimately to the 1916 rising and the creation of a separate Irish state from 1922, most Scots and Welsh then seemed content with their participation in the industrial growth and imperial expansion of the British state, from which, it could be argued, they profited economically and politically. Although a strong consciousness of separate national identities persisted which had some basis in real differences, a distinctive religious, legal and educational system in Scotland and a surviving Welsh language and culture, this national consciousness did not develop then into demands for national independence as it had done in Ireland and over much of the continent of Europe. Substantial support for nationalism in the sense of full independence for Scotland and Wales is very recent. Plaid Cymru was only founded in 1925 and the Scottish National Party (SNP) in 1928 (Marr, pp. 1992, 63–7) and neither achieved much electoral success before the late 1960s.

The British or UK state made some concessions to national sentiment in Scotland and Wales. Thus Scotland, which already had its own system of courts, local government and education, acquired a Secretary for Scotland from 1885, while Scottish administration was progressively reorganised and rationalized under a largely autonomous Scottish Office in the course of the twentieth century. Wales, which had (and still has) similar administrative legal and educational systems to those in England, did not acquire a minister until 1951, and a full Secretary of State with a separate Welsh Office only in 1964. Yet from the late nineteenth century onwards there were also concessions to Welsh national feeling on religion, temperance, education and the use of the Welsh language in administrative and judicial proceedings, and on television.

The rapid loss of empire and great power status after the Second World War relegated Scotland and Wales to the declining periphery of a shrunken British state. Moreover, partly because of their peripheral location, both suffered disproportionately from the decline of the United Kingdom's manufacturing industries. The decline of textiles, shipbuilding and coal mining hit the Scottish economy, while South Wales was similarly damaged by the run down of iron and steel and mining. 'UK Ltd' no longer appeared a successful enterprise. British decline was doubtless one factor in stirring nationalist currents in Scotland and Wales. The SNP and to a lesser extent Plaid Cymru made a political breakthrough in the late 1960s and early 1970s; the SNP won 30.4 per cent of the vote and 11 seats in October 1974, when the Welsh nationalists won over 10 per cent of the Welsh vote and three seats. Since then support has fluctuated, but the nationalists are now firmly established as the second largest party and the main opposition to Labour in both Scotland and Wales.

Welsh nationalism, however, was not essentially a question of economics. It has not flourished in the valleys of South Wales which were hardest hit by industrial decline, but in the core Welsh-speaking areas of the north-west where preservation of the Welsh language and culture has been the key concern. Education in Welsh, Welsh television, and Welsh as the language for legal and administrative business have been important issues, although supplemented to a degree by concerns over English immigration, which is partly related to the protection of Welsh culture but also has an economic dimension (particularly in terms of housing). Yet Wales is essentially divided rather than united by the language issue which helps to explain both the consistency of support for Welsh nationalism, but also its failure to grow, at least until the 1999 Assembly elections.

Support for nationalism in Scotland has been stronger but also more volatile. There, language is a negligible issue, enabling the SNP to make a wider appeal based on national sentiment and Scottish economic and political interests. The negative part of this appeal is a perceived neglect of Scottish issues by a remote and (in 1979–97) politically alien United Kingdom government, responsible for the imposition of the poll tax and privatization measures strongly opposed in Scotland. At the same time, the SNP could plausibly claim that an independent Scotland would be economically better off because of North Sea Oil. 'It's Scotland's Oil' became a potent election slogan, although the force of it diminished with the depletion of oil reserves and the fall in world oil prices.

Such naked appeals to Scottish self-interest provided some ammunition for critics who denounced the nationalists as narrow and materialist. Since then the SNP have sought to counter charges of narrow chauvinism by campaigning on the platform, 'Scotland in Europe', aligning themselves with progressive tendencies favouring closer European integration. This involved a marked policy reversal from earlier opposition to EC membership, yet it is logical that Euro-federalists and separation nationalists should make common cause against the entrenched power of existing European states.

There were formerly some significant differences in the location of Scottish and Welsh nationalism on the political spectrum. Whereas Plaid Cymru was firmly associated with the left and socialism, a common gibe by Labour opponents of the SNP was that they were 'Tartan Tories'. The rapid growth of the SNP in the 1970s and the defection to it of some erstwhile Labour politicians has weakened that charge, although it is still true that the SNP covers a wider range of views on domestic and economic policy than Plaid. Yet it is now easier for socialists like Nairn (1981, 2000) to identify Scottish and Welsh nationalism with progressive civic nationalism rather than a more exclusive ethnic nationalism.

Nationalism and devolution

British politicians and parties from time to time proposed some transfer of political power to Scotland and Wales. The notion of Home Rule for Scotland and (to a more limited extent) Wales, began to appear on the political agenda in the late nineteenth century, largely as a consequence of the bitter controversy over Irish Home Rule. 'Home Rule all round' was one attempt by Liberals to popularize a cause which did not greatly appeal to the British electorate, and they and their Liberal Democrat successors have fairly consistently supported it. Labour's record has been more erratic. They favoured Home Rule up to 1945, then opposed it, becoming reconverted in 1974 when they promised Scottish and Welsh Assemblies but failed to secure sufficient support for their devolution proposals in referendums in 1979. The Conservatives occasionally flirted with some concession to nationalist feeling but remained in name and spirit a Unionist party.

By the mid-1970s there was, for the first time almost since its establishment, serious doubts about the long-term survival of the British state, with Northern Ireland in turmoil and nationalism on a steep upward curve in Scotland and Wales (Birch, 1977). After 1979, however, the separatist tide briefly appeared to recede, and British nationalist sentiment was stimulated by the 1982 Falklands War, a generally more assertive foreign policy and a reaffirmation of commitment to the Union under the premiership of Margaret Thatcher. John Major strongly opposed the Labour and Liberal Democrat commitment to devolution in 1992 and 1997, arguing that this threatened the break-up of the UK, a point also made by some Labour dissidents like Tam Dalyell (Marr, 1992; Harvie, 1994).

Yet the fundamental problems of the British state remained, involving uncertain and changing internal loyalties and questions over the United Kingdom's external relationships, particularly with Europe. Labour's landslide victory in 1997 led to the rapid implementation of plans for devolution conceived in opposition, and a Scottish Parliament and Welsh Assembly were instituted following referendums in 1997 and elections in 1999. A Labour–Liberal Democrat coalition took control of the Scottish executive and, ultimately, the Welsh executive, after a troubled period of Labour minority rule. Meanwhile a devolved assembly and executive was rather more precariously established in Northern Ireland.

The long-term implications for the British state are as yet unclear. The Acts establishing the new devolved assemblies insist that the sovereignty of the Westminster Parliament is unaffected, but this position seems difficult to maintain in the longer run. One possibility is evolution into a quasi-federalist or fully federalist state. An alternative is the break-up of the British state into independent nation states, a future already confidently predicted by nationalists (Nairn, 1981, 2000, 2001).

Changes in the European political map since 1989 make it easier to contemplate a Scottish or Welsh state. If Slovakia, Slovenia and Latvia, why not Wales? What actually constitutes a nation, and how far in practice might the process of national separation go? Hobsbawm (1989, p. 120ff) suggests that requirements of political and economic viability for states in the nineteenth century provided some restraint then on political fragmentation or 'Balkanization'. The development of an international economy on the one hand, and an (albeit imperfect) European and global political order on the other has rendered outmoded old assumptions about economic self-sufficiency and defence capability, enabling tiny states to emerge and survive in the modern world. Thus there is no practical brake on nationalist aspirations. The Basques or the Bretons, like the Scots and Welsh, can reasonably aspire to full sovereign independence; but if an independent Scotland, why not an independent Shetlands?

Nairn (1981, 2000) argues that the break-up of Britain could have a progressive, beneficial effect, enabling all its former constituent parts, including England, to rediscover or develop separate national identities and a civic republican nationalism which could coexist and cooperate fruitfully in a European or global environment. Hobsbawm (1989, pp. 134–5) considers reactionary consequences more likely. One possibility is a narrow exclusive chauvinism, which would discriminate against non-Welsh speakers in Wales, English settlers in Scotland, and all kinds of ethnic minorities in England, with bitter inter-state disputes over assets, debts, off-shore fishing and mineral rights. Interpretations and expectations rest heavily on different perspectives on the nature of nationalism.

It is the implications of nationalism and the possible break-up of Britain for English national identity and English politics which has inspired most speculation recently. A rising tide of Euro-scepticism is fed by a narrowly nationalist press and an increasingly anti-European Conservative Party. There is also the prospect of an 'English backlash' against devolution, incited not only by parties on the political fringe but increasingly by the Conservatives – former champions of the United Kingdom but now more than ever an English Party advocating English interests (they won no seats in Scotland or Wales in 1997, and only one Scottish seat in 2001, although a more proportional voting system led to better fortunes in the elections for the devolved assemblies). A vociferous section of English football fans mix sport and politics in chanting 'Two World Wars and one World Cup' and 'No surrender to the IRA'. The resurgence of white racism, evident in and around the 2001 General Election is another disturbing development. Significantly, the preferred symbol of both football hooligans and the racist right is now the 'Cross of St George' rather than the Union Jack.

Europe, regionalism and nationalism

The growth of the European Union runs counter to traditional nationalist assumptions. European integration appealed to many precisely because it would transcend and render redundant the old national rivalries within Europe which had culminated in two world wars. It involved a different vision and a distinctive political programme. From the beginning the founders of the European Community envisaged a political as well as an economic union, which implied the development of a European consciousness and identity.

Yet despite the hopes of Euro-enthusiasts and the loudly voiced fears of British Euro-sceptics the European Union is hardly yet a 'superstate'. While its developing institutions involve in embryo all the apparatus of a sovereign state – an executive in the shape of the European Commission, a legislature (potentially at least) in the European Parliament, and a judiciary in the Court of Justice in Luxembourg – these institutions coexist with others – the European Council and Council of Ministers – which reflect the national interests of the member states. These increasingly seem more influential in decision-making despite formal progress towards integration.

In the long debate over British membership of the European Community from the early 1960s onwards, there has been some discussion on the implications for sovereignty, an issue particularly raised by opponents such as Enoch Powell. Supporters of British membership then and since largely played down the political implications, and emphasized instead the economic advantages. In so far as they addressed the issue of sovereignty, it was to deny that it was affected.

The term sovereignty is used to describe two linked concepts – sovereignty, or independence, in relation to other states, and supreme power within the state, involving 'parliamentary sovereignty' in the case of the United Kingdom. Both have been affected by British membership of the European Union. As with membership of other international associations, such as the United Nations or NATO, membership of the European Union effectively constrains UK freedom of action in relation to other states. It also has implications for the traditional constitutional doctrine of the sovereignty of Parliament, as European law overrides state law and is automatically applied within member countries. It may be argued that parliamentary sovereignty is unaffected, as a vote of the Westminster Parliament took Britain into Europe and a similar vote could take Britain out again; yet as the real possibility of withdrawal recedes, the argument weakens.

The European Union thus has considerable consequences for existing European states, and for the ideology of nationalism. The idea that nations should constitute independent sovereign states does not sit easily with the concept of European unity in which such sovereignty may be 'pooled' or 'shared'. Nationalism may be reconciled with a relatively loose and weak form of political association – a 'Europe des Patries' in De Gaulle's formulation, or 'confederalism' rather than federalism, a solution which some British politicians have implicitly or explicitly favoured. Thus strong independent sovereign states cooperate with other members, but retain the right to protect their own separate state interests.

Equally, a rather stronger form of European unity involving a federal structure is quite compatible with a form of nationalism which does not necessarily demand full sovereign independence. Indeed the European Union may give some tacit encouragement to 'peripheral nationalism' within existing member states. The existence of the Union weakens old objections to such nationalism on the grounds of lack of viability or economic dependence. Moreover, it enables nationalists to avoid accusations of narrow chauvinism; they can proclaim their national and European loyalties together, as in the slogan 'Scotland in Europe'.

Even if the European Union does not give overt encouragement to 'peripheral nationalism', there is certainly some institutional pressures towards regional devolution which have implications for existing states and nationalist assumptions (Keating, 1998). In England this has involved the establishment of Regional Development Agencies, and the more contentious prospect of directly-elected regional assemblies. Both local and regional governments have long sought direct links with Brussels, and regional subsidies have become a growing element of the European budget. The Committee of Regions set up by the Maastricht Treaty further institutionalizes this strong regional element in European policy-making. Regional institutions potentially bypass the national state level, which is thus eroded from above and below. The principle of 'subsidiarity', used to justify taking decisions at the national rather than European level, can equally be employed to devolve decision-making further to regional or local bodies. Thus there is some commonality of interest between those advocating closer European union and more devolution of decision-making within states.

So far it has been assumed that the European ideal is incompatible with older more aggressive and exclusive forms of nationalism within Europe, but the debate over enlargement has revived some awkward questions about European identity. Some who originally opposed the European Community did so because they perceived it as a narrow group of rich capitalist nations banding together in a protectionist association against threatened competition from poorer countries. European federalists have tended to counter such arguments with reference to European Union aid and special trade arrangements with the developing world, yet the critics have a point, at least up to and including the 1995 enlargement. In the new century, ongoing negotiations with (mainly poorer) applicant members from Central and Eastern Europe raise not only economic concerns but more fundamental issues over Europe's boundaries and identity, not dissimilar in essence from issues raised by traditional nationalism. The 'natural frontiers' of Europe suggested by geography may not be the same as those indicated by language and culture. While the European Union has always been multilingual, awkward questions remain over the very nature of European culture and civilization. A Christian Europe would rule out Moslem states or communities. More significantly, while several EU states contain substantial black or Asian minorities, it is questionable how far they share in the European dream. The rules governing citizenship, of several member states, and hence European citizenship are implicitly racist. It is easier for immigrant Russians of German descent to claim German citizenship than for Turks who have lived in Germany all their lives (Schlesinger in Hutchinson and Smith, 1994). European unity, like national unity, poses questions of identity which can be interpreted in an exclusive or inclusive way. The European ideal has not been wholly successful in overcoming the narrow nationalist assumptions it theoretically transcends.

Globalization, decentralization and the future of nationalism

The movement towards European unity is just one among many trends in the modern world which appear incompatible with nationalist doctrines. Just as the rise of nationalism was connected with industrial modernization and associated economic developments, so it can now be argued that in the modern post-industrial world nationalism is outdated. Global markets on the one hand, and pressures towards decentralization on the other, have combined to render nationalism redundant. It is increasingly clear that nation states can no longer immunize themselves from the international economy (if indeed they ever could). Movements in money or security markets in

New York or Tokyo have immediate repercussions for London, and the operations of multinational corporations have massive implications for domestic economies. Interest-rate policy and, increasingly, fiscal policy are heavily constrained by international pressures. There are tight rules governing trade restrictions and direct and indirect subsidies for domestic industries.

Similarly, developments in communication technology are rapidly creating a global culture. Just as industrialization in the nineteenth century helped create a national culture instead of diverse regional and local cultures in many European states, so post-industrial society has created cultures which transcend national boundaries. Much popular music now finds an international audience. Television programmes may have a global market, particularly with the development of satellite and cable television. Regimes determined to preserve a distinctive national culture find it more difficult. While France still tries to restrict Anglo-American imports into its language and culture, former Communist regimes and the former apartheid regime in South Africa both failed to immunize their people from alternative perspectives and implicit promises held out by the western media.

But if nationalism is apparently being undermined by globalization, it is also threatened by decentralization. 'Fordist' assumptions about economies of scale, mass production and standardization have given place to a 'post-Fordist' economy and society, where small is once again beautiful, and where the emphasis is on flexibility and meeting customers' requirements. Government and public services as well as the private sector are affected. In most European countries there has been a significant devolution of power from central government to regional and local authorities. In Britain and other western countries the introduction of increased competition and quasi-markets into the public sector has transformed patterns of service delivery. Whether power is really devolved to consumers is questionable, but there has been some decentralization of decision-making to institutions, managers and professionals away from centralized bureaucracies. The 'free economy' has after all undermined the 'strong state' despite the Thatcherite attempt to combine them (Gamble, 1988). On the left, few desire a return to bureaucratic central control, or older models of centralized state socialism, despite continuing criticism of market individualism. More emphasis instead is placed on the values of community and locality.

The implications for mainstream nationalist ideology should be manifest. Nationalism suggests that national communities should have their own political and governmental framework in the form of sovereign independent nation states, perceived as the only level of government which ultimately counts. Yet increasingly the trend is towards multi-level governance where different levels of public institutions work with private and voluntary organizations, 'steering' or 'enabling' rather than 'rowing' (Rhodes, 1997; Pierre and Peters, 2000). Multilevel governance may be mirrored by multiple identities as 'a natural feature of the human condition' which increasingly may involve dual or multiple national, regional and civic loyalties (Davies, 1999, p. 874). Such developments reflect changes in the economy, society and technology which may prove irreversible. On this analysis, nationalism, the most potent political ideology of the nineteenth and twentieth centuries, is doomed to extinction.

Yet there is now little sign of the impending demise of nationalism. On the contrary, nationalism seems as vigorous as ever in most parts of the world, and has flourished in extreme forms particularly in former communist countries where a counter ideology stressing universalism and international working-class solidarity has been inculcated for half a century or more. 'Peripheral' or 'separation nationalism' continues to thrive in parts of the western world and remains manifest over much of the third world also. While nationalism appears logically redundant in the post-modern, post-industrial, post-Fordist world, it continues to defy predictions.

Further reading

The literature on nationalism is extensive and growing. A useful brief critical survey is provided by Calhoun (1997). Contrasting interpretations are offered by Kedourie (4th edn, 1993), Gellner (1983), Anderson (1983), Breuilly (2nd edn, 1993), Hobsbawm (1990), Smith (1991), Greenfeld (1992) and Alter (1994). Extracts from nearly all these and much else besides can be found in a reader on nationalism by Hutchinson and Smith (1994). Hobsbawm's four volumes on modern history also contain valuable material on nationalism. Schwarzmantel (1991) illuminates the troubled relationship between nationalism and socialism, while Hutchinson (1994) is good on nationalism in the modern world, and Keating (1998) is essential reading on the 'New Regionalism'.

It is more difficult to find books which can be confidently recommended on nationalism in Britain. Davies (1999) provides a stimulating corrective to Anglo-centric history. On the issue of national identity Crick (1991) has edited a collection of essays, while there has been a spate of books on English identity (for example Paxman, 1998). On Scottish nationalism McCrone (1992), Marr (1992) and especially Harvie (1994) are useful, while Nairn (1981, 2000, 2001) provides a provocative nationalist commentary on the continuing devolution process.

6

Fascism, Racism and Multiculturalism

Introduction: racism and fascism

It may be questioned whether racism qualifies as an ideology and whether it rates a separate chapter in a book on political ideologies in Britain. It depends on how ideology is defined, itself a contentious issue (see Chapter 1). If, however, ideologies are 'action-oriented', their significance may be assessed more in terms of their implications for political behaviour than their degree of intellectual sophistication. Racism is an ideology with very significant political implications manifest in other societies past and present where overtly racist doctrines have been extensively promoted, sometimes officially by the state as in Hitler's Third Reich (Kershaw, 1993), or under the apartheid regime in South Africa. In contemporary Britain, by contrast, overt racism has been long-excluded from elite political discourse. Mainstream politicians and respectable organs of opinion publicly repudiate racism, and public and private-sector organizations officially pledge themselves to combat racial prejudice and discrimination. Some forms of racist expression are punishable by law, and the accusation of racism is a serious charge to be hotly denied.

Yet although overt racism is an ideology which is officially 'beyond the pale', racist beliefs are widely held. In a 1997 survey, 32 per cent of British people described themselves as very or quite racist (Parekh, 2000a, p. 227), while politicians who publicly denounce racism have sometimes employed coded language to appease (or appeal to) racist sentiment, and pursued policies which are racist in effect and intention. However, it is the incontrovertible evidence of the persistent and extensive discrimination and disadvantage suffered by ethnic minorities which continues to provides the clearest evidence of the deeply-rooted prevalence of racism in Britain. For most blacks and Asians, racial prejudice and discrimination is a routine and inescapable element of their everyday lives.

Even so, general surveys of political ideologies rarely offer any extended discussion of racism. In so far as racist ideas are examined at all, it is commonly as a component of other ideologies, particularly fascism, or extreme variants of nationalism. This is partly because the concept of race no longer appears to have scientific validity, and racism seems intellectually threadbare. Fascism offers more substance for analysis. It was once presented as a serious and comprehensive ideology, with pretensions to offer a middle way between liberal capitalism and bolshevism. Its culmination in the horrors of the holocaust may have totally discredited fascism for the bulk of humanity, but also provided a dire warning of where racism can lead. So it appears logical to examine racism within the broader context of fascism.

Yet to examine racist ideas largely or exclusively within the context of fascism is to risk underestimating their importance. Racism existed before fascism (and was not even a key element of Mussolini's fascism originally) and survived fascism's defeat. In Britain the full fascist ideology was an alien creed which never presented a serious threat to the political mainstream. British fascists did not create racism, although they sought to exploit racist feelings and exacerbated racial tensions. Yet ultimately it is racism rather than fascism which remains a significant feature of domestic British politics. In this chapter, therefore, the main focus will be on racism, and fascism will be examined (briefly) in the context of racism.

Racist ideology: critical issues

Racism has been very variously defined, but virtually all definitions stress the implications of racist beliefs for behaviour. Thus, on one formulation, racism is 'any political or social belief that justifies treating people differently according to their racial origins' (Robertson, 1993, p. 404). Racist doctrine does not bear close examination, for it is now accepted that there is no scientific basis for the division of humanity into distinct races. Even so many people still cling to racist assumptions and for some 'race' remains the key political divide which informs their whole political outlook and behaviour.

Moreover the study of ideologies is not only concerned with the consequences of political convictions, but how people come to hold those convictions. Even if racism is regarded as intellectually untenable and morally repugnant, it is still important to analyse how and why people come to hold racist views. Is racism the consequence of the deliberate stirring of racial, ethnic or religious fears by politicians (mainstream or fascist) for their own ends, or the byproduct of religious convictions or prejudices (such as anti-Semitism, Islamophobia), or the legacy of imperialism and slavery, or the consequence of inequality and deprivation? Is racism essentially about 'colour' prejudice, or can racial conflict involve communities with similar skin colours? Is it largely or exclusively a white problem (as has sometimes been suggested), or can blacks and Asians be racist?

Different explanations for racial prejudice clearly may have different policy implications, if one indeed assumes that public authorities are committed to combat rather than appease racism. There are important questions about the efficacy of outlawing discrimination, about the scope and limits of educational policy, and over the advisability of 'positive discrimination' in favour of ethnic minorities. More fundamentally there has been a shift from past 'colour-blind' policies designed to promote the integration and assimilation of ethnic minorities, towards the acceptance of difference and the perceived benefits of multiculturalism. Multiculturalism itself may be regarded as a political doctrine, philosophy or ideology which suggests that peoples of different 'races' or cultures may live together to their mutual advantage. Ethnic and cultural diversity need not lead to the 'rivers of blood' foretold by the former Conservative politician, Enoch Powell, but to an enriching exchange and blending of ideas and energies. Multiculturalism, however, also raises important ethical issues, particularly where the beliefs and practices of ethnic minorities run up against the settled convictions of the majority or even against what are proclaimed as universal human rights.

The origins and development of racism

Theories of the division of humanity into distinctive races were not elaborated until the eighteenth and nineteenth centuries. However, from the earliest times human societies have observed distinctions between themselves and others, particularly when they came across people with different physical characteristics, such as skin colour, hair or height. Such physical differences were easily identified, but perceptive observers such as the ancient Greek historian Herodotus also noted that other peoples held markedly different beliefs and behaved differently. Thus, from the start, perceptions of peoples involved both physical and cultural distinctions. Other civilizations sometimes evoked interested curiosity and even admiration, but more commonly differentiation was accompanied by negative evaluation, and sometimes fear. Ancient Greeks and Romans looked down on, but also feared, 'barbarians' outside their Greco-Roman civilization, with some reason because of the military threat they presented, but they did not normally perceive other cultures or more specifically other religions as a threat. Indeed, the gods worshipped by other peoples were commonly seen as different versions of their own divinities.

Yet many of the great religions which came to dominate the world were rather more exclusive in the demands they made of their followers, and 'other peoples' might often exhibit a mix of different physical and cultural characteristics, generally evaluated extremely negatively. Thus medieval Christians scorned and feared 'heathens', Jews and Moslems. 'The Islamic Other was portrayed as barbaric, degenerate and tyranni-cal, and these alleged characteristics were considered to be rooted in the character of Islam as a supposedly false and heretic theology' (Miles, 1989, p. 18). Yet Christianity and Islam were competing creeds and the 'threat' from Islam was real enough to Christians in parts of Europe, while Christian 'crusades' posed a similar threat elsewhere to Islam. By contrast, the 'threat' from Jews was almost wholly imagi-nary. Jews were targeted as an 'enemy within' partly on religious grounds (the rejection and crucifixion of Christ), but also partly because of their involvement in banking and finance which rendered them both useful but resented. Fantastic stories of secret Jewish practices fed anti-Semitism which periodically led to persecution and violent attacks on the Jewish community in many countries, including Britain, where Jews were eventually expelled by Edward I.

Exploration and trade brought Europeans into more extensive contact with other peoples and civilizations. Much of this led to negative and pejorative assessments of other people as 'cruel', 'savage' and 'heathen', although there was also a minority more positive assessment, sometimes associated with notions of 'lost innocence' and the 'noble savage'. Exploration and trade often led in turn to colonization and western imperialism. This is now (understandably) almost universally condemned, although it is important to recognize the diversity of the colonization process. Some European settlers were 'asylum seekers' – victims of religious persecution in their country of origin – and sought a new life of freedom in the 'new world'. Some were convicts deported as a punishment. Some were 'economic migrants' driven by relative poverty and lack of opportunity. Some were adventurers on the make. Some even saw imperialism as a noble and inspiring cause – a 'white-

man's burden' to bring the benefits of western law, religion and education to less fortunate peoples (although the reality was generally otherwise). The attitudes of colonists to indigenous peoples likewise varied.
Some were regarded as heathen savages, who might be exploited or
even enslaved, but equally might, more paternalistically, be 'converted'
and 'civilized'. Other cultures (for example India) were sometimes initially treated with more respect (Saggar, 1992, p. 17)

White racism is often plausibly attributed to the past history of
European colonial exploitation, and more particularly slavery. Thus, it
is suggested, slavery was both a product of western assumptions of
black racial inferiority and reinforced those assumptions. Moreover, the
ideology of imperialism and the linked assumption of white superiority
was spread and reinforced through education and popular culture in the
nineteenth and early twentieth centuries. Today the sizeable black and
Asian minorities in the UK population are clearly a legacy of empire
(or the 'colonial diaspora'), in that most of them are descended from
immigrants from the 'new commonwealth' or old empire. To that
extent, tensions between the majority white population and ethnic
minorities might also be fairly regarded as a product of empire. Yet it is
questionable whether modern white racism in Britain today is largely
the product of past imperialist assumptions rather than contemporary
experiences and misconceptions. Britain's former empire is now
recalled with more shame than pride, but is generally shrouded in
collective amnesia.

Thus it seems misguided to relate racism largely or exclusively to
imperialism. Racist attitudes preceded the European colonial period and
have survived its collapse. Anti-Semitism, one of the most persistent
and extreme forms of racism, owes nothing to colonialism and the past
domination of Blacks and Asians by whites. Some contemporary
racism is directed against peoples who were never colonized in the conventional sense – against Turkish *gastarbeiter* (guestworkers) in
Germany and Eastern European asylum seekers in Britain. Moreover,
as these examples suggest, although 'colour prejudice' is a familiar
form of racism, racist attitudes are not always linked to distinctions
based on skin colour. Anti-Irish prejudice and derogatory observations
on the Irish 'race' have a long history Britain, although this 'anti-Irish
racism' has often been ignored or downplayed (Mac an Ghaill, 1999,
pp. 77–80). The linked contention that racism is largely or exclusively a
'white' characteristic also seems untenable in the face of fairly extensive evidence of prejudice between, for example, blacks and Asians
(Phizacklea and Miles, 1980, pp. 181–3). Rather, it seems that what

would now be called racism is a long-standing and widespread aspect of human beliefs and behaviour, although its precise form is influenced by specific historical experiences.

'Scientific' racism

Much of this racism was, however serious its effects, not extensively rationalized nor related to any systematic theory of racial difference. Indeed, in so far as attempts were made to explain observable differences between peoples in physical appearance or behaviour, these were commonly linked to environmental factors such as climate rather than attributed to innate biological differences. This changed with the development of 'scientific racism' from the late eighteenth century onwards.

The application of science to the previously rather arbitrary and imprecise concept of race led to extensive measurement, racial classification and theorizing. Much of this work seems to have been inspired by genuine scientific curiosity, rather than aimed merely to legitimate racial prejudice. There were observable physical differences between peoples, and cultural differences also, and it seemed a reasonable object of scientific enquiry to determine more precisely the extent of these differences and the links between them, and to produce a more comprehensive scientific theory of racial differences. Some of this work appeared to confirm that there were a number of distinctive human races whose differences were innate. Scientific theorizing was extensively supported by measurements of head shapes, hair colour and structure, eye colour and, most significantly, cranial capacity, which implied some races might naturally be more intelligent than others. Unsurprisingly perhaps, 'science' seemed to confirm the expectations of European investigators, and was used to support some of the racist doctrines which were beginning to circulate, including the notion of a Nordic/Aryan master race which was destined to rule over other 'inferior' races.

Later in the nineteenth century Darwin's theory of evolution was misapplied to indicate that some races had evolved to reach a higher level than others, although Darwin's work really made nonsense of the whole notion of fixed and innate biological differences which underpinned scientific racism (Miles, 1989, p. 36). Darwin's concept of the survival of the fittest was misused to serve racist ideas by its adaptation to justify a necessary and inevitable struggle between human races for supremacy in which victory validated claims to superiority. Thus the race or people who conquered in war or secured the largest empire 'proved' they were the highest race. In this way 'social Darwinism' served to justify imperialism.

The assumption that there were distinct races hierarchically ordered also implied that a superior race might be damaged or weakened by intermingling with an inferior race. This reinforced preexisting prejudices against immigration. Thus the purity of the Anglo-Saxon or Aryan race might be undermined by the increasing presence in their midst of Jews, Irish or Poles. Among the consequences of these fears, apparently legitimated by science, were increasing restrictions to immigration on implicitly and often explicitly racist grounds, such as the Aliens Act passed in Britain in 1905.

By the time scientific racism was to receive its most complete endorsement in Hitler's Third Reich, the scientific world was retreating fast from the whole concept to the extent that race was declared a pseudo-scientific term. Scientists concluded that classification of people by racial type was subjective rather than objective, and 'race' did not determine mental or physical ability, or behavioural characteristics. After the Second World War scientific or biological racism was totally discredited. Yet this did not mean the end of notions of race and racist ideas, which had existed before scientific racism, and survived its refutation.

Fascism and Nazism

Any analysis of racism can hardly avoid some reference to fascism, as it was notoriously Hitler's Nazi regime which most systematically adopted and applied racist doctrine. The horrors of the 'final solution' have become so inseparably linked with fascism to marginalize other elements of the ideology.

Yet fascism, in Mussolini's original form, was not particularly racist; it was always a strange amalgam of ideas. Linz (in Laqueur, 1979, p. 15) has referred to 'the essential anti-character of its ideology and appeal', and indeed it is easier to describe it in terms of what it was against rather than what it was for. Thus fascism can be seen as involving a reaction against the rationalism, individualism, liberalism and parliamentarism which constituted the mainstream European tradition from the eighteenth-century Enlightenment onwards. It stood for national loyalty rather than class loyalty, the state rather than the individual, action rather than intellectual debate, leadership, discipline, order and military virtues rather than the mundane liberal democratic values of bargaining and compromise. It looked back to an imagined heroic past which emphasized traditional values, but it also gloried in and exploited modern technology, particularly the modern mass media. It claimed to offer planned economic growth and higher living standards through a 'middle way' between liberal capitalism and revolutionary communism, in which labour and capital would be brought together in corporations to serve the interests of the whole state and people. In practice the boasted achievements of fascism were more cosmetic than real, and Mussolini's regime was always a rather squalid dictatorship which involved the silencing of opposition by brutal intimidation and violence.

However, while Mussolini was certainly an aggressive nationalist, he was not in the usual sense of the term a racist, and indeed he initially referred rather contemptuously to the racial doctrine of the German Nazis, and spurned the eager admiration of Hitler (who came to power a full decade later). Fascism was Mussolini's creation and he regarded imitators with some suspicion. Yet, effectively, Nazism has absorbed fascism in the public mind. Although some academics would still prefer to distinguish between fascism and Nazism, the two terms have come to be used interchangeably. While Hitler's Nazism certainly shared many of the key characteristics of Mussolini's fascism, its distinguishing feature was the racist theory and practice with which it will ever be associated. Against the deliberate policy of the wholesale genocide of Jews, and the subjugation and exploitation of the 'inferior' races of the Poles and Slavs of Eastern Europe, other elements of fascist ideology have paled into insignificance (Kershaw, 1993). It was ultimately Hitler's version of the ideology which came to define what fascism was about. Fascism became racism, and racism pushed to hitherto unimaginable extremes.

While fascism and Nazism did not create racism and anti-Semitism, the preexisting conscious and unconscious racial prejudices of many were legitimated, encouraged and employed in the service of a state in which racism was the official orthodoxy. Anti-Semitism had certainly been a feature of German society before Hitler came to power, but Germans had not been markedly more anti-Semitic than Poles, Russians, French or British. Indeed the German Jewish community had appeared more fully and successfully integrated into German society than Jews in many other countries. The apparent ease with which the Nazis applied race hate and ultimately genocide in an apparently advanced and civilized country suggests that other societies might be equally vulnerable. This was demonstrably true in many of the countries occupied by the Nazis, where willing collaborators helped round up Jews for transportation to death camps, and sometimes were directly involved in atrocities. Had Britain been defeated and occupied there is little doubt that similar collaborators would have been found, particularly perhaps from those who had openly espoused fascism, or who had expressed sympathy for Hitler.

British fascism

The roots of British fascism lay in a number of small extreme right-wing nationalist and racist groups founded before, during and immediately after the First World War (Thurlow, 1987, pp. 1–61). Some of them were established to campaign against immigration, particularly of Jews from Eastern Europe, which led to the racist Aliens Act of 1905. Anti-Semitism, long a feature of British society, became particularly virulent amid fears of British decline and the degeneration of the Anglo-Saxon 'race'. During the war those perceived to be of foreign origin (including both Jews and Germans), were suspect as potential traitors. After the war there was a ready market for international Jewish conspiracy theories, commonly inspired by forged documents such as the notorious *Protocols of the Elders of Zion*. Jews were convenient scapegoats, indiscriminately blamed for the excesses and failures of capitalism on the one hand and Bolshevism on the other, for fears of the 'socialist menace' were another major concern (Benewick, 1972, ch. 2; Thurlow, 1987, pp. 62–91). Some right-wing groups labelled themselves 'fascist' following Mussolini's rise to power in 1922. However, the British Fascists consciously or unconsciously followed Mussolini in being 'insufficiently anti-Semitic' for the taste of some right-wing nationalists (Thurlow, 1987, p. 53). Another organization, the Imperial Fascist League, was strongly anti-Semitic from the start.

It was only when an already established politician with a national reputation was converted to fascism that it was briefly taken seriously. Oswald Mosley had pursued a chequered career across the party political spectrum, starting as a Conservative MP before crossing the floor to become briefly a Labour Minister, and finally the leader of the British Union of Fascists, (BUF) which quickly absorbed most of the tiny older fascist groups (Skidelsky, 1990). Mosley's capabilities have perhaps been exaggerated, but he was certainly (like Mussolini and Hitler) a gifted platform orator, capable of whipping up a crowd. Yet although the activities of Mosley and the BUF for a time alarmed the authorities, they never in retrospect represented a significant threat to the British

political scene. It would be comforting to assume that the BUF's
increasingly strident anti-Semitism was unacceptable to most Britons,
but the relative failure of British fascism was more down to other
factors. Unlike Germany, Britain had not been defeated and humiliated
in the 1914–18 War. As compared with Italy or Germany, parliamentary democracy was longer and more securely established, society less
deeply divided, economic difficulties, although severe enough, less cat-
astrophic. A particular problem was that fascism drew on extreme
nationalism, but in Britain the fascist role models, Germany and Italy,
were increasingly viewed as enemies. Support for fascism (never
very significant) crumbled once it appeared incompatible with British
patriotism, particularly after war with Germany was declared.

Yet if fascism never caught on in Britain, racist ideas were (and
remain) widespread in British society. In so far as fascism achieved any
temporary appeal it was not because of the attractions of totalitarianism, elitist theory, the corporate state, autarchy, or other elements of
fascism as propounded by Mussolini's tame philosophers, but because
of its anti-Semitism and racism. Mosley himself does not seem to have
been particularly anti-Semitic or racist in his earlier political career,
and even in his fascist phase generally avoided openly racist or anti-
Semitic language. Yet his leading henchmen were far less restrained
and his movement became increasingly anti-Semitic and racist, in imitation of the Nazis, because this played well in areas such as the East
End of London where there was long-established hostility to the Jewish
community. But it was not British fascism which created racism, rather
it was preexisting racism which sustained for a time British fascism.

The same is true after the Second World War, when Mosley himself
formally renounced the fascist label, although his new Union Movement
was little more than a renamed BUF, and his reformed creed, which
included support for European unity, was not unreasonably described as
'Euro-fascism'. His occasional forays into British politics owed little to
these refinements of his political message but essentially involved exploiting racism – against 'coloured immigrants' rather than Jews – in the East
End and areas such as the West Midlands. Similarly, although some of the
leading activists of other far-right parties such as the National Front or the
British National Party (BNP) endorsed the full fascist ideology and had a
predilection for dressing up in Nazi uniforms, their appeal was essentially
confined to racism (Walker, 1977; Taylor, 1982). Indeed the fascist and
Nazi associations were a distinct handicap, as anti-racists recognized
when they set up the Anti-Nazi League and campaigned on the effective
slogan 'The National Front is a Nazi Front'.

Although labelling all racists as fascists involves good political tactics in that it deters support for explicitly racist parties, it also tends to understate the true extent of racist feeling in Britain particularly if it is measured in terms of votes attracted by fringe right-wing parties dubbed 'fascist' or 'quasi-fascist'. No such party has remotely threatened to win a single parliamentary seat. In 1997 the average vote secured by 57 BNP candidates was 1.3 per cent. In 2001 although the BNP secured votes of 16 per cent and 11 per cent in two Oldham constituencies where there had been recent riots, elsewhere they generally did no better than in 1997. One might comfortably conclude that racism has been comprehensively repudiated by the British public. However, the extent of racism in contemporary Britain is not to be measured by the tiny proportion of the electorate who vote for overtly racist or neo-fascist parties.

Immigration and race in modern Britain – a new racism?

Indeed, racism remains widespread in Britain, despite the discrediting of the whole concept of race as 'an idea that should be explicitly and consistently confined to the dustbin of analytically useless terms' (Miles, 1989, p. 72). Miles, indeed, only uses the term 'race' in quotation marks, and insists that the focus of analysis should be on the ideology of racism and the process of racialization rather than the bogus concept of race. He further argues that the official use of the term in Britain, in for example, 'Race Relations Acts', legitimizes differences which have no scientific validity. Thus racism is unwittingly reinforced by policies ostensibly designed to combat it. Some have continued to use the term 'race' as a concept familiar in modern everyday usage, but linking it primarily with culture rather than biology. Others have preferred the broader, more culturally oriented term 'ethnicity', but while this avoids the bogus scientific overtones of race, it lacks precision (Kohn, *New Statesman*, 30 July 2001, p. 12).

However, much of the official public debate in the decades after the Second World War did not refer to the forbidden discourse of 'race' but to immigration. Britain had over centuries experienced waves of immigration, so it was hardly a new phenomenon or a new concern, but it had a fresh focus in the increasing numbers of immigrants from the British Empire and Commonwealth who were officially UK citizens with a right of entry to the 'mother country' (Saggar, 1992, pp. 66–85). Ostensibly the concern was with the numbers of immigrants entering Britain in the postwar period, but as ministers privately admitted, they were not worried about immigrants from the old (white) Commonwealth but only about immigrants from the 'new' (or black and Asian) Commonwealth. The real concern was over what was then termed 'coloured' immigration, and the resulting 'racial tension' which could result. An uglier populist and explicitly racist rhetoric lurked behind the bland elite debate. A Conservative candidate won a seat against the general Labour swing in the 1964 election on the slogan 'If you want a nigger neighbour, vote Labour' (Butler and King, 1965, p. 361).

Immigration controls from 1962 onwards were effectively and intentionally racist and pursued by both Conservative and Labour governments, yet they were accompanied by measures to outlaw racial discrimination and promote good 'race relations' and integration. This 'twin-track' approach reflected a bipartisan political consensus on race issues for much of the 1960s and 1970s. That consensus was challenged by Enoch Powell who dramatically prophesied 'rivers of blood' from continuing immigration in 1968. Although Powell acquired a populist following, he effectively destroyed his own political prospects as he was sacked from the Conservative Shadow Cabinet by Ted Heath (Saggar, 1992, pp. 109–13). Subsequently, some leading Conservative politicians employed more coded language to express sympathy with the fears of 'ordinary people' that increasing numbers of 'immigrants', 'ethnic minorities' or 'asylum seekers' threatened their own traditional values and ways of living. Thus Margaret Thatcher in 1978 referred to a 'fear' that the 'British character' might be 'swamped' by 'those coming in', while Norman Tebbit aroused concerns over the allegiance of ethnic minorities through his 'cricket test' (Kingdom 1999, p. 189). More recently, William Hague's Conservative Conference 2000 vision of a future Britain as a foreign land was widely linked to Conservative-exploited fears of asylum seekers, although the speech was more obviously directed against a European 'superstate'.

This racism which was covertly or overtly expressed in Britain has sometimes been termed a 'new racism', based not on biology but on perceived differences in culture between communities. The new racism reflected an assumption that humans naturally seek to form bounded communities or nations, which they perceive as different from other communities of nations, and which they wish to protect (Barker, 1981, p. 21). This new racism is linked closely with a form of nationalism. 'Its focus is the defence of the mythic "British/English way of life" in the face of attack from enemies outside ... and within' (Solomos and Back, 1996, p. 18). Thus 'Peter Simple' of the *Daily Telegraph* laments that the people of England ... have seen everything that is distinctively English suppressed and derided... They have seen their decent manners and customs corrupted... They have seen part of their country colonised by immigrants and been forbidden by law to speak freely of the consequences. (Quoted in Paxman, 1998, pp. 70–1)

Yet although the new racism is supposed to relate to cultural rather than physical differences, the two are often implicitly or explicitly linked. Indeed, most idealized images of Britain and more particularly England relate to a past not shared by ethnic minorities, so that 'Englishness' and a black skin seem almost mutually exclusive. Powell denied that a 'West Indian or Indian' born in England could become English: 'In law he becomes a United Kingdom citizen by birth; in fact he is a West Indian or Asian still' (quoted in Saggar, 1992, p. 113). Margaret Thatcher was less explicit, but her patriotic rhetoric at the time of the Falklands War waxed lyrical on the British 'island race'. Thus according to Miles (1993, p. 75) 'English nationalism encapsulates racism'. Miles denies that modern racism is essentially new, arguing, firstly, that crude 'scientific' racism survives in contemporary expression despite its official discrediting, and, secondly, that cultural racism is still underpinned by implicit notions of biological inheritance and physical differences.

Racism, class and religion

Racism has been persuasively associated with economic deprivation and class relations under capitalism (Phizacklea and Miles, 1980). Although some 'Asians' (particularly Indians and East African Asians) are middle-class and relatively integrated and successful in British society, the majority of the black and Asian ethnic minorities are employed in manual work, and many live in racially segregated and economically deprived urban areas. As a 'fraction' of the working class, they are perceived to be in competition for jobs, houses and services with members of the white working class inhabiting the same deprived urban environment. Both working-class white racism, and the aggressive response of young black Asian males to racism can be seen as the consequence of economic decline and deprivation. 'Racial' conflict is a symptom rather the cause of the problem.

Such an (essentially Marxist) analysis provides a convincing explanation not only of the recent 'race riots' in British towns and cities, but also of working-class anti-Semitism in the East End of London, and much anti-Irish racism over the last two centuries in Britain. Moreover, such examples underline the point that it is not necessarily colour, or other observable physical differences, or even necessarily clear cultural differences which drive racism. Yet if economic conflict and deprivation provides a substantial explanation for racism, it hardly provides a sufficient explanation. While anti-Semitism flourished in working-class areas, it was also common among the middle classes (who often attempted to exclude Jews from their golf clubs and other social institutions) and particularly among the upper classes.

Differences in religious observance were obviously an element behind this cross-class anti-Semitism, and they have become an increasingly evident aspect of racism directed against 'Asians' today. Much of the early postwar racism in Britain was directed against black West Indian immigrants who shared many aspects of British culture, including Christianity. In the 1950s and 1960s the 'Asians' who 'kept themselves to themselves' were less often perceived as a 'cause of trouble' and were less conspicuously victims of white racism. By the late twentieth and early twenty-first centuries it was the 'Asians' who had become the main target for white racists, and relations between whites and Asians became the focus of much anguished analysis. In part this simply reflected the growth in numbers of Asians as opposed to Afro-Caribbeans, and the particularly severe economic problems of industries and towns into which Asian migrants had been drawn, but it was exacerbated by increasingly manifest religious differences. Islamophobia has become a marked aspect of anti-Asian racism.

One catalyst for Islamophobia was the Rushdie affair (see below) which served to reinforce existing prejudices but also alienated many liberals. As one Muslim has sardonically observed,

> while 'Asian' and 'Indian' suggest amorphous yet containable differences, 'Muslim' describes a specific and volatile difference. Muslims are not simply a brand of believers: they are rampant, dangerous and impenetrably different believers. (Sardar, *New Statesman*, 30 July 2001, p. 16)

Yet this may exaggerate the capacity of most 'whites' to discriminate between 'Asians'. Indeed, 'Asian' and 'Muslim' have become so associated in popular consciousness that it is widely assumed that an 'Asian' is a Muslim, when they may be Hindu, Sikh or Christian. Religion rather than skin colour has become the defining mark of the community, although colour provides a ready, if highly misleading, means of identification.

Thus brown skin means 'Muslim', and 'Muslim' means 'Islamic fundamentalist', regardless of distinctions between and within faiths. This has become more evident since the destruction of the World Trade Centre in New York September 2001 leading to 'revenge attacks' on the moderate British Muslim community and even non-Muslim Asians.

To that extent religious differences have become bound up with racism and have fuelled prejudice. That religion can be an element in racism or ethnic conflict is evident from anti-Semitism, as well as the experience of northern Ireland and many other parts of the world. Yet strongly-held religious convictions and divisions within and between faiths can present difficulties in any liberal pluralist society without necessarily involving a 'racial' or 'ethnic' element', as indicated by some Christian fundamentalists in the US 'bible belt'.

Institutional racism

It remains difficult to equate the relative absence of overt racism in mainstream British politics and polite society with the continued evidence of extensive discrimination and disadvantage suffered by ethnic minorities in their everyday lives. The concept of institutional racism provides one possible answer – racist assumptions are so embedded in society and societal institutions that racist outcomes result, even in the absence of overt racist attitudes. The concept was developed by race theorists in the United States who suggested that racism was deeply ingrained in American society as a consequence of the historical experience of slavery and racial segregation. Thus the dominant white group continued to exclude and disadvantage the black subordinate group, without necessarily deliberately intending that outcome.

Miles (1989, pp. 50–61) has argued that this interpretation of institutional racism involves 'conceptual inflation'. As institutional racism 'denies that intentionality or motivation are measures of the presence or absence of racism' it does not constitute an ideology in Miles' own understanding of the term. Miles himself (1993, p. 74) confusingly employs the term institutional racism to mean institutionally or officially recognized racism. Thus, he argues that British legislation on immigration involved an 'institutionalization of racism' by the British state which 'legitimated common-sense racism'. Yet for Miles this 'institutional racism' not only in practice discriminated on grounds of 'race' or 'colour', but intentionally discriminated on those grounds without acknowledging a racist purpose.

Other British scholars have employed the term 'institutional racism' in a sense broadly derived from the American use of the concept, but have sometimes applied it more narrowly to specific institutions whose practices might be 'unwittingly discriminatory' against black people. The term became more widely familiar as a result of the Macpherson inquiry (1999) into the conduct of the police in response to the murder of the black teenager, Stephen Lawrence. An internal police inquiry found no evidence to support the allegation of racist conduct by officers, who 'roundly denied racism or racist conduct'. The Macpherson Inquiry agreed that it had not 'heard evidence of overt racism or discrimination' but did nevertheless conclude that the Metropolitan Police Service (MPS) was 'institutionally racist' according to the Inquiry's own definition of the term:

> The collective failure of an organisation to provide an appropriate and professional service to people because of their colour, culture, or ethnic origin. It can be seen or detected in processes, attitudes and behaviour which amount to discrimination through unwitting prejudice, ignorance, thoughtlessness and racist stereotyping which disadvantage minority ethnic people. (Macpherson, 1999, p. 28)

Other evidence to the Inquiry accepted that institutional racism was a feature of police forces elsewhere in the country and reflected 'racism which is inherent in wider society which shapes our attitudes and behaviour' (Macpherson, 1999, p. 31), a perspective which comes closer to the American use of the term. However, the Inquiry's conclusion that the Metropolitan Police Service was institutionally racist was widely interpreted in the media and the police service to mean that all police officers who belonged to the MPS were themselves racists, almost the opposite of the argument advanced in the report. Indeed, one criticism of the whole concept of institutional racism is that it too readily acquits individuals of responsibility for racist attitudes and behaviour. The acknowledgement that 'we are all guilty' often means in practice that no-one is.

Anti-racism

Anti-racist ideas would not need to be articulated in a society which did not recognize racial differences nor discriminate on racial grounds. It is only the prevalence in British society of racist ideas which seriously and adversely affect ethnic minorities which has provoked the dissemination of a counter ideology of anti-racism. Perhaps inevitably, the emphasis of anti-racism has been negative rather than positive – to attack politicians, groups or parties disseminating racist ideas, to root out racist discrimination and prejudice, and ban racist language. Anti-racism has been successful in securing formal commitments to anti-discrimination and equal opportunities policies from public and private sector bodies, and the establishment of special committees and units to combat racism on local councils.

Yet it is questionable how far anti-racism has really changed ideas and lessened ethnic conflicts. Indeed, to many it is anti-racism rather than racism which is perceived as the problem. Because racism is so embedded in the majority culture, its manifestations are ignored or downplayed, while the expression of anti-racist ideas is widely noticed and criticized as unnecessary and exaggerated. An official anti-racist discourse has sometimes had the perverse effect of reinforcing a popular misconception (against all the evidence) that ethnic minorities are especially favoured by officialdom and thus secure more than their fair share of jobs and public services. In practice, although such positive discrimination is sometimes advocated to reverse the substantial persistent disadvantage and inequality suffered by members of ethnic minorities, it is actually illegal under equal opportunities legislation. Even so, the 'race relations industry' and 'politically correct' attitudes are routinely denounced and mocked in the tabloid press.

A more fundamental criticism of anti-racism has been its neglect of the importance of culture, identity and difference. Anti-racism tended to focus on what has been called 'black–white dualism' neglecting differences within the majority and minority communities, and ignoring racism which was not based on skin colour (such as anti-Semitism or anti-Irish racism). Anti-racism similarly downplayed differences in culture and religion (such as Islamophobia) which did not fit its theoretical assumptions derived from the liberal universalism of the Enlightenment and the materialist class focus of classical Marxism. The anti-racist strategy was to deny racial differences in emphasizing a common economic interest, as in the slogan 'Black and white unite and fight'. Anti-racism thus attracted criticism not only predictably from the New Right, but also from sections of the left for its neglect of differences within and between ethnic groups, and for its rationalistic rejection of felt identities (Mac an Ghail, 1999, pp. 105–16). Some of this criticism was echoed within ethnic minority communities.

Ethnic-minority community mobilization

Many of the anti-racist organizations such as the Campaign Against Racial Discrimination or the Anti-Nazi League were white-dominated, and ethnic minorities were sometimes slow to organize in their own defence. The first generation of immigrants from the West Indies or the Indian subcontinent often preferred not to 'cause trouble' by directly confronting prejudice or discrimination. Nor did they make much use of the formal political process to defend their interests. Although Asians in particular used their votes, they were not initially active within political parties and they long remained grossly underrepresented in both the council chamber and parliament. When they did become more directly involved they often faced discrimination and prejudice. Some parties at the local level were openly racist and a few local Labour Clubs even operated a 'colour bar' in the 1960s. Later, black members were recruited and even actively sought, but even then the local political culture was characterized as a 'patron–client relationship' in which white politicians looked after ethnic minority interests in return for their loyal support in the internal affairs of the local party (Solomos and Back, 1995, p. 74). Later still, black party members became more assertive, often seeking to influence party policy directly and become candidates for the council or parliament, principally through the Labour Party. To become more effective some sought to organize black sections within the party, which became a major issue from the mid-1980s onwards (Solomos and Back, 1995, pp. 85–91). Although this battle was lost, an increasing number of black and Asian candidates were selected and subsequently elected to play a growing role in the mainstream political process. Even so, blacks and Asians remain grossly underrepresented at every level.

Alongside this growing involvement in the party and electoral process, ethnic minorities have also played an increasingly important role in pressure group politics. Organizations representing ethnic minorities have sought influence and often funding from the council and other public bodies, and have engaged in the policy networks which now characterize the modern local governance process. Yet this cannot conceal their relative lack of political clout both within organizations and in policy bargaining between them. Nor has it ensured that ethnic minorities secure a better deal at local or national level.

The children and grandchildren of black and Asian immigrants, born and raised in Britain and speaking English with local accents, appear less willing to accept the discrimination and prejudice which their parents and grandparents have more docilely suffered. Educated along- side white children they are only too aware that they cannot compete on equal terms with them, particularly when it comes to seeking employ- ment. Increasingly living in deprived, segregated communities where education and employment prospects are poor, where they routinely suffer harassment and prejudice from the police, and where they are provoked by the racial taunts and violence of gangs of whites, it is hardly surprising that some are drawn into violent demonstrations and riots, which are almost guaranteed to provoke a serious political response and focus more attention on the problems of the area than years of patient consultation.

One reaction of disaffected members of ethnic minorities is to deny allegiance to the national community of which they legally form a part, and focus their loyalties on their own community. Thus some blacks and Asians have sought to imitate the 'black power' movement in the United States, pursuing their own version of racial pride and loyalty and displaying a form of racist ideology which mimics that of the white majority. While some would see racism as solely a white ideology, reflecting the majority power of the white community, it is also clear that ethnic minorities can display prejudice and practice discrimination towards each other, as well as showing a more understandable 'racist' reaction against white prejudice.

A trivial but symbolically significant illustration of the latter has been expressed in the support of young British-born Afro-Caribbeans and Asians for West Indian, Pakistan or Indian cricket teams in matches against England. Faisal Bodi (*Guardian,* 21 June 2001, p. 28), a Muslim journalist, has argued that underlying the show of allegiance to Pakistan is,

> a malaise of identity. Many of the revellers will never have been 'back home'… They are only nominally Pakistani … [but in sup- porting Pakistan] they are underlining and celebrating their alien- ation from mainstream society. Rejecting those who don't accept you is a common reaction of excluded groups.

Indeed, exclusion and separation, once forced on ethnic minorities, is now often freely chosen. This further reinforces a segregated pattern of housing, education and employment in which there is very little social contact across the 'racial' divide. Already it is claimed that there are virtual 'no-go areas' for both whites and ethnic minorities in some urban areas, and some physical barriers have even been erected between communities. The dangers of such segregation for inter-communal incomprehension, hostility and conflict hardly requires emphasis. If extremist racist 'solutions' are to be avoided, the only viable alternative would seem to involve a willing acceptance of a non-racist multicultural society in which people's ethnic origins did not determine their life chances.

Multiculturalism

Multiculturalism involves a more positive message than anti-racism, stressing the benefits of ethnic and cultural diversity. It thus directly confronts and counters the old racist fears of racial mixing, but also presents a challenge to ethnic nationalism. A common assumption in many modern nation states is that there is a single national culture which all citizens should share. New immigrants may be allowed in, and even in some circumstances encouraged, but they are expected to assimilate into the existing society and culture. Thus the United States of America long welcomed immigrants but insisted they should be for-mally instructed and thoroughly assimilated into the American way of life and become loyal American citizens. The British approach was less formal, but still assumed a process of naturalization and assimilation, which was fairly rapidly achieved with some immigrant groups such as the French Huguenots.

The idea of multiculturalism developed in the United States out of the black struggle for civil rights in the 1960s, which led to demands for the recognition of their black culture 'as an affirmation of their dis-tinct ethnic identity'. This led in turn to Hispanics and others insisting on affirming their own distinctive ethnic and cultural identity in a mul-ticultural society, while Australia and Canada similarly embraced mul-ticulturalism in the 1970s (Parekh, 2000b, p. 5).

Multiculturalism was a term employed in Britain in the 1970s and 1980s to describe an alternative policy approach to the previously 'colour-blind' strategy of encouraging assimilation and integration. Rather, difference should be accepted and respected. Children from minority ethnic communities, it was suggested, should have pride in their own language, religion and culture which should be part of their own school curriculum, and also part of the wider community's cur-riculum to encourage mutual understanding. This in turn provoked something of a backlash from those who claimed that English culture and Christian values were being sacrificed on the altar of 'political correctness', and from others who alleged that the new multicultural curriculum involved the neglect of vital skills which young blacks would need if they were to prosper in the British labour market and British society.

More recently, multiculturalism has been advanced more positively as a political doctrine which celebrates cultural diversity and emphasizes the mutual gains to be derived from contact between communities and cultures. Thus, it is argued, British society and culture has gained immeasurably from the influx of new skills, new ideas, different art and music, fashions and cuisine. If chicken tikka masala, now Britain's favourite dish, owes more to the ingenuity of Asian restaurants in catering to British taste than to authentic Indian cuisine, that is taken as further evidence of the benefits to be derived from a cultural mix.

There are some problems involved in this celebration of diversity and difference. 'Unfortunately the right to be different can all too readily be conceded without allowing for equality of opportunity and perhaps positively reinforcing inequality of opportunity' (Rex, 1986, p. 120). Moreover, multiculturalism involves some awkward implications for liberalism, when universal human rights conflict with the prevailing values of particular communities. According to Parekh (2000b), liberals wrongly assume their own values have universal validity, and thus accord insufficient respect to cultures which involve different beliefs and practices. Thus liberal western ideas and values are embodied in universal declarations of human rights, which might conflict with other (for example Asian) values of 'social harmony, respect for authority, orderly society, a united and extended family and a sense of filial piety'. Human beings are not the same everywhere, but 'culturally embedded in the sense that they are born into, raised in and deeply shaped by their cultural communities'.

Barry (2001) argues that this approach 'is liable to be harmful to women and children in minority communities and to those within them who deviate from prevailing norms' (Barry, p. 2001, 58). Thus respecting the values embedded in a particular culture might entail accepting discrimination on grounds of gender or caste, and legitimizing prejudices on sexual orientation. Cultural norms can be employed to trump minimal universal norms (as for example enumerated in declarations of human rights) including women's rights, gay rights and even rights to freedom of speech. Barry goes on to argue that the appeal to abstract universal principles has been the driving force behind the transformation of the legal status of women in Britain and elsewhere. He similarly points out that the advance of the rights of American blacks depended on similar abstract universal principles, whereas hitherto prevailing cultural norms would have justified the continuation of discriminatory racist practices.

Parekh (2000b, p. 196) acknowledges the inevitable tensions between the norms of the majority and of minority communities. Any political society, he argues:

> should foster a strong sense of unity and common belonging among its citizens, as otherwise it cannot act as a united community able to take and enforce collectively-binding decisions and regulate and resolve conflicts.

The problem is how to resolve the apparently conflicting needs for both unity and diversity. What happens when the strongly held values and practices of a minority culture run against the values, practices and sometimes deepest convictions of the majority? Parekh explores a number of controversial issues – including female circumcision, polygamy, Muslim and Jewish methods of slaughtering animals, arranged marriages, initiation ceremonies, and exemption from legal or school requirements on matters of dress. Yet while Parekh discusses such problems sensibly and sensitively, the balance he strikes between unity and diversity seems more pragmatic than principled, and as Barry (2001, p. 64) observes 'in every case broadly supports the status quo in Britain'. Ultimately there is no easy criterion for deciding which norms are universally applicable human standards and which are culturally variable.

The difficulties were dramatized in the Rushdie affair. The publication of *The Satanic Verses* (Rushdie, 1988) caused deep offence to the religious convictions of Muslims, and was perceived as a deliberate assault on the identity and pride of the Muslim community. Yet the reaction of sections of that community, extending to book-burning and threats on the life of the author and others, outraged the basic liberal values of toleration and freedom of speech, thus alienating those who would normally stand up for the rights of minorities, while reinforcing the anti-Islamic prejudices of others with no great attachment to universal human rights.

The politics of race and anti-racism are sometimes linked with the politics of gender and feminism, and indeed both find expression in anti-discrimination and equal-opportunities policies. In the 1980s some on the political left hoped to construct a 'rainbow alliance' of feminists, ethnic minorities, gays and disabled with traditional working-class trade unionists and socialists. Yet this alliance of oppressed minorities failed to constitute a cohesive political major-ity. The assumed natural coincidence of interest and values between those who were disadvantaged on grounds of class, race, gender or sexual orientation proved an optimistic assumption. Just as some trade unionists could be both sexist and racist, victims of racism might be sexist and homophobic. 'Race' or 'ethnicity' is ultimately a contentious social category which cuts across other classifications, interests and values. Clearly, the interests of black or Asian middle-class women may not coincide with those of black working-class men (Mirza, 1997). Multiculturalism is a political ideology which assumes a pluralist multi-ethnic society with crosscutting interests and values. As such it certainly contradicts the assumptions of racism. Yet the demand for respect for different cultures, if treated as an absolute value, has potentially damaging implications for some within those cultures.

Further reading

The literature on fascism and Nazism is formidably large. Kitchen (1976) provides a useful general introduction, while Carsten (1967) and Eatwell (1996) provide good brief histories. Kershaw (1993) is illum-inating on Nazism. Laqueur (1979) has edited a thought-provoking col-lection of essays which discuss some of the main theoretical issues. On British fascism, Thurlow (1987) has written a useful general history which takes the story beyond Benewick's (1972) earlier illuminating study. For Mosley, see the scholarly but rather too sympathetic biogra-phy by Skidelsky (1990). Walker (1977) provides a good (if now dated) general account of the National Front, while Taylor (1982) is particu-larly useful on their ideology.

The literature on racism is similarly large and complex. Saggar (1992), Solomos (1993) and Skellington (1996) provide broad surveys of race and politics in contemporary Britain. Key texts which focus on theory from different perspectives include Rex (1986), Miles (1989, 1993), Solomos and Back (1996) and Mac an Ghaill (1999). Bulmer and Solomos (1999) and Back and Solomos (2000) have edited sub-stantial readers on racism which include extracts from many key writers. Other required reading includes several landmark reports on racism in Britain which discussed theoretical issues including Scarman (1981), Macpherson (1999) and Parekh (2000a). Parekh (2000b) has also furnished a substantial theoretical exploration of multiculturalism, which provides an extended underpinning of the analysis of the report he chaired.

7

Feminism

Introduction

Like other ideologies, feminism involves a critique, an ideal and a programme. The critique contains an analysis of the discrimination and injustices suffered by women in existing society; the ideal is justice for women, generally but not exclusively interpreted to mean sexual equality. The practical programme has included action to achieve political and legal rights, equality in the economic sphere, the elimination of sexual discrimination in education, the workplace and the home, and protection against physical and sexual violence. All political ideologies contain implications for political action, but feminism is markedly action-oriented.

Feminism clearly differs from most of the other political ideologies discussed in this book. It is not a party ideology. Moreover, many of its concerns are with the private sphere of family and interpersonal relations rather than the public sphere of government and conventional politics. Yet the definition of what is and what is not political is itself an essentially ideological question. While many conservatives or liberals would distinguish between state and civil society, and between a public and personal sphere, feminists have argued that 'the personal is political'. Thus issues of identity and interpersonal relations, the exploitation of women within the family, or the sexual abuse of women are political questions, just as more conventionally political issues such as civil and political rights, and equal opportunities. Feminism involves a distinctive and radically different perspective which has important implications for politics in its broadest sense.

Analysis of feminism, as with other ideologies, has tended to involve distinctions and classifications into periods and sub-categories. Thus the literature commonly refers to two main 'waves' of feminism – the first from the late eighteenth century until around 1920, and the second from the 1960s onwards. Largely cutting across this time dimension there is also a conventional distinction between three main varieties of feminism – liberal feminism, socialist/Marxist feminism, and radical feminism – to which other sub-categories are now sometimes added such as eco-feminism, or black feminism or post-modern feminism. Such classifications are helpful, particularly to students struggling to make sense of a complex range of feminist thinkers, ideas and issues, and some use is made of them here. However, categorization always involves oversimplification and often distortion. There are feminists who are difficult to pigeon-hole and newer strands of feminist thinking which cut across or lie outside the conventional categories.

Feminism transcends national boundaries. Feminists would argue that women are everywhere exploited, regardless of economic, political and cultural differences between societies. Thus a focus on British politics appears problematic for an analysis of feminism. However, the problems of women in advanced western capitalist societies like Britain have distinctive aspects, and some British feminists question whether even American feminist analysis is necessarily applicable to 'the state of feminism in Britain' (Linda Grant, *Guardian,* 11 May 1995). Action to remedy discrimination and exploitation in Britain inevitably relates to the specific economic, social, political and legal context (Carter, 1988; Lovenduski and Randall, 1993), and this context also affects theory. Thus while this chapter will draw on feminist thought from other countries, it will concentrate principally on British feminism.

The origins and development of feminist thought – liberal feminism

Much early feminist writing involved the application of liberal assumptions and values to the position of women. Although liberals initially were reluctant to extend the 'rights of man' to woman (Arblaster, 1984), a few men and rather more women brought up within the liberal tradition argued that women could and should compete on equal terms with men. These liberal feminists sought the same education for women as for men, and the same civil rights and economic opportunities (Tong, 1989, pp. 13–22). Among writers who contributed to the predominantly liberal 'first wave' of feminism were Mary Wollstonecraft, John Stuart Mill and Harriet Taylor, while modern liberal feminists include Betty Friedan, Susan Moller Okin and Janet Radcliffe Richards.

Mary Wollstonecraft's *A Vindication of the Rights of Women* (ed. Tauchert, 1995) is still widely regarded as the first key feminist text. It was written in 1792, soon after the outbreak of the French Revolution and the 'Declaration of the Rights of Man', and the appearance of Tom Paine's *Rights of Man*. Its fundamental assumptions were those of liberalism – the rights, freedom and equality of the individual – applied specifically to the position of women. Wollstonecraft argued that women were as capable of reason as men, and should be educated in the same way as men. They should be free to exercise their reason and choose their role in life. An equality of worth between men and women implied an equality of rights, including political rights.

John Stuart Mill as a young man championed women's political rights, and his feminist convictions were strengthened by his long intellectual partnership and subsequent marriage to Harriet Taylor, who was herself largely responsible for the essay *The Enfranchisement of Women* (ed. Pyle, 1995) published in 1851. Mill's own *The Subjection of Women* (ed. Okin, 1988) is still widely regarded as 'one of the landmarks of British feminism' (Pyle, 1995, p. ix). Although not published until 1869, it was actually written in 1861, the year of the beginning of the American Civil War in which slavery was a central issue. Many women who joined the eventually successful campaign for the abolition of slavery in the United States came to appreciate the irony of their own exclusion from political rights and privileges. Writing as an English opponent of slavery, Mill provocatively claimed that 'no slave is a slave to the same lengths and in so full a sense of the word, as a wife is' (ed. Okin, 1988, p. 33), detailing the extent of a woman's legal subjugation to her husband. While admitting that most women were treated better than the law permitted, Mill also wrote of the physical abuse some women suffered at the hands of men. Mill's remedies involved principally political and legal equality for women, which he hoped would lead to a partnership of equals between the sexes, to their mutual benefit.

Mill also demanded women's 'admissibility to all the functions and occupations hitherto retained as a monopoly of the stronger sex', although he still assumed a choice between career and marriage, and that most women would prefer the latter. Here he differed not only from modern feminists but also from his wife. Her expectation that women could and should combine marriage and career, however, depended on 'a panoply of domestic servants', 'presumably', as one historian of feminist thought tartly observes, 'working class females' (Tong, 1989, p. 19).

The second wave of feminism produced some notable additions to liberal feminist literature. Betty Friedan's work (1963, 1977, 1982) appealed to a generation of American and British women who wanted careers and fulfilment outside the home, without necessarily wishing to reject the traditional values of motherhood and family. Janet Radcliffe Richards' *The Sceptical Feminist* (1982), involved a reaffirmation of the traditional liberal feminist appeal to reason, equality and social justice in the face of modern radical feminist criticism of liberalism. Susan Moller Okin (1990) has extended the theory of justice of John Rawls to the family, and has also incidentally edited a modern edition of *The Subjection of Women* (1988), supplying a vigorous defence of Mill's work

Before we proceed to a more critical analysis of liberal feminism generally it is important to record that its achievements were far from negligible. In feminism's 'first wave', educational advances and legal reforms of benefit to women were secured, new careers were opened up and votes for women finally won (in 1918 in Britain). It was the perceived shortcomings of some of the achievements of 'first-wave' feminism – continued inequality at work and women's underrepresentation in management and the professions – which further helped to drive essentially liberal reforms in the second wave of feminism from the 1960s. An Equal Pay Act was passed in 1970, and a Sex Discrimination Act in 1975. A new body, the Equal Opportunities Commission, was established to monitor implementation of both Acts and to investigate allegations of discrimination. While such changes in the law did not ensure equal pay or equal opportunities, it did entail some significant advances, particularly for middle-class career women.

Modern feminist criticism of liberal feminism

Modern feminism is not predominantly liberal, and many second-wave feminists have regarded the 'whole liberal approach' as 'flawed and inappropriate for feminist purposes' because it accepts 'without criticism a set of values that are essentially male', particularly 'the importance that liberalism attaches to rationality, self-determination and equal competition' as opposed to the qualities of 'empathy, nurturing and cooperation' associated with women (Bryson, 1999, p. 12). Liberal feminists are criticized for assuming that women's nature is much the same as man's, while radical feminists today are more concerned to emphasize female difference.

Liberal feminists are also criticized for failing to provide an adequate explanation for the injustices so universally inflicted on women. If the case for women's emancipation was as clear as the liberals suggested, how could their subjection for so long and in so many parts of the globe be explained? Liberal feminists assumed that rights for women would be secured by rational persuasion and specific legal reforms, and were not drawn to analyse the prevailing power relations which denied those rights in practice (Coole, 1988: ch. 6; Bryson, 1992, pp. 58–64). Many radical feminists today would argue that men enjoy too much the fruits of their power over women to surrender it without a struggle.

To critics this central failure to explain women's inequality meant that the liberal strategy for tackling it was inadequate. Legal reforms were insufficient, and the evidence of continued discrimination in Britain after the achievement of formal legal equality was extensive and damning. Thus women remained considerably underrepresented in Parliament and local government long after their formal political enfranchisement (Lovenduski and Randall, 1993, pp. 165–6). Similarly, even after the passing of an Equal Pay Act in 1970, average earnings for women in full-time employment remain only 80 per cent of male earnings (Bruley, 1999, p. 165). Despite the outlawing of discrimination on grounds of sex, and the establishment of the Equal Opportunities Commission, only relatively few women have reached the highest levels in the civil service, the judiciary (Lovenduski and Randall, 1993, pp. 166–9), the professions and company boardrooms. Neither rational persuasion nor legal compulsion seemed adequate to secure justice for women.

Particularly glaring were the continuing and perhaps increasing differences among women themselves. While a minority of largely white middle-class women signally gained from the changes in the legal and cultural climate, the majority of women hardly profited. Those who, like Mrs Thatcher, succeeded exceptionally in what was still so evidently a man's world, did little to assist women generally. Indeed, the opportunities opened up for a minority of professional career women were often dependent on the provision of child care, catering and cleaning services, performed by other women, commonly among the most exploited in terms of pay and conditions of employment. The majority of women were still largely confined to low status and low-pay jobs in manufacturing, retailing, catering, cleaning and that ubiquitous category, caring. Increasingly, economic necessity forced many women to combine the dual role of low-paid wage earner and unpaid domestic worker.

Finally, some modern feminists criticize liberals for concentrating on discrimination and injustice in the public sphere of the law, politics, school and work, and neglecting women's role in the private world of home and family, to many feminists the very centre of women's

exploitation and subordination. As a consequence of the liberal separation of public and private spheres, of state and civil society, behaviour
within the private world of the home and family was not regarded as a
legitimate field for state intervention (although, as we have seen, Mill
and other liberal feminists were concerned with justice within marriage
and the family).

Yet while both their analysis and prescription has been subjected to
extensive criticism, and formal legal and political rights have failed to
produce equality between the sexes, the liberal feminists secured real
gains for women. Moreover, changes in UK law fostered changes in
discourse, and much of the liberal feminist agenda has been incorpor-
ated into mainstream political ideology. Thus liberal feminists have
been more successful in realizing their admittedly limited agenda in
comparison with the more ambitious but largely unachieved programmes of socialist and radical feminists.

Socialist and Marxist feminism

Socialists and liberals start from different assumptions. For the liberal,
society is the sum of its individual parts, and social change is the cumulative consequence of free choices made by individuals. For the socialist, individual men and women are severely constrained by social
pressures outside their control. While the liberal relates the position of
women to fundamental underlying assumptions about individual liberty
and formal equality, the socialist naturally attempts to explain woman's
exploitation in terms of broader social processes.

For Marxists this entails an analysis involving inevitable conflict
between economic classes, shaped by the dominant mode of production
– capitalism in the modern western world. Thus the position of women
can only be understood in terms of capitalism and class. The exploitation of women in modern society is a consequence of the exploitation
of the industrial working class under capitalism; the unpaid domestic
labour largely performed by women in modern western societies is
related to the requirements of capitalism. Women may also be exploited
in the labour force – used as part of the industrial reserve army of
labour to swell the ranks of workers in times of boom and to undercut
the wages of male workers more generally. It follows that liberal
remedies are at best mere palliatives and that the emancipation of
women can only be truly achieved by abolishing capitalism and those
bourgeois social relations associated with capitalism.

By no means all socialist feminists are Marxists. There were pre-Marxist socialist thinkers who addressed the position of women, such as, notably, William Thompson (1775–1844) in Britain (Coole, 1988, pp. 158–65). Subsequently, there were many other writers and active socialists and social democrat politicians who put forward arguments and practical proposals to advance the position of women. These included both Keir Hardie and Ramsay MacDonald in the British Labour Party, the indefatigable campaigner for family allowances Eleanor Rathbone, and more recent mainstream Labour socialists. Yet while some writers distinguish between Marxist feminism and other socialist feminism, the line between them is in practice blurred, and it is difficult to construct a distinctive socialist or social democratic feminism which comprehends all the various feminists who were socialists but not Marxists.

However, socialist feminists of all kinds differ from liberal feminists in the importance they attach to class. Most women, it is argued, suffer from a double exploitation, belonging both to a subordinate class and disadvantaged by their sex. The link between class and gender is more problematic. Marxist analysis suggests that the exploitation of women both in the workplace and the home is the consequence of the class conflict associated with capitalism. Thus it is assumed that it is class conflict rather than gender conflict which is ultimately fundamental (Coole, 1988, p. 193).

The social class of women is itself a contentious issue. Married women were once conventionally assigned to class categories based on their husband's occupation, and this is still the case if they are not themselves in paid employment. Yet although such women may be officially defined as middle-class, their lifestyle may more closely resemble that of their working-class counterparts, while their husbands enjoy business perks, including prestigious company cars, expense account meals and corporate hospitality. Some feminists have tried to solve the knotty relationship between class and gender by simply declaring that women constitute a distinctive class.

Laying aside problems of analysis and classification, all socialist feminists share a practical concern for the condition of ordinary women, and specifically for women in paid employment, particularly those in low-paid casual and part-time employment who lack even the more basic legal protection afforded to most full-time workers. Socialist feminists not only seek extend rights to part-time and casual workers, but also to empower female workers themselves through organization, unionization and consciousness raising. A characteristic practical concern has been the provision of adequate childcare for ordinary women workers for whom the facilities commonly utilized by professional women are unavailable, unsuitable or simply too expensive. Thus socialist feminists commonly demand the availability, as of right, of day nurseries, nursery schools and workplace creches.

Some socialist feminists would argue that the provision of childcare for women in paid employment does not assist those women who, either through circumstances or choice, are obliged to perform housework and childcare services unpaid in the home. This practical concern was linked with a long-running theoretical debate among Marxist feminists over domestic labour, which was seen as providing a crucial underpinning for the whole capitalist system. Some argued that the low dependent status of domestic labour could only be significantly improved by acknowledging the value of the services performed through regular payment – hence the demand for wages for housework. This campaign was not supported by all feminists, partly because it condoned and legitimized traditional gender roles within the family and the unfair burden of domestic tasks undertaken by women.

Marxist and socialist feminists played a leading role in the Women's Liberation Movement in Britain which did so much to raise women's consciousness and stimulate action, particularly in the early 1970s. The demands of the founding conference at Ruskin in 1970 in large part reflected the socialist feminist agenda: equal pay, equal education and opportunity, 24-hour nurseries, and free contraception and abortion on demand (Bruley, 1999, p. 149). British Marxist feminists also made a rich contribution to feminist theory. Yet their analysis and prescription increasingly diverged from some of the new radical feminists who prioritized gender relations over class relations, and the movement which the Marxists had done so much to create and develop became fragmented (Lovenduski and Randall, 1993, pp. 93–100).

Criticism of Marxist and socialist feminism

Socialism and feminism do not invariably go together. Some feminists have learned from bitter experience that male socialists and trade unionists can display as much male chauvinism as their counterparts on the right. However, many feminists are also socialists, and are thus often faced with a conflict of loyalties or priorities. Aware that the treatment of women is only one, and not always the most important, of the manifestations of 'man's inhumanity to man', they are sometimes accused by other feminists of not giving sufficient priority to women's issues.

This criticism is linked with a more fundamental questioning of the theoretical assumptions underpinning Marxist feminism. In so far as the injustices suffered by women are linked with capitalism, there is a tacit assumption that the end of capitalism would entail the end of women's subjection. Ultimately, it is implied, inequality of the sexes derives from the inequalities between different economic classes. Thus issues of class are primary, and issues of gender secondary. This hardly provides an adequate explanation for the extensive evidence of women's oppression across time and cultures. As Coole (1988, p. 193) points out, although Marxism is relevant to women 'because of its general analysis of the dynamics of oppression', it is also 'problematic... because it cannot account for a specifically sexual form of oppression except in so far as it is functional to private property and production'.

There has been some anguished reassessment of *The Unhappy Marriage of Marxism and Feminism* (Sargent, 1981). Many Marxist feminists themselves would today acknowledge that male domination and the exploitation of women is a feature of most if not all known societies, which implies at least a need to extend Marxist analysis by borrowing from other approaches. Thus Juliet Mitchell (1971, 1974, 1984) has combined a Marxist class analysis with insights drawn from psychology and psychoanalysis to explain the subordination of women within the family and domestic sphere. Through childhood socialization, gender roles are learned which have an enduring significance. Other Marxist feminists have acknowledged a need to incorporate the radical feminists' theory of patriarchy into their analysis. Thus women are exploited because of their class position within a capitalist society, but also because they are women and generally subject to male domination. This does raise the question of the connection, if any, between capitalism and patriarchy, and of the fundamental source of women's oppression. MacKinnon (1983) has argued that while Marxism focuses on work, feminism focuses on sexuality, which is the real basis of women's subordination according to those described as radical feminists.

Radical feminism

Marxist feminism involved a widening of the focus of the woman's movement away from specific legal and political concerns of the liberals towards an analysis of the underlying economic and social causes of women's oppression. At first sight, the work of the radical feminists implied, by contrast, a drastic narrowing of horizons to sexual and personal relations between men and women. However, if the focus appeared to be narrow, the radicals argued it had a universal relevance. Moreover, their central concept of patriarchy, rule by the father or the male head of the household, provided feminism with a theory which was not essentially derivative, not just an application of theories like liberalism and Marxism. For radical feminists the nature of the problem is neither an inadequate political and legal framework, as liberal feminists imply, nor capitalism, as Marxist feminists suggest, but just men. Everywhere men exploit women. It is the sex war, not the class war, which is fundamental.

Who are the radical feminists? Several key texts first appeared around 1970: Kate Millett's *Sexual Politics*, Germaine Greer's *The Female Eunuch*, Eva Figes' *Patriarchal Attitudes* and Shulamith Firestone's *The Dialectic of Sex*. What these books had in common was a preoccupation with the biology and sexuality of women. Indeed, the term 'woman's liberation' was closely linked with what was seen as a sexual revolution in the 1960s. These writers were all less concerned with the discrimination against women in the political and public sphere, and more concerned with the everyday relations between men and women in the home, family and bedroom. They illustrated their themes of feminine exploitation with examples from literature, journals and popular culture.

This radical focus on male–female relations in the home involved not so much a retreat from politics as a deliberate widening of the political sphere. The title of Kate Millett's book *Sexual Politics* was not accidental; the implication was that sexual relations involved power and were inherently political, hence the radical feminist slogan, 'The personal is political.'

Another characteristic of much radical feminism is its style: they freely use the language of revolution rather than reform; they challenge and set out to shock. The prevailing tone is anger and outrage, and there is a clear difference in approach from that of the liberals. The enemy was male power, embodied in the universal institution of patriarchy. Patriarchy may be variously defined, but is a term most usually employed by radical feminists to signify, simply, male dominance. The power of the husband over his wife, the power of the father over his children, and the power of the male head of the household over everyone within in it was seen as the ultimate symbol and source of male power in politics and society. Justice for women could thus never be achieved unless the institution of patriarchy was destroyed. In this context the absence of legal rights and privileges were beside the point. These were not the cause of injustice for women, only its visible manifestation. Likewise a socialist revolution which ended the oppression of one class by another would not by itself end the oppression of women by men.

For radical feminists it was in the sexual relations between men and women that male domination and female subjugation were most evident. A prime practical concern of radical feminists was violence against women, and most particularly rape, which was not perceived as a rare and aberrational act of violence but as a widespread and typical aspect of male sexuality. Thus radical feminists drew attention to the extent of unreported rape, 'date rape' and rape within marriage (Brownmiller, 1977). Another target was pornography which involved degrading images of women, reinforced their role as sex-objects, and arguably incited sexual violence against women (Dworkin, 1981). Radical British feminists involved in Women Against Violence Against Women (WAVAW) argued that 'pornography is the theory and rape is the practice', and led direct action attacks against porn shops and cinemas (Bruley, 1999: 155), although other feminists opposed censorship (Lovenduski and Randall, 1993, pp. 337–51).

Radical feminists revolutionized thinking on gender relations. Liberal feminists had sought as far as possible to eliminate the differences between men and women, and to enlist male aid in the emancipation of women. They aimed to open up the existing all-male bastions to women to allow free and equal competition, regardless of gender differences. Mill and others argued that the equality of women would ultimately be to the benefit of men and society generally (Mill, 1869, 1983). Radical feminists assumed by contrast that the advantages men enjoyed by virtue of their power over women would not be readily surrendered. Thus the women's movement would have to depend on women. Indeed it might entail the positive exclusion of men. Moreover, many radical feminists celebrated women's difference; they did not want to be like men.

A subject of debate among feminists was the extent to which male nature and behaviour might be modified. Thus a 'new man' could emerge to be a fitting equal partner to a liberated woman. Others suggested that the new man was a myth. For a few radical feminists the rejection of the whole male sex was a logical corollary – a factor in the emergence of the hostile caricature of the typical feminist as a lesbian man-hater. Although lesbianism has been an issue for feminists and sometimes a source of division between them (Lovenduski and Randall,

1993, pp. 67–78), the rights of individuals, both male and female, to pursue their own sexual preferences as long as these do not involve harm to others is essentially a different issue from women's rights.

Another closely associated target for radical feminists was the conventional family, perceived as the centre of the inequitable burden of domestic work and childcare imposed on women. In contrast to the arguments of liberals like Betty Friedan, or of the Marxist feminists who sought wages for housework, many radicals denied that women would be able to achieve fulfilment outside the home while they were fettered by domesticity. A meaningful career could not realistically be combined with traditional institutions of motherhood and family. Thus the emancipation of women appeared to some to entail the abolition of the family.

A problem here was that greater involvement of women in child-rearing was clearly in some sense biologically determined. Shulamith Firestone (1979) tried to tackle this problem head-on, arguing that women would not be free until they were liberated from the tyranny of their biology. Pregnancy, she declared, was barbaric, and she looked forward to its ultimate replacement by artificial reproduction. These views have provoked some ridicule, but they do pose in stark form a dilemma for women. Modern forms of contraception have already revolutionized sexual behaviour. Developments in baby care have facilitated earlier weaning and this and other changes have allowed mothers to leave their babies earlier with child carers. Test-tube babies are already a reality. All such developments enable or oblige choice. Further scientific developments might render human reproduction outside the womb feasible, and enable women to escape from 'the tyranny of reproduction'. As Firestone suggests, 'development of the option should make possible an honest reexamination of the ancient value of motherhood'. While many women might reject the kind of future suggested by Firestone, there can be no certainty unless and until such options are available.

Faced with the diversity within radical feminism, it is difficult to sum up its achievements. Certainly the style of the radicals has provoked a reaction. Arguably, the anger and shock tactics of some radical feminists has had a signal effect on the climate of opinion towards women, and the treatment of women. There is now a greater consciousness of the implicit and often quite explicit sexist assumptions behind many advertising and media images of women. This has led to some attempt to avoid old stereotypes and provide new more appropriate female role models. Similarly, the campaigns focusing on rape and the general issue of violence against women have contributed to a significant shift in public attitudes and some changes in practice. The issue has been forced onto the political agenda, recognized as a serious problem, and is now treated more sensitively by the police than hitherto, encouraging more women to report rape and physical abuse although it remains very difficult to secure convictions. More support is provided for the victims of violence, both in terms of counselling and in the provision of refuges (Lovenduski and Randall, 1993, pp. 302–34).

Criticism of radical feminism

The main strength of radical feminism has perhaps always been in action rather than theory, although only radical feminism can lay claim to a really distinctive political ideology, liberal and Marxist feminism both being essentially derivative. However, radical feminism has perhaps been more impressive in exposing the shortcomings of alternative theoretical foundations than in developing new theory. While there have been attempts to explore the implications of the concept of 'patriarchy', it has more commonly been employed as a catch-all definition and explanation of male dominance. The involvement of some radicals with environmentalism on the one hand or post-modernism on the other (see below) clearly involves other theoretical connections, but these have contributed to some fragmentation of feminist theory rather than offering a body of ideas which might be generally acceptable to radical feminism.

Feminists from Wollstonecraft onwards have stimulated a hostile reaction from many men and often also women, so the anti-feminist backlash provoked by the radicals is perhaps scarcely surprising. Yet criticism is not confined to anti-feminists. Thus the liberal feminist Betty Friedan (1982) claims that the shock tactics of the radicals has also alienated support, not least from many women. In particular she suggests that 'sexual politics has been a red herring', a diversion from the real issues of political and economic exploitation. Janet Radcliffe Richards (1982) argues that exaggeration of the feminist case and neglect of the traditional liberal ideals of reason, justice and fairness have spoiled the legitimate demands of women for fair and equal treatment. She provides a spirited defence of traditional liberal reason in the face of the deliberate rejection of 'male' logic in favour of feeling and intuition by some radical feminists. She denies that feminism is 'the primary struggle', as some radicals would assert, and rejects the claim of the Redstockings Manifesto that 'All other forms of exploitation and oppression (racism, capitalism, imperialism etc.) are extensions of male supremacy.' Natasha Walter (1999) has urged that the new feminism should be 'less personal and more political', an explicit criticism of the central thrust of radical feminism.

Some of this is a criticism of style rather than substance, but there are more fundamental points which go to the heart of the universalist claims of the radical feminists. Thus the preoccupations of some western upper-middle-class feminists, particularly their outright rejection of the institutions of marriage and the family, and even maternity, do sometimes appear remote from the lives and experience of the majority of women, particularly working-class women, black women and women from other cultures. The rejection of patriarchy need not necessarily entail the rejection of motherhood, but some feminist writing has involved a rejection of maternal values (Freely, 1995). Scorn for motherhood is often accompanied by an overidealized perception of the liberating value of a career, which does not recognize that for most women (as for many men) work involves endured tedium, undertaken from financial need, with little prospect of releasing creative energies.

Radical feminists from a relatively privileged background have sometimes been accused of universalizing their own highly specific and untypical circumstances as if these were the problems of women everywhere. Yet women may experience very different forms of oppression and have very different needs in different social classes, communities and cultures. The preoccupations of white middle-class feminists do not necessarily coincide with those of black women (ed. Mirza, 1997). In some cultures women are more exercised over the right to bear children, free from pressures towards family limitation, unsafe contraception, abortion or sterilization, than they are over the right to abortion. Black and Asian women in Britain have pointed to the distinctive problems and injustices they suffer, leading to claims that 'the Women's Liberation Movement as a whole is irrelevant to the needs and demands of most black women' (quoted in Lovenduski and Randall, 1993, p. 81).

Eco-feminism

Some feminists have moved in quite a different direction from those radicals who rejected traditional roles associated with motherhood and the family. Traditional feminine attributes are celebrated rather than spurned. Thus child-rearing, far from being stigmatized as demeaning, is perceived as the most obvious manifestation of the caring cooperative nature of women, compared with the aggressive, competitive behaviour of men. Far from competing with men, or seeking to be like men, as the liberal feminists appeared to suggest, women should be themselves and maintain their own distinctive characteristics, values and priorities. This did not necessarily entail a retreat from the political sphere back to the privacy of domesticity, but the promotion of a distinctive alternative female politics of love, peace and care for the environment. The women peace campaigners who symbolically hung baby's bootees and similar objects from the barbed wire surrounding nuclear missile bases were asserting a different female-oriented value system. Women's involvement thus changed the style and content of politics.

One possible outcome of this kind of radical feminist thinking is what is sometimes referred to as eco-feminism (Plant, 1989; Mies and Shiva, 1993). There is perhaps no logical reason why feminism should entail a concern for the environment. Indeed some forms of environmentalism have involved a markedly conservative view of the relations between the sexes. The fundamentalist cry 'back to nature' might seem to entail a return to a 'natural' division of labour between the sexes, but the image of the earth mother, sometimes associated with eco-feminists, is not one which all feminists find helpful or appealing. Indeed, fascists combined a mystical reverence for the land with some very old-fashioned ideas about the position of women.

Even so, it is clear that women are prominently involved in the Green movement, and for many there is a clear link between their feminist values and their Green commitment. There is a strong female presence likewise in the associated animal rights and vegetarian movements. It may be that experience of pregnancy, giving birth and child nurture do give women a closer sense of kinship with the natural and animal world. Concern for the health of their children entails perhaps a greater awareness of the possible dangers in the environment and in the food chain. Women's nurturing role also gives them a greater felt stake in the future.

Yet the involvement of some feminists in environmentalism has revealed some fissures within the woman's movement. There is not a great deal in common between the radical feminism of Shulamith Firestone and that of some of the eco-feminists. The issue of abortion serves to illustrates some of the divisions which have emerged. For many radical feminists of the 1960s and 1970s the demand for abortion on demand was central to female emancipation; women could not be free unless they had control over their own bodies. Yet for some eco-feminists respect for the life in the unborn foetus was part of their respect for the life of all created things, aligning them (on this issue) with the pro-life 'moral majority' associated with the neo-conservative New Right.

The impact of the New Right – Conservative feminism?

This raises the more general question of the impact of New Right ideas on feminism, which has usually been associated predominantly with the left of the political spectrum. Mary Wollstonecraft mixed with French revolutionaries and married the anarchist William Godwin. Many nineteenth century American feminist women were closely involved with the anti-slavery movement. Similarly, the second wave of feminism was bound up with civil rights and anti-war protest movements. Thus feminism was associated with other progressive or socialist political causes.

By contrast, the right tended to ignore, scorn or completely reject the demands of feminists for justice and equality. This was most manifest on the extreme right. The Nazis persecuted feminists, outlawed birth control, condemned women's involvement in politics and recommended a return to the traditional female concerns of *kirche, kuche, kinder*. Conservatives were less overtly hostile, but generally showed little sympathy for demands for the vote, equal pay and equal opportunities until after they were formally achieved. The British Conservative Party has certainly welcomed women into its ranks, but with a few marked exceptions, of which Mrs Thatcher is the most obvious, has generally assigned them a subordinate role as party workers and fund-raisers, and wives and unpaid political help-mates of male MPs. Thus feminism would seem to have little in common with the right of the political spectrum.

Yet it would be strange if the ideas of the New Right, which have had such a marked effect on British and western culture generally in recent years, had not also influenced the women's movement. The initial mainstream feminist reaction was dismissive or hostile to both the neo-conservative and neo-liberal strands of the New Right (Tusscher and Waylen, in Evans et al., 1986); however, some women, and even a few feminists, have been less antagonistic to elements of New Right thought.

Neo-liberal free-market individualism has some obvious implications for the position of women in the labour market. Discrimination against women appears not so much unjust as downright inefficient, involving interference with the operation of the free market and leading to the employment of less able and less-productive workers. The increased employment of women, and large-scale unemployment among men is in part a consequence of the greater flexibility of the female workforce, and a greater readiness to accept the competitive market rate for the job (that is, lower pay), characteristics applauded by neo-liberal economists, although likewise deplored by many feminists as exploitation. However, there are arguably positive aspects for women in this restructuring of the labour market. The world of employment is no longer preeminently a man's world. Women are not only breadwinners in their own right, but often the main breadwinners in the household. A small proportion of women, moreover, have spectacularly benefited from the new meritocratic competition for career advancement. The economic position of women generally has been transformed; their purchasing power in the economy is increasingly evident not only in the advertising of traditional female products, but in the promotion of cars, banks and insurance policies.

The neo-conservative aspects of the New Right have other implications for women. The reaction against 'permissiveness', the proclaimed concern for the silent or moral majority, and the 'back to basics' campaign have involved a reaffirmation of traditional and particularly family values. Thus the breakdown of marriage and the traditional family have been widely deplored. As gender relationships within marriage and the nuclear family have been a major target for radical feminists, it might be imagined that the attitudes of feminists and neo-conservatives are diametrically opposed. Indeed, this is still largely the case. However, radical feminists have sometimes found themselves in the same camp as neo-conservatives, notably over pornography which many feminists have vigorously denounced. Such feminists find themselves aligned with neo-conservative opponents of sexual permissiveness, once commonly associated with women's liberation. Indeed, men were arguably the main beneficiaries of sexual liberation, while many women were literally left 'holding the baby', forced into the dual role of sole breadwinner and carer in lone-parent households.

Betty Friedan, who encouraged a generation of American women to careers outside the narrow confines of conventional domesticity has in a later book (1982) reaffirmed the values of the family and marriage. For Friedan, who was always a liberal feminist with a reformist agenda, this was only a shift of emphasis. Rather more surprising perhaps, Germaine Greer, who remains a scathing critic of the western nuclear family, has become an enthusiast for the extended family as a source of comfort, support and fulfilment for women. Other feminists, while seeking a broader, more inclusive and more tolerant definition of the family, have cautiously endorsed family values. Thus they have sometimes appeared as ideological bedfellows of New Right neo-conservatives. Indeed there are some female Conservative politicians for whom the term 'conservative feminist' may not be inappropriate, in that they combine traditional family values with a concern for women's issues.

For most feminists any ideological fellow-travelling with the New Right is strictly limited. While some policy prescriptions may coincide, underlying assumptions remain very different. To many neo-conservatives the institution of the family is valued for its presumed capacity to restore the authority and social order which they see as lacking in society. It is a means of disciplining the young, and the restoration of paternal discipline is a key facet of this neo-conservative agenda. Hence it is urged that 'families need fathers'. At another level, support for the traditional two-parent family is a means to limiting the escalating social welfare budget. Family break-up and single parenting is perceived as a significant burden on the state and the taxpayer. By contrast, feminists seek increased support for lone parents. While they too advocate more help for families, that presupposes a broader conception of the family.

Thus Conservative feminism remains somewhat problematic. Although Natasha Walter (1999, p. 40) strenuously argues that feminists can be Conservative, she concedes that 'Individual women who are both Conservative and feminist feel isolated and misrepresented by a culture that denies the compatibility of the two creeds'.

Feminism and post-modernism

Feminism has always appeared a particularly action-oriented ideology, with immediate practical concerns generally taking priority over the elaboration of feminist theory, which indeed has sometimes been criticized as relatively thin or essentially derivative. Some feminists have found in the ideas associated with post-modernism new theoretical insights.

Post-modernism is difficult to pin down and define. Its major thrust is to question the whole search for meaning and purpose in art and life, and essentially it involves a reaction against the post-enlightenment faith in rationalism and progress. The enlightenment was sceptical in the sense that it rejected traditional authority, particularly the 'revealed truths' of religion. Yet it was not sceptical over the search for truth itself through the exercise of human reason and science. Post-modernism, by contrast, rejects all 'meta narratives', or universal explanations, including those derived from post-enlightenment science and rational enquiry. It undermines the assumptions of truth and authority in male-oriented western culture, and even the assumptions of both Christians and humanists of a universe centred on the human species. Just as sceptical post-enlightenment rationalism was a critical weapon in the struggle against the received wisdom of the age, so post-modernism is a useful intellectual tool for anyone (including feminists, Greens, and post-colonial opponents of cultural imperialism) who wishes to challenge prevailing mainstream (or 'malestream') thinking in the modern world.

It is therefore unsurprising that many feminists have been attracted to post-modernism. Women have not always conspicuously benefited from the progress entailed in industrialization and modernization. Some feminists have seen rationalism as 'male logic', antipathetic to feminine feeling and intuition. Moreover, well before post-modernism became fashionable, feminists spelled out in some detail the unfavourable image of women presented both in 'serious' literature and popular culture, while others pointed to a persistent male bias in conventional estimates of literary worth. Post-modernist literary criticism has provided feminists with a powerful conceptual framework to reveal the gender-bias in the use of language, to uncover new messages in and behind texts, and to attack traditional male-oriented canons of literary excellence.

Some feminists have undoubtedly found the debunking thrust of post-modernism stimulating and liberating (McRobbie, 1994). Women, they argue, can only benefit from the rejection of received intellectual authority, from the undermining of old assumptions and the breaking down of old barriers between disciplines. Moreover, the rejection of 'meta-narratives' is useful for those feminists seeking to escape the universalist assumptions of Marxism and older forms of radical feminism, with their neglect of women's needs and feelings in other cultures. In this intellectual atmosphere new diverse ways of thinking can flourish.

Yet others have been more cautious. The relativism implicit in post-modernism is ultimately, they argue, not only destructive of 'malestream' assumptions but of any alternative, including feminism itself, which may be perceived as just one other subjective perspective with no claim to universal validity. Thus feminists 'must be wary of throwing out reason and justice in their entirety' (Bryson, 1992, p. 229), although the same author has come to accept that 'handled carefully, post-modernist insights can be helpful to feminist analysis' (Bryson, 1999, p. 9).

Post-feminism or new feminism?

At the beginning of a new millennium it may appear that women have achieved many of the goals sought by feminists. Most notably, the movement of women into the labour market has been massive and almost certainly irreversible. Formerly male-monopolized or male-dominated occupations have been increasingly opened up to women. Gender segregation in employment has been significantly reduced, and there has been a narrowing of the pay gap. Women are consequently more financially independent than ever before. They have also achieved more political power, with increased representation in local government and Parliament (although despite a substantial increase in the number of women MPs, they still only amount to 18 per cent of the House of Commons after the 2001 General Election, below the level in most of Western Europe). Women also have increased control of their own fertility and increased choice over relationships and family commitments. All this has been accompanied by a significant shift in the media portrayal of women. The 'new woman' has seemingly arrived, although it is questionable how far there has been a commensurate emergence of the 'new man'. Indeed there has been some agonizing over male roles and male identity in this new world of gender equality.

Thus it is sometimes claimed that we now live in a post-feminist era in which feminist aims have already been substantially achieved, and it is men rather than women who have the problems. Feminists would not agree. They concede that some of the gains for women have been real enough, and even acknowledge that some men have legitimate grievances (for example on divorce, child custody and support). Yet they point to the extensive evidence of persistent discrimination and exploitation – inequalities in pay and opportunities, lasting gross inequalities in domestic and child-rearing responsibilities, and continuing violence against women. Feminists still have much to achieve.

If the future of feminism now seems more problematic, this reflects differences among women themselves, which partly reflect cross-cutting divisions of class, race and sexuality. The relationship between gender and class has long been problematic for socialist feminists. The gap between rich and poor women in Britain is now as marked as ever, with the high-profile success of a few professional career women like

Cherie Blair contrasting with the limited opportunities and low pay which is the lot of most working-class women. Race and ethnicity clearly cut across the gender divide. For many black women the injustices they suffer have more to do with their colour than their gender, and thus the primary struggle involves standing alongside black males to combat racial discrimination and disadvantage, although they are generally only too aware of their own exploitation by black menfolk. Lesbians similarly unite with gay men to assert their rights to pursue their own sexual orientation without facing discrimination and prejudice from the 'straight' majority of men and women.

Thus for feminists 'an important starting-point must be a recognition of the diversity of women's experiences and the specificity of the oppressions that particular women face' (Bryson, 1999, p. 66). Connections and tactical alliances may be made between the victims of different forms of oppression, yet 'solidarity between oppressed groups cannot, however, be assumed' as 'those who are disadvantaged in one system do not automatically empathise with or support other oppressed groups' (Bryson: 1999, p. 68), as indeed some in the Labour Party discovered when they tried to construct a 'rainbow alliance' of economically deprived male manual workers, women, blacks and gays in the 1980s. Bryson urges engagement with 'the politics of solidarity', while arguing that 'this does not preclude separatist activity by particular groups of women'.

Above and beyond the issue of engagement with other oppressed groups remains 'the problem of men' (Bryson, 1999, pp. 195–216). While liberal feminists like Mill argued that men, too, would benefit from female emancipation, radical feminists saw men as the problem and insisted that women would have to rely on their own efforts to secure justice for women. Indeed, some have seemed to turn their backs on the whole male sex (for example the Leeds Revolutionary Feminist Group, in Evans, 1982, pp. 63–72). Thus 'the popular ideas of feminism' is that 'to be a feminist you must believe that all men are irredeemably bad' (Walter, 1999, p. 145). Admittedly the charge sheet against men is a long one. Besides exploitation, abuse and violence in the domestic sphere, in the wider community men are far more involved with crime and acts of violence (including rioting), and men bear the major responsibility for wars and their consequences. Yet if 'male nature' presents a problem, as the radicals have always pointed out, women have to engage with men if only to prevent them destroying the communities and ultimately the planet which women and men inhabit together. As Bruley (1999, p. 180) observes, 'Radical feminists

Table 7.1 Varieties of feminism

	Liberal feminism	*Marxist/socialist feminism*	*Radical feminism*
Who	(First wave) M. Wollstonecraft J. S. Mill, H. Taylor Suffragettes (Second wave) B. Friedan J. R. Richards S. M. Okin	(First wave) W. Thompson F. Engels (Second wave) J. Mitchell M. Barrett	G. Greer K. Millett S. Firestone E. Figes S. Brownmiller A. Dworkin Ecofeminists
Ideas	Extension of liberal principles to women – emancipation, equality, civil and political rights	Application of Marxist/socialist principles to women – economic exploitation, industrial reserve army, domestic labour, reproduction of labour force	Patriarchy and male dominance; 'The personal is political'; Sexual politics; Celebration of women's difference?
Practical concerns	Votes for women; legal rights; Outlawing of discrimination; equal opportunities; education for women; equal pay	Unionization and politicization of women; child care for working women; wages for housework? Positive discrimination?	Alternatives to traditional nuclear family; abortion; violence against women – rape, date rape, rape within marriage, pornography, lesbian rights, green issues

Table 7.1 Varieties of feminism   cont.

	Liberal feminism	Marxist/socialist feminism	Radical feminism
Problems	Endorsement of male values; Limitations of legal remedies; Failure to explain or remedy continuing sexual inequality; Focus on middle-class, professional career women, neglect of working-class women?	Assumption that end of capitalism and class domination would entail end of exploitation of women. Problematic link between gender and class. Continued discrimination against women in 'socialist' societies	Insistence on primacy of gender differences over other forms of injustice. Remoteness from concerns of 'ordinary' women? Neglect of concerns of black and third world women? Neglect of the 'problem of men'

who will not engage with men... cannot help to transform the gender system.'

One starting point for feminists is to recognize the diversity among men as well as women, not only that men too are divided by class, race and sexual orientation, but also that masculinity, like femininity, is socially constructed. Thus 'there may be competing models of masculinity in society' and dominant forms of masculinity 'may be experienced as oppressive by some men'. Accordingly, feminists should 'welcome and strengthen non-oppressive forms of masculinity', and 'attempt to move beyond the binary divisions of a gendered society' (Bryson, 1999, p. 203). While Bryson is well aware of the 'damaging effects of dominant forms of masculinity', she argues that feminists may be able to 'form alliances with some men in pursuit of egalitarian social goals.' There may, as Mill argued, be benefits for both sexes in a relationship based on a partnership of equals, yet for many men 'the alleged long term benefits of greater equality may be intangible, while the immediate threat to their own privileges feels very real and their loss of centrality deeply disturbing' (Bryson, 2000, p. 8). Thus justice for women will still not be won without a fight in which women will have to continue to rely mainly on their own efforts.

Further reading

Good introductions to feminist politics in Britain are provided by Randall (1987), Carter (1988) Lovenduski and Randall (1993) and Bruley (1999). For a lucid analysis of feminist political theory Bryson (1992, 1999) is invaluable, while Tong (1989) offers an incisive (although American-oriented) thematic survey, and Caine (1997) concentrates on English feminism. Coole (1988) focuses enlighteningly on women in the history of traditional political theory, from Plato onwards. There are several readers which offer a sample of the range of feminist thinking, including those edited by Evans (1982), Lovell (1990), Humm (1992) Jackson et al. (1993) and Mirza (1997) – the last covering black British feminism.

Liberal feminism may be explored through the classic texts of Wollstonecraft and Mill, and the more recent work of Friedan (1977, 1982, 1986), Richards (1982) and Okin (1990). Aspects of Marxist feminism are examined by Mitchell (1971, 1974, 1984), who combines psychological analysis with a Marxist framework, and Barrett (1980). Sargent (1981) has edited a collection of essays on *The Unhappy*

Marriage of Marxism and Feminism. The modern radical feminist classics by Millett, Greer, Firestone and Figes are all still readily available. Other important texts are Brownmiller (1977) on rape and sexual violence, and Dworkin (1981) on pornography.

The diversity of modern feminism is further demonstrated by the eco-feminism of Plant (1989) and Mies and Shiva (1993), Freely's (1995) defence of motherhood, and Walter's (1999) lively and provocative *New Feminism.* Ramazanoglu (1989) points to the different preoccupations of women from ethnic minorities and the third world, while Bacchi (1990) critically examines the debate over sexual equality and difference. The implications of post-modernism for feminism are explored critically by Bryson (1992, 1999) and Grant (1993), and more enthusiastically by McRobbie (in Perryman, 1994).

8

Green Ideology

Introduction

Any survey of modern ideologies would be incomplete without an examination of Green thinking, which now clearly constitutes an important and distinctive political philosophy, presenting a profound challenge to longer established political creeds. While its roots can be traced back a long way, to pantheism, romanticism and the rediscovery of nature, Malthusianism, elements of anarchism, and even aspects of fascism, it is essentially a new ideology. It has brought together a number of more specific concerns – over, for example, conservation, pollution, energy, population growth and animal rights – and woven these together into a coherent and distinctive political philosophy, which, in a comparatively brief period, has achieved a remarkable impact over much of the world.

Inevitably, as with other ideologies, there are problems of definition and terminology. The label 'Green' is a broad one, and is not easily adapted into an 'ism'. Thus some commentators have preferred the terms 'environmentalism' or 'ecologism' to describe the political ideology which is here simply described as 'Green'. Yet these alternatives are not only awkward and less familiar, but also carry their own baggage of associations. The term 'Green' by contrast is freely adopted by pressure groups and political parties, and both the name and the colour has become powerfully associated in the public mind with specific environmental concerns and a more general political outlook. All familiar labels involve problems and ambiguities, but there seems no compelling reason to substitute another term for one which is so universally recognized. Here the term 'Green' is applied not just to specific causes, groups or parties commonly described as 'Green' but to the underlying political philosophy which relates humanity to its environment.

Political ideologies are expressed at various levels and involve sharp internal tensions and conflicts. The Greens are no exception, and there are considerable internal differences over analysis, prescription and strategy. Distinctions have been drawn between dark Greens and light Greens (for example Porritt and Winner, 1984) deep and shallow Greens, ecologists and environmentalists (Dobson, 1995), radicals and reformists (Garner, 1995), ecocentrics and technocentrics (O'Riordan, 1976), fundamentalists and realists (among German Greens). The pairs of terms overlap, but each has particular connotations, and they are not necessarily interchangeable. Most are relative terms implying a spectrum of attitudes, not sharp distinctions, and some have specific environmental concerns which gives their general political outlook a greenish tinge. At the other end there are those who hold a coherent and distinctive Green philosophy which determines their whole personal and political behaviour.

This Green philosophy is clearly marked off from other political ideologies. All other political creeds focus on the presumed interests, needs or rights of humanity, or sections of human society – such as a particular race, nation, class or gender. The Greens effectively relegate all these interests (and most of the issues of traditional political theory) by focusing instead on the universe or the planet. Mainstream political ideologies are dismissed as anthropocentric – they assume that humankind is the centre of the universe, rather than one species among countless others. To Greens the overriding political issue is the relationship of the human species with its environment.

The Green message is a stark one. It is that a continuation of unthinking and unlimited human exploitation of the natural environment spells disaster for the planet and for its human inhabitants. Impending disaster can only be averted by a sharp change of direction, preserving rather than destroying the environment, using renewable rather than non-renewable resources, and adopting sustainable rather than non-sustainable lifestyles. There are massive implications for all areas of public policy, but particularly industrial and agricultural policy, energy policy and transport policy.

Green and other ideologies

One way of classifying older or more established mainstream political ideologies is by locating them on the familiar left–right political spectrum, although, as has been seen, there are some difficulties in placing nationalism and feminism. The Greens are similarly awkward to place. Indeed many Greens would argue the old classifications are irrelevant; they are 'neither left nor right but forward'. Yet attempts to relate Green ideas to other ideologies are unsurprising.

In the first place, no ideology can be wholly new. Ideas derive from somewhere, and in exploring the roots of Green thinking, connections are inevitably made with thinkers, values and interests more familiarly associated with other ideologies or traditions of thought. Secondly, virtually all political creeds now proclaim some environmental concerns, which in turn requires some analysis of their Green credentials. Thirdly, even those who reject older ideologies and identify themselves as 'Green' generally also have views on political issues which are not essentially or exclusively Green, and associate them with the 'left' or the 'right'. Finally, in pursuit of practical political objectives Greens may form tactical alliances with other interests and parties, and are thus linked with the political company they keep.

Aspects of Green thinking can be derived from a very diverse range of sources. A pantheistic concern for the universe can be found among Greek stoics. The revolt against rationalism, industrialism and modernism can be discerned in such thinkers as Rousseau, Carlyle, Ruskin or Disraeli. The notion of limits to growth was famously articulated by Malthus. A preference for the small scale and community values can be derived from Kropotkin or William Morris. Thus some Green ideas can be derived from conservative, liberal, socialist and anarchist thinkers and there are also links with some forms of nationalism and even fascism. More recently, there is a marked compatibility with a significant strand of feminism, sometimes called eco-feminism (Warren, 1994).

Greens and the Right

At the Conservative Party Conference of 1988, Mrs Thatcher startled commentators by proclaiming her party's Green credentials (McCormick, 1991, ch. 3). This was surprising in the sense that the free-market strand of conservatism with which Mrs Thatcher has been particularly associated has generally seemed the political ideology least obviously compatible with green ideas (Hay, 1988). The freedom of market forces and legitimacy of profit maximization does not sit easily with controls over pollution and environmental exploitation. Yet private interest and ownership may be more conducive to environmental preservation than common ownership (Hardin, 1968), and some neo-liberal economists argue for free-market solutions to problems of resource depletion and pollution. Thus market pressures will oblige entrepreneurs to find innovative alternatives to scarce resources, while experience has demonstrated the profit potential of environmentally friendly goods. Moreover, ways can be found of making polluters pay (Ashford, 1989). Yet the free market does not provide easy answers to either long-term resource depletion and pollution issues (such as climate change), or sudden environmental disasters (for example floods, earthquakes and famine). Such problems commonly involve more interference with free-market forces than neo-liberals are generally prepared to countenance (Martell, 1994, pp. 63–72).

Traditional Conservatism has rather more affinities with Green thinking, as it involved a reaction against post-enlightenment rationalism, science, industrialism, modernism and faith in progress, much of which is shared by modern Greens. Almost by definition, conservation is a key value, and traditional Conservatives have had a strong interest in the land and the preservation of the environment. In some cases this has taken the form of support for groups such as the Council for the Protection of Rural England, the National Trust or more recently the Countryside Alliance. Further to the right on the political spectrum, some extreme nationalists or fascists would proclaim an almost mystical association between race and environment, of 'blood and soil'.

There are indeed some Greens whose views are compatible with the traditional or even the fascist right. However, many Greens would argue that the Conservative interest in the land is essentially self-interested and exploitative. The concern is for the rights of landowners, including their rights to exploit the land for their own profit and pleasure, conserving game, for example, so they can subsequently hunt or shoot, and restricting access to the countryside. Many Greens, moreover, would reject the assumptions of natural hierarchy and inequality associated with the right. In terms of practical politics, although Greens might sometimes enter tactical alliances with local right-wing preservation groups opposed to new roads, housing or retail developments, the grounds of Green concern are fundamentally different from those of self-interested NIMBYs (Not In My Back Yard). Thus although Greens share some conservative values, they are not essentially defenders of the status quo, but radicals, seeking a very different future.

Greens and the Left

In practice, Green activists are more commonly associated with the left rather than the right, with anarchists, socialists, social democrats and radical liberals. 'Red-greens' are a more familiar phenomenon than 'blue-greens', at almost every level of political activity. There are socialists with a strong green commitment; some Greens were previously members of left-wing parties or groups, and retain an affinity with their former political allegiance. Other Greens have worked closely with socialists of all kinds in the peace movement or the women's movement. In terms of analysis, Green concerns with certain aspects of industrialism overlap with the fundamental socialist critique of capitalism. Some Marxists have argued that not only are Marx's ideas compatible with environmentalism, but that his analysis is highly relevant to modern Green thinking (Pepper, 1993). In terms of prescription both socialists and Greens seek radical change.

Yet some strands of socialism are clearly more compatible with Green ideas than others. Greens tend to be individualist rather than collectivist, with a mistrust of large bureaucratic organizations, whether these are major industrial unions or government departments. Anarchism, and the bottom-up decentralized approach of Owen, William Morris or the Guild Socialists have more in common with Green thinking than the centralized state socialism or labourism dominant on the British left. Moreover, for all their critique of capitalism, most socialists (including Marx) belong firmly to the modernist, rationalist and essentially optimistic post-enlightenment tradition. Their objections to the private ownership of capital does not extend to the industrialization associated with capitalism. On the contrary, they tend to be fervent believers in modernization, progress and growth. Indeed, the leading socialist revisionist, Crosland (1956), hoped to promote greater equality in large part through redistributing the product of economic growth. At a practical level the interest of the labour movement in jobs and living standards is not easily compatible with Green concerns.

Thus the Labour government elected in 1997 initially promised a new commitment to the environment, but in practice concentrated on traditional Labour issues such as employment, health and education. Greens have been particularly critical of Labour's record on biotechnology and transport. While Blair favoured trials of genetically modified crops, many Greens feared the risks of irreversible damage to the environment. On transport, Labour's initial commitments to improve public transport and restrain the growth of car use were given insufficient priority even before they were undermined by chaos on the railways (caused by safety restrictions following crashes) and the fuel protests of autumn 2000. The latter in particular dramatized the difficulty for any government in pursuing unpopular policies to restrict car use. A blockade by hauliers which initially neither the police nor the oil companies took steps to break enjoyed substantial public support and ultimately forced a modification of taxation policy. The Green case for higher fuel taxes gained little attention while the crisis lasted (Carter, 2001).

For both conservatives and socialists, Green issues have a lower priority than core ideological concerns, for private property and the free market on the one hand, or social reform and equality on the other. Thus, for Greens, the environmental concerns of other political creeds involve only relatively shallow and cosmetic 'greenspeak'. Only for the Greens are environmental issues central and fundamental rather than essentially peripheral. Only the Greens (or perhaps some Greens) articulate a coherent alternative ecological ideology.

Key elements of Green thinking

It is now necessary to identify the core ingredients of this Green ideology. The key elements of Green thinking have been variously identified. Lists of core principles generally include the assumption that there are limits to growth, and the corollary of 'sustainability', an eco-centric rather than anthropocentric view of the relationship between humans and their environment, and a 'holistic' rather than piecemeal approach to the analysis of environmental issues and problems. Some would add a preference for small-scale and local organization and activity. Other principles sometimes mentioned might be regarded as essentially derivative – thus limits to population might be seen as an application of sustainability (Kenny in Eccleshall *et al*, 1994; Dobson, 1995; Garner, 1995).

While all the above have been regarded as core Green principles, they are principles of different kinds. The holistic approach is a fundamental methodological assumption which suggests that problems cannot be tackled in isolation, but are only explicable as parts of a whole. The notion of 'limits to growth' can be interpreted, by contrast, as a scientific hypothesis, in principle susceptible to empirical investigation. The ecocentric view, crudely expressed in the slogan 'Earth first', asserts a moral principle although it may also be interpreted as a means to the anthropocentric end of human survival. The emphasis on the small-scale and the local might be interpreted as a fundamental political principle or alternatively as a means to an end.

Green thinking is sometimes associated with post-modernism, naturally enough, as the targets of post-modernists are largely targets of Greens also – post-enlightenment assumptions over science, reason and progress (Pepper, 1993, pp. 55–8). Yet post-modernism implies a moral relativism which is at odds with the Greens' essentially ethical message.

Moreover, post-modernism rejects all 'meta-narratives' or universal explanations, and ecologism is above all a meta-narrative. While Greens reject current orthodoxies, they have their own truths to proclaim. It is now necessary to explore these truths in rather more detail.

Limits to growth – sustainability

Greens challenge the near universal modern assumption of the benefits to be derived from economic growth. The Green notion that there are limits to growth can be derived from Malthus *Essay on Population,* (1798, ed. Flew, 1970) and his theory of diminishing returns, which was particularly applicable to agricultural society. However, the experience of the industrializing western world in the nineteenth century suggested, by contrast, that virtually limitless improvements in growth and living standards were possible. Since then, high growth has become a tacit and often explicit objective of governments across the ideological spectrum, and a crucial component of a revisionist social democratic creed which sought to promote greater equality without making anyone worse off through distributing the products of growth.

Modern Greens have rediscovered the essentially Malthusian assumption that there are limits to the increases in productivity to be derived from the exploitation of finite natural resources. They have also identified significant costs associated with the pursuit of growth, in terms of damage to the environment and risks to health. The limits to growth were vividly dramatized in some celebrated attempts to predict the consequences of present trends, such as the Club of Rome report (Meadows *et al*, 1972). While the more pessimistic doomwatch scenarios have been partially discredited (Maddox, 1972), Greens would argue that the fundamental point remains unchallenged and unchallengeable – that non-renewable resources such as fossil fuels are finite and will ultimately be exhausted.

The Green alternative to the pursuit of growth is the principle of sustainability. Humanity should only adopt those policies which can in the long run be sustained without irreversible damage to the resources on which the human species and other species depend. The practical implications, however, are more contestable, although there is a school of thought known as 'ecological modernization' which suggests that environmental protection and sustainability is compatible with real growth and improvements in living standards (Weale, 1992, ch. 3).

One issue at stake here is what 'growth' actually involves, and how it should be measured. Another line of argument suggests that western consumerism is ultimately not fulfilling for human beings, who increasingly prize a quality of life which involves environmental protection. Indeed, the involvement in Green parties and causes of a growing section of the middle classes in advanced industrial societies provides some supporting evidence for this assumption (Martell, 1994).

Yet if economic growth is measured in conventional economic terms, many Greens would concede that sustainability can only be achieved with (for developed nations at least), zero or negative growth, with lower material living standards, and a reduction in population levels. This is, needless to say, a difficult message to sell. Politicians have generally sought power by promising to make people better off in material terms. Greens are effectively promising to make people worse off (although they argue that a reduction in material consumption could involve a better quality of life). On the assumption, particularly by neo-liberals, that human beings are naturally self-seeking and acquisitive, it is difficult to see how they can be persuaded to forego current consumption in the interests of generations yet unborn, still less other species or the long-run survival of the planet. Thus even if the economic case for long-run limits to growth is accepted, there seems little prospect that individual human beings will reduce consumption from self-interest. Green solutions require either more altruistic behaviour from citizens and voters, or, alternatively, the imposition of a superior Green morality through a more authoritarian political system. The first seems unlikely, while the second is unpalatable.

Ecocentrism

Some would argue that an ecocentric rather than an anthropocentric approach is the defining characteristic of a distinctive Green philosophy (Eckersley, 1992). An anthropocentric view puts humankind firmly at the centre of the universe. Green policies of pollution control and resource conservation are justified in terms of human interests – both present and future generations. An ecocentric view does not accord any priority to humanity, but emphasizes the intrinsic value of the natural world, and the need of men and women to live in harmony with the universe. The distinction seems clear, but in practice, like other attempts to categorize Greens, involves a subtle gradation of positions. Further subdivisions can be discerned within both anthropocentrism and ecocen-trism (for example Eckersley, 1992, ch. 2) and, moreover, there are some Greens who would reject anthropocentrism without endorsing a pure ecocentric position. Supporters of animal rights occupy an impor-tant intermediate position (Martell, 1994). As they argue animals should be valued for their own sake they are clearly not anthropocen-tric, but in confining their concerns to sentient beings which can experi-ence pain and pleasure they fall far short of the ecocentric perspective which values the whole universe, including non-sentient nature (e.g. trees) and inanimate objects (e.g. rocks).

It can be argued that ecocentrism is ultimately a moral principle, requiring human beings to place the interests of the planet above their own self-interest. It is a moral principle which runs counter to key assumptions of post-Renaissance humanism, Baconian science and post-Enlightenment modernism, and indeed to most religions and philosophi-cal systems which have held sway in the world, although some attempt has been made by Green writers to relate their ethical principles to those of 'primal' peoples, such as pre-Christian Celts or American Indians, or to women rather than men (Mies and Shiva, 1993; Warren, 1994).

Mainstream religion and mainstream political thought is anthro-pocentric – it focuses on humanity and human needs. It is implicitly and often explicitly assumed that the rest of the natural world exists to serve the needs of humankind, and it follows that men and women are free to exploit natural resources in which ever way they please to suit their own interests. Scientific advances have enabled humanity to over-come specific problems and exploit the resources of the natural world more effectively, and industrialization and modernization has involved the apparent taming of nature in the service of man.

In place of this anthropocentric approach, the ecocentric view places the human species in the context of its environment. 'Earth first' is a shorthand slogan which requires humans to consider first and foremost the future of the planet rather than their own immediate requirements. They have no claim to primacy over other species. Indeed, some Greens argue, it is the human species which has provided the main threat to the long-run survival of the planet. If the earth is to survive, human beings must learn to live in harmony with their natural environ-ment, rather than seeking to exploit it.

One version of the ecocentric approach is the Gaian hypothesis, which suggests that the earth – personified as the Goddess Gaia – is a complex super-organism which requires other organisms to operate so as to keep the planet fit for life (Lovelock, 1979). Greens who oppose spiritual values to the materialist values they see embedded in modern society have sometimes tended to deify nature, providing a quasi-religious foundation for their ethical assumptions. Yet defining exactly what is 'nature' or 'natural', and identifying right with nature involves familiar philosophical difficulties. Another militant interpretation of the injunction 'Earth First!' is provided by extremists within the American group of that name who have sometimes employed violent direct action techniques to protect the environment from man.

The notion of animal rights might be considered as either an important subsidiary application of the ecocentric principle, or a distinctive political perspective. While all Greens would share a concern for animal welfare, and support the aims of established pressure groups such as the RSPCA and the League Against Cruel Sports, not all would go further to endorse animal rights. Greens in practice adopt a variety of positions with regard to the treatment of animals (Singer, 1976; Regan, 1988; Garner, 1993, 1995; Martell, 1994). Thus many, but by no means all, Greens are vegetarians or vegans. For some this is a matter of simple preference or health or efficient resource utilization. For others it is a critical ethical issue – 'meat is murder'; they view the rearing and killing of animals for human consumption as morally on the same level as the deliberate murder of fellow humans. Similarly, the use of animals in experiments to test new beauty treatments or medicines is regarded by some animal rights activists as akin to Nazi medical experiments on the Jews. A few who take this view have been prepared to indulge in acts of violence, including even murder, against those who are perceived to abuse animals

Ultimately 'Earth first' or 'Animal Rights' are fundamental moral principles not susceptible to scientific verification or falsification, to be held irrespective of their consequences. Clearly they are moral principles which some people hold and at least try to act upon. Yet such principles are not widely held, and it is difficult to see how the majority of humanity might be persuaded to adopt them, particularly in the absence of religious sanctions. In practice, despite their explicit rejection of the anthropocentric approach, in order to persuade others, and perhaps also to persuade themselves, many Greens tend to fall back on human-centred justifications for their injunctions. Thus human beings should refrain from exploiting and polluting in their own long-term interests, or those of their children and grandchildren.

The holistic approach

The holistic approach requires that problems should not be analysed in isolation but related to the whole of which they are a part; The whole in question here is the universe or the eco-system. Thus holism might be derived from the ecocentric perspective. Yet although it has moral overtones, it is essentially a matter of methodology.

The need to analyse environmental problems in context is sometimes seen as the defining characteristic which marks off genuine ecologists, deep or dark Greens, from those who have particular and limited environmental concerns. Thus light or shallow Greens are commonly associated with particular single issues, such as live calf exports, or new roads, or nuclear power, while deep or dark Greens have a holistic concern for the environment of which such specific issues are at best only a part, and at worst a dangerous diversion from more fundamental objectives.

This can be illustrated by reference to the campaign for lead-free petrol, which demonstrated and publicized the harm caused to children's health by lead additives to petrol. At one level it was a textbook example of a successful single issue campaign, which ultimately persuaded government to encourage lead-free petrol through a tax incentive (Wilson, 1984). From a light Green perspective the problem was virtually solved. Yet 'dark Greens' perceive the problem against the general context of resource conservation, waste and pollution. From this perspective the removal of lead from petrol is at best a palliative which does not tackle the fundamental problem of resource depletion, waste and pollution associated with human dependence on the motor car. At worst it might be regarded as ecologically counterproductive, encouraging false assumptions about green fuels and green motoring.

In one sense the need to see problems in context and relate issues to the wider whole is simply common sense, and may help to avoid counterproductive strategies. Yet taken to extremes it might inhibit any action, because it would be impossible to calculate all the possible environmental implications and side-effects of any policy initiative compared with all the alternatives. Moreover, any personal or local initiative might be regarded as 'a drop in the ocean' and irrelevant to the real issue.

In practice, even those Greens most insistent on a holistic approach tend to become involved in single-issue campaigns, which can often be justified not only in terms of incremental reform but also for raising environmental consciousness. Thus pure or dark greens may become involved in tactical alliances with others whose commitment to a wider green agenda is vestigial. Indeed any specific environmental issue, such as opposition to a new road, tends to attract a coalition of interests, including NIMBYs with little or no general concern for the environment, people seeking to preserve particular areas of countryside or wildlife habitats, specialist pressure groups such as Transport 2000, as well as committed Green activists for whom the proposed new road is only an illustration of much wider issues of pollution and resource depletion. For Greens, such tactical alliances present awkward questions of political strategy which might be perceived as particularly problematic for the Green movement generally.

Small is beautiful?

Sometimes regarded as a core principle, sometimes seen as an issue of strategy, is the widespread green preference for the small-scale, decentralized and local. An influential text was Schumacher's (1973) 'Small is Beautiful' which challenged the then fashionable presumption in favour of large-scale enterprise. Since then the mass production associated with Fordism has increasingly given way to the small-scale and flexible high-tech and service enterprises considered characteristic of a post-Fordist economy. To that extent the previously heretical assertion 'small is beautiful' has become the new orthodoxy.

Schumacher was an economist, and much of the argument can be couched in terms of economic theory. Conventional economic theory suggested that there were economies of scale to be gained from larger-scale production, although it was always recognized that beyond a certain point there might be diseconomies of scale. Theory seemed to be abundantly confirmed by the expansion of manufacturing industry through the mass production of standardized products, such as the family Ford car, which in western capitalist societies brought previous luxury items into the reach of those on average income. Standardization and large-scale operations also seemed to yield benefits in such areas as retailing and catering, and even in government where it was suggested that larger departments, larger local authorities and larger units for administering specific services such as education, health or police would likewise yield economies of scale.

There were always those who held a more sceptical or hostile perspective on this trend towards larger-scale production and organization in the modern world. Burke spoke eloquently of the love of the little platoon. Toulmin Smith fulminated against the centralizing tendencies of the Victorian era. William Morris reaffirmed the value of individual craftsmanship in an age of mass production. Anarchists rejected the growing power of the modern centralized nation-state.

These often appeared as minority voices vainly protesting against the onward march of progress and modernisation. Yet modern Green preferences for the small-scale and local seem rather more consistent with prevailing trends. Thus the Fordist assumptions behind mass production, standardization, specialization and the division of labour have given place to a post-Fordist emphasis on innovation, flexibility and autonomy in the workplace. To an extent, small has become fashionable. Mainstream analysis accords a leading role to small to medium-sized enterprises in fostering economic development, and modern management theory suggests the need for flatter hierarchies which accord more autonomy to front-line staff. And current political wisdom reaffirms the need for government close to the people through decentralization.

All this would seem to abundantly justify the common Green preference for community-based action at the local level, and bottom-up rather than top-down political strategies. Indeed, Green political activity seems largely to fit neatly into a post-industrial, post-Fordist, post-modern world. Their own organizational structures tend to be decentralized, with few concessions to the conventional requirements for discipline, unity and leadership. Thus the British Green Party has shown a marked reluctance to recognize leaders, and a distaste for actual or potential political stars. Green activists generally follow the injunction to 'think global, act local.'

A possible corollary of decentralization is greater self-sufficiency or autarky. Indeed, unless there is to be considerable cooperation among self-governing small-scale communities, an increased level of self-sufficiency is essential. Yet some Greens would also point to substantial positive benefits from greater self-sufficiency in terms of resource conservation. Less fuel and other resources would be needed to transport goods and people. One version of this approach is described as 'bioregionalism' (Eckersley, 1992, pp. 167–70; Martell, 1994, pp. 51–3; Dobson, 1995, pp. 112–17) which seeks the integration of human communities within their distinctive regional environment. Thus the inhabitants of a particular region would utilize the specific resources of the region at a sustainable level, rather than relying on international trade to fulfil their needs. Bioregionalism rejects the general assumptions of the benefits to be derived from specialization and comparative advantage in conventional economic trade theory. It also incidentally involves a critique of mass travel and tourism.

Although many Greens seem to favour greater decentralization and self-sufficiency, there are some who would deny that it is or should be an integral element of a Green ideology (Eckersley, 1992; Goodin, 1992; Martell, 1994). The preference for the small-scale, decentralized and local is reminiscent of anarchism, and indeed there are close links in theory and practice between Greens and anarchists (Bookchin, 1971). Yet for anarchists the decentralization of power is clearly their fundamental principle – it is what anarchism is essentially about. For Greens the ultimate objective is saving the planet, and 'small is beautiful' would seem an essentially subordinate principle to this overriding end.

Decentralization, particularly if combined with increased self-sufficiency, has for some Greens uncomfortable implications for the distribution of resources between different regions and communities. Thus 'insisting too emphatically on decentralization, local political autonomy, and direct democracy can ... compromise the ecocentric goal of social justice' (Eckersley, 1992, p. 175). It is difficult to see how considerable inequalities between regions could be avoided; those from poorer underdeveloped regions of the world would be effectively prevented from benefiting from the only assets they could offer richer areas – cheap raw materials and cheap labour.

Moreover, it may be questioned whether decentralization is a political strategy which is likely to further other, more fundamental Green objectives. It is at least arguable that if drastic and urgent action is needed to save the planet this may be more effectively achieved by centralized and even dictatorial methods. Most modern Greens seem temperamentally averse to such an approach. The issue does, however, raise in acute form the problem which has already been alluded to in the above analysis: what is an appropriate strategy for the Greens?

Green strategy

It has been suggested that all political ideologies contain (implicitly or explicitly) three main elements – a critique of existing society, a vision of the future, and a strategy for moving from the present to the desired future, what is often termed the problem of agency. The first two are very clearly evident in Green thinking, but Green strategy often appears relatively weak and undertheorized (Dobson, 1995, p. 124).

Strategy is particularly problematic for those ideologies which assume a need for radical change. For example, many socialists have envisaged a future society very different from the world in which they lived, which inevitably raises acute questions over the means of achieving objectives, the agency for change. Indeed socialists have often been more bitterly divided over strategy rather than ultimate ends. Greens similarly seek a very different future. They seek massive economic and social change, and their political philosophy has far-reaching implications for industrial policy, agricultural policy, energy policy, transport policy and taxation policy. Virtually all Greens, apart from the most optimistic reformists, believe that radical changes in government policy and human lifestyles are urgently required. Indeed many Greens would argue that the Green revolution they seek is more fundamental and far-reaching than a socialist revolution. Nor, if their analysis is correct, do Greens have time on their side. Those who subscribe to the Green ideology readily proclaim that change is urgent now if catastrophe is to be avoided in the future. This is scarcely compatible with the kind of gradualism acceptable to a Fabian socialist.

Yet it is not just the radical and urgent nature of the change envisaged which makes strategy particularly problematic for Greens. The early socialists portrayed a potential future which was very different, but in many ways attractive to the mass audience at which it was directed, if threatening to established wealth and power holders. They were promising a better life. Greens, by contrast, seek a future which is widely perceived as involving a worse rather than a better life for the majority of humanity. It is an intrinsically difficult message to put across.

A variety of strategies, not necessarily mutually exclusive, are adopted in practice, including personal commitments to a green lifestyle, education and rational persuasion, grassroots community action, single-issue and broader pressure group campaigns, and involvement in party politics. Most of them neglect or skate round the problem of power; all of them raise awkward questions.

Green convictions may clearly involve some implications for personal behaviour. Just as high living seems inconsistent with socialist views, so Greens indulging in conspicuous consumption and environmental degradation invite charges of hypocrisy. Many Greens in practice agonize over the concessions and compromises which they make to modern consumerism. Others prefer to express their convictions almost entirely through their lifestyles, giving up their cars and reducing their consumption of non-renewable resources, becoming vegetarian and growing organic food. Some join communes of like-minded people.

Like medieval monks or nuns, they have opted out of conventional values and materialistic lifestyles (Eckersley, 1992, pp. 163–7). However, their individual commitment, while affording some personal satisfaction, is unlikely by itself to promote any wider change beyond the limited influence of their example.

Broadly compatible with the politics of personal commitment is involvement in local initiatives within the immediate community. This sometimes involves a conscious rejection of conventional national politics for a bottom-up grassroots political strategy, much as some of the early socialists sought to fulfil their ideals through self-help friendly societies, cooperatives, and educational projects. The question here is the extent to which the cumulative impact of such local initiatives can possibly achieve the extent and pace of change required by Green analysis. 'Think global, act local' is an appealing slogan, but if the scale of the problem is global rather than local, it seems unlikely that local initiatives can produce global solutions.

Another strategy, similar to that adopted by some early socialists, is to rely essentially on education and rational persuasion. While Green thinking often appears antipathetic to the post-enlightenment rationalism, some Greens in practice place a heavy dependence on the power of reason, assuming that people will be convinced of the need for massive changes in their current materialist lifestyles if they can only be persuaded to grasp the facts. Yet of course the 'facts', however persuasive to Greens, involve assumptions and projections which are disputable. There are optimistic as well as pessimistic perspectives on the future, and most human beings may understandably be inclined to accept interpretations which have less uncomfortable implications for their own well-being. Thus concerns that greenhouse gases were causing climate change, in particular global warming with increased risk of floods, led to the 1997 Kyoto agreement to reduce emissions in which the British Labour Government played a prominent role. However, it has proved difficult to persuade major countries, particularly the USA, to keep to the modest targets agreed. One problem is that much of the scientific case remains contestable, and key politicians and the wider public remain unconvinced of the need for restraints which might adversely effect industry, employment and existing lifestyles. Thus Greens may be doomed to play the role of Cassandra, perhaps accurately forecasting the future, but disbelieved or ignored. Alternatively, in order to dramatize their case more effectively they may be tempted to exaggerate risks and dangers, risking loss of credibility if their claims are disputed or disproved (Maddox, 1972).

At the other extreme to the employment of rational persuasion is the use of direct, sometimes illegal and even violent action by a minority of Greens. Examples include the attacks on the Huntingdon Life Sciences laboratory designed to secure its closure, the trashing of trial GM crops, the occupation of tunnels and trees to prevent the building of new roads or airport runways, and the more general demonstrations against global capitalism. Such tactics are sometimes successful in delaying or halting developments or activities which are opposed. They may also serve to raise public consciousness of wider environmental issues, yet 'extremist' action may sometimes prove counterproductive by alienating public sympathy.

Pressure group politics involve some familiar dilemmas, whether for example to seek increased influence on government through securing insider status, involving some compromise of ideals and possible incorporation, or to maintain ideological purity at the expense of effective exclusion from the decision-making process. In Britain the environmental organizations with most members are the highly respectable National Trust and the Royal Society for the Protection of Birds, and these are both influential within their limited conservationist spheres, in part because they rarely challenge established interests. More radical are Greenpeace and Friends of the Earth, which both operate at an international level. Their activities have certainly raised public consciousness of green issues, and have often seemed to influence both business practice and government policy. While Greenpeace has generally maintained its provocative radical outsider stance, and has sometimes operated outside the law, Friends of the Earth has become more involved in the consultative process. Only time will tell which is the more effective strategy in terms of changing policy.

Pressure group politics is almost by definition the politics of influence rather than the politics of power. Indeed, it could be argued that none of the approaches discussed above really address the problem of political power. Greens need some effective leverage on centres of power if they are to have any hope of forwarding their extensive and urgent agenda for change, perhaps some involvement in conventional electoral and parliamentary politics, either through existing political parties, or through the relatively new Green Party.

The extent of the compatibility of Green ideas with older established political ideologies is a contentious issue, and the potential for working through existing parties will depend in part on the view taken. Indeed there are Green (or Greenish) groups operating in all major British parties, although the extent of their influence is contentious (Robinson, 1993). There are others of course who would argue that Green convictions are fundamentally inconsistent with the established political parties and their underpinning ideological assumptions. The logical corollary for those who accept, nevertheless, the need for involvement in electoral and parliamentary politics, is a separate Green Party.

Yet Green Parties, unless they can win power on their own (which no Green Party anywhere has remotely approached), can only have any effective influence if they combine with others. Thus the German Greens, after enjoying some electoral success in local, state and federal elections, finally entered a coalition with the Social Democrats under Gerhard Schröder, while Greens have also joined coalition governments in Belgium, Finland France and Italy (Carter, 2001, p. 121) Such relative success in conventional politics inevitably forces some hard choices and compromises which are not always palatable to Green purists, and indeed the political record of the German Greens has not always won the approval of Greens inside and outside Germany. Yet such bargaining and compromise are a necessary party of electoral and parliamentary politics.

In Britain, familiar problems of competing with established parties are compounded by an electoral system which effectively penalizes national parties without a strong regional base. The Greens achieved a remarkable 15 per cent of the poll for the 1989 European elections, which would have secured respectable representation in Strasbourg in any other country in the European Union, but resulted in no MEPs, and proved something of a false dawn as the party has achieved nothing remotely comparable since. However, the Blair Labour government's introduction of more proportional electoral systems for the European Parliament, new Scottish Parliament and Greater London Authority have led to modest representation for the Greens – one Green MSP (May 1999), two Green MEPs (June 1999), and three members of the London Assembly (May 2000). Yet without electoral reform for Westminster and local elections the Green Party will remain confined to the margins of British electoral politics.

Lack of success should not perhaps be blamed solely on the electoral system. The Green electoral cause has scarcely been helped by their disregard for the conventional imperatives of party politics, for which some Greens have a marked distaste. While the party's avoidance of hierarchical organization, discipline and leadership is true to their decentralist philosophy, it scarcely assists their electoral appeal in an environment where politics is personalized and is increasingly about

Table 8.1 Varieties of Green strategies

Strategy	Examples	Problems
Personal	Green lifestyle, no car, etc. Grow food, make clothes, vegetarianism, join commune	Monastic withdrawal? Lack of impact on environmental problems
Local or community	'Think global, act local'. 'Small is beautiful', local initiatives, self-help anarchism	Difficulty in coordinating local initiatives. Negligible impact on global environmental problems
Pressure group activity – orthodox	Rational persuasion, Education, Lobbying Parliament, Whitehall, parties, public etc. Seek insider status for purposes of consultation	Unpalatable messages not believed or rejected. Short-term horizons of public, politicians, etc. (but over-dramatizing or exaggerating may be counterproductive). Danger of incorporation
Pressure group activity – direct action	Demonstrations, obstruction, sabotage, damage to property, violence to people (e.g. those involved in experiments on animals)	May be counterproductive, alienate sympathy etc. Gives cause a bad name. Remedy worse than problem?
Regional strategy	Regional government? 'Bio-regionalism', autarky, limits on travel and trade, encourage close relationships between people and region, regional diversity	Cuts across conventional wisdom on free trade. Challenges existing economic and political interests. Would lead to unacceptable inequalities between regions

Table 8.1 Varieties of Green strategies *cont.*

Strategy	Examples	Problems
National strategy	Involvement in conventional electoral politics. Either seek to convert major parties to Green ideas, or to support Green Party	Strength of vested interests in traditional parties – Green policies only cosmetic? Electoral system and other factors hinders Green Party
International strategy	'Think global' – influence and involvement on international organizations and multinational corporations, international pressure groups. Protests against globalization, WTO, etc.	Lack of political clout. Problems of coordination. Differences between rich and poor nations – western paternalism

image and presentation. Indeed the whole approach to politics of many Greens is schizophrenic. They reject not only conventional political parties and their associated philosophies, but the whole existing political process as outdated and morally bankrupt, yet their own ideas have massive political implications which require active involvement in that political process.

However, the real problem for any Green Party is that the message they seek to present is at odds with prevailing materialist values, with the immediate apparent interests of the bulk of the electorate, and with dominant assumptions about political motivation. For most people, it seems, the good life is about increased income and wealth, and the enjoyment of more and better consumer goods and services. Parties, it is assumed, win votes by appealing to the self-interest of individuals, groups and classes, promising to protect or raise living standards, reduce taxation, improve benefits and services. Even when politicians demand sacrifices in immediate consumption, this is usually on the expectation of some tangible benefit in the not too distant future, such as stable prices, increased employment, steady growth. The Greens, by contrast, are effectively promising to make people worse off in material terms. The sacrifices they call for are not for an immediate better future, but to avert a potential environmental catastrophe which might not affect current voters. It is not an easy political message to sell.

Other political ideologies are linked to a particular social class or an identifiable sectional interest within society. Indeed, as has been noted, an influential interpretation is that political ideologies are essentially rationalizations of interest. Now there are some who would link environmentalist concerns with class interests; and some Greens have indeed seen the middle classes in advanced capitalist countries as credible agents of change, providing the political muscle for a transition to a green (or greener) society. By contrast, critics of Greens from both the left and the right have sometimes sought to portray preservationists as selfish well-heeled people concerned to protect their own property values and lifestyles against the poor or aspiring. On a global scale it is sometimes alleged that western concern with destruction of the Amazonian rain forests or pollution in the third world reflect neo-colonial attitudes designed to keep other countries poor and underdeveloped. There is something in the allegation. Green politics would seem to appeal more to the haves than the have-nots, both within and between countries.

Yet, ostensibly, in so far as the Green ideology serves an interest at all, it would appear to be an interest which transcends present society or even humanity itself. It is concerned with generations yet unborn, with other species, and with the future of the planet. While this is a noble and unselfish concern, it poses a problem for conventional politics; there is no mechanism for taking into account the interests of future generations, still less threatened fauna and flora, in either the economic or political marketplace. The radical Greens require a collective sacrifice of current consumption and immediate aspirations on the part of humanity in the interests of an unknown and unknowable future. Such heroic unselfishness does not fit easily with the assumptions about humankind which are implicit or explicit in mainstream western political ideology. Yet unless these assumptions prove mistaken, it is difficult to see a realistic political strategy for the Greens.

Further reading

There are useful introductory short chapters on what is variously described as ecologism, environmentalism or Green politics in Heywood (1997), Vincent (1995), Eccleshall *et al.* (1994), Adams (1998) and Eatwell and Wright (1999). There are a number of longer but accessible accounts of green politics, including Porritt (1984), Porritt and Winner (1988), McCormick (1991) and Garner (1995). Garner has a particularly useful chapter on 'Green thinking' a topic which is explored in more detail in Goodin (1992), Eckersley (1992) and Dobson (1995). More specialist books include Weale's *The New Politics of Pollution* (1992), Pepper's *Eco-socialism* (1993), Robinson's *The Greening of British Party Politics* (1993) and Martell's *Ecology and Society* (1994).

Among books which have almost acquired the status of modern Green classics are Carson's *The Silent Spring* (1962), the Club of Rome's *The Limits to Growth* (Meadows et al., 1972), Goldsmith's *A Blueprint for Survival* (1972), Schumacher's *Small is Beautiful* (1973), O'Riordan's *Environmentalism* (1976) and Lovelock's *Gaia: A New Look at Life on Earth* (1979). Extracts from most of these and much else besides can be found in *The Green Reader* edited by Dobson (1991).

9

The New Right, Thatcherism and Contemporary Conservatism

1975: a change in direction?

In 1975 Margaret Thatcher became leader of the Conservative Party. Her victory was unexpected, and arose because the bulk of the parliamentary party wished to be rid of Ted Heath, not primarily for reasons of policy or philosophy but because of personality factors and electoral failure (he had lost three elections out of four). Most of her new Shadow Cabinet had been members of Heath's Cabinet, of which Mrs Thatcher had been a loyal and fairly junior member. Thus no sharp change of party direction was anticipated. Some assumed the new leader would not last long. In the event, Mrs Thatcher was to remain party leader for 15 years and was to serve as Prime Minister for 11, longer than any predecessor since Lord Liverpool. Moreover, she presided over a marked change in the direction of British conservatism.

The reasons for separating modern and traditional conservatism have been lightly sketched in a previous chapter, although the case for continuity was also conceded. What marked Prime Minister Margaret Thatcher off from most of her predecessors and the mainstream conservative tradition was her overtly ideological approach to politics, her populism, and her radicalism, in contrast with past pragmatism, elitism and cautious gradualism. She was first and foremost a conviction politician, determined to put ideas and principles into practice and consequently averse to traditional conservative compromise and consensus. She was a populist in the sense that she sometimes appeared the champion of ordinary people against established interests (although she was not always particularly popular, and aroused some marked antipathy). Finally, many of the changes she began were not of the 'small and limited' nature associated with conservative gradualism, but very radical. Nigel Lawson (1988) observed that she had 'transformed the politics of Britain – indeed Britain itself – to an extent that no other Government has achieved since the Attlee Government of 1945–51.'

Yet 'Thatcherism' is hardly an ideal term to describe the ideology associated with Mrs Thatcher. While she took ideas seriously, she was never herself an original thinker. She had absorbed her convictions from many sources, some long dead, others still active and influential. Academics and think-tanks played a larger role in the dissemination of ideas. Even the policies pursued by her governments owed much to energetic colleagues such as Geoffrey Howe, Nigel Lawson, Nicholas Ridley and Norman Tebbit, who all contributed significantly to aspects of 'Thatcherism'. Thus some commentators from the start preferred the less personalized description 'New Right', which can also be employed to cover similar ideas advanced in other countries.

Indeed, many of the political developments described under the heading of 'Thacherism' in Britain show similarities to changes over much of the western world in the last quarter of the twentieth century. Thus 'Thatcherism' might be seen as a UK manifestation of a wider transition to a post-modern, post-industrial, global economy. Even so, Mrs Thatcher herself made such an impression not only on British politics but on the western world that the term 'Thatcherism' has survived her personal fall, and is not entirely inappropriate.

The ideas associated with 'Thatcherism' or the 'New Right' involved an interesting mix, and there were two principal strands. Firstly there were the free market ideas derived ultimately from classical liberalism, but more recently expressed by thinkers such as Hayek and Friedman who were dubbed neo-liberals. Secondly, there was a neo-conservative strand which emphasized more traditional Tory and Conservative themes such as authority, sovereignty, law and order and the national interest. Clearly neither strand was really new, although both seemed relatively novel in the context of the dominant 'One-Nation' strand of post-Second World War conservatism. Mrs Thatcher herself did not even pioneer the blend of neo-liberal and neo-conservative ideas: Enoch Powell had articulated a mixture of pure free-market liberalism and ultra-traditional Toryism a decade or so earlier. Mrs Thatcher's version was less provocative than Powell's, although it still contained tensions and contradictions which have posed problems for the Conservative Party under Mrs Thatcher herself and her successors.

Classical liberalism, neo-liberalism and the free market

Capitalism and Freedom was the title of an influential book written by the American economist Milton Friedman in 1962, which propounded the virtues of the free market. Neither the free market nor the term capitalism were then fashionable in Britain, even with Conservatives. Conservative governments had embraced the welfare state, Keynesian demand management and the mixed economy. Indeed, in the same year, 1962, as Friedman's book appeared, Harold Macmillan had established the National Economic Development Council, and embraced a form of planning. This was fully consistent with Macmillan's earlier career as a Conservative left-wing rebel, an advocate of a 'Middle Way' between free-market capitalism and communism, and a former Housing Minister who had depended substantially on council house building to achieve his proclaimed target of 300,000 houses a year. Macmillan had never believed in unrestrained capitalism or free-market forces, and his government was generally unreceptive to Milton Friedman's free-market message, although it did contain at least one heretic, Enoch Powell, who was to become a prominent exponent of free-market capitalism, and a future heretic, Keith Joseph, who was then however as keen on state housing and public spending as his chief. Well outside the Cabinet there was a recently appointed young, very junior minister, Margaret Thatcher, whose ideological leanings were as yet unrevealed to the wider political world.

Friedman's advocacy of the free market derived from the classical liberal economic theory of Adam Smith (1776). Smith had argued that wealth was created by the pursuit by individuals of their own self-interest in the free market which guided production like an 'invisible hand'. Those governments did best which governed least. This became the economic orthodoxy of classical liberalism. A passionate belief in free markets and free trade became the key characteristic of the 'Manchester Liberalism' of Cobden and Bright, and subsequently Gladstonian Liberalism. Conservatism, meanwhile, was committed to protection in the early and mid-nineteenth century, 'fair trade' (rather than free trade) subsequently, and imperial preference and tariff reform in the early twentieth century. It was also beginning to be associated with paternalist social reform (see Chapter 3). As we have seen (Chapter 2), classical free-market liberalism gave place to the more interventionist New Liberalism in the British Liberal Party, and these reforming ideas also took root in the twentieth-century Conservative and Labour Parties. Two world wars, the depression and the rise of new state-centred ideologies marginalized the old free-market orthodoxies.

Friedrich von Hayek was one important thinker who unfashionably attempted to turn back the collectivist tide. All state planning, he argued, involved a *Road to Serfdom* (1944, 1976), whether undertaken by fascist, communist, moderate social democratic, or even Conservative governments. Another key influence on Thatcherism was the public (or rational) choice theory of a school of American writers including Downs, Tullock, Buchanan and Niskanen who applied classical liberal economic analysis to government and the public sector. Thus Niskanen (1971) argued that public sector bureaucrats would pursue their own interests rather than that of the public they were supposed to serve. Instead of profit maximization they would seek 'bureau maximization' – the growth of programmes, employment and spending associated with their own department or bureau – as this would favour their own status, pay and prospects. This would always tend to produce a higher level of provision and public spending ('bureaucratic over-supply') than would be demanded and supplied in the free market. Thus public bureaucracies were inherently inefficient and wasteful. These ideas were to influence the Thatcher government's reforms of the civil service, local government and National Health Service.

More immediately influential were the increasingly vocal critics of Keynesian orthodoxy, including Friedman himself and the economists Alfred Sherman and Alan Walters. They argued that Keynesian budgeting was inflationary. and that control of inflation required tight control of the money supply. 'Monetarism' was thus the label initially associated with Mrs Thatcher's brand of conservatism but it was never a satisfactory label. It was actually the Labour Prime Minister Callaghan and his Chancellor Healey rather than Mrs Thatcher who first adopted monetary targets, while her political philosophy was always about much more than controlling the money supply (which received less emphasis subsequently).

All these free-market ideas belonged more to the liberal than the conservative tradition, although Greenleaf (1973, 1983) has associated them with a 'libertarian' strand of Conservative thought. Significantly, Hayek considered himself a liberal rather than a conservative although he carefully distinguished his own liberalism from what he described as the 'constructivist rationalism' of Voltaire, Rousseau and the English Utilitarians. Milton Friedman similarly described himself as a 'Liberal of the nineteenth-century variety', which was how he also described Mrs Thatcher herself:

> Mrs Thatcher is not in terms of belief a Tory. She is a nineteenth century Liberal. But her party consists largely of Tories. They don't really believe in free markets. They don't believe in free trade. They never have, as a party. They believe in an elite governing,

which is a very different conception to hers. (Friedman, *Observer*, 26 September 1982)

Yet before she became leader these ideological convictions were less evident. Although she claimed to have read Hayek's *Road to Serfdom* as a student at Oxford, she showed few signs that she was a disciple in her early political career. Her biographer Hugo Young (1989, p. 56) observes 'What is striking about this period is how small and tentative were her contributions to the debate which raged about the future of Conservatism.' She was a loyal member of Heath's team in opposition and later as a junior Cabinet Minister at the Department of Education and Science where she was 'responsible for the abolition of more grammar schools than any Secretary of State before or since' (Young, 1989, p. 68) as well as fiercely defending educational spending. Nor did she indicate any criticism of the general direction of government policy under Heath, although scorn for Heath's 'U-turn' in 1972 subsequently became Thatcherite orthodoxy. Following Heath's election defeats in 1974 it was Sir Keith Joseph who took the lead in advocating free-market rather than Keynesian policies, with Margaret Thatcher giving quiet support.

It was only after Mrs Thatcher emerged as the unlikely winner from the leadership contest in 1975 that her own free-market convictions became manifest in speeches where she extolled Victorian virtues of self-reliance, attacked collectivism, and dismissively referred to 'bourgeois guilt', a phrase widely interpreted as a criticism of Tory paternalism as much as socialism. She also acknowledged the influence of two celebrated neo-liberals, Friedman and Hayek, and, behind them, the virtual founder of classical economics, Adam Smith (Thatcher, 1977).

Detailed analyses of the policies of the Thatcher governments can be found elsewhere (Young, 1989; Kavanagh, 1990; Gilmour, 1992). Here it is sufficient to indicate how far free-market ideas informed the broad direction of policy. Control of the money supply, early seen as the very essence of the new approach, was found to be difficult in terms of definition and execution and was accorded less priority. There was a more determined attempt to 'rein back the state' although the state and public spending was effectively restructured rather than cut back. The sale of council houses and the privatization of most of the former nationalized industries marked, however, a significant transformation of the hitherto mixed economy. A shrunken public sector was systematically overhauled through the injection of competition and free-market principles. A managerial revolution challenged the old administrative culture of the civil service, which saw most of its tasks and personnel transferred to semi-autonomous Executive Agencies. Compulsory competitive tendering was imposed on a range of services, transport was deregulated and internal markets introduced into reorganized health and education services.

All this amounts to a formidable redirection of policy inspired by what might be described as neo-liberal free-market ideas. Even so, the Thatcher government did not go as far or as fast as some of the free-market enthusiasts would have liked. While the administration of health and education was reorganized, the principle of state provision of those services was substantially unaffected. The fashionable New Right notion of vouchers for education and health were considered but not implemented. The state was still substantially funding 'social housing' but through voluntary housing associations rather than local councils. Even privatization disappointed some critics because many of the newly-privatized services involved little effective competition, while the state retained an extensive regulatory role.

Moreover, despite the free-market rhetoric which emphasized decentralization to consumers, customers and patients, the reality often seemed to involve increased centralization. Thatcherite reforms appeared to strengthen rather than weaken the authority of the state, which did not match liberal or neo-liberal assumptions although it did sit comfortably within the mainstream Tory or conservative tradition and the neo-conservative strand of Thatcherism.

Neo-conservatism

Early accounts of Thatcherism and the New Right played down its traditional conservative or neo-conservative elements in emphasizing its roots in liberal and neo-liberal free-market ideology (Bosanquet, 1983; Green, 1987). Even while Mrs Thatcher was still in opposition, her liberal rhetoric disturbed both critics and some admirers within the Conservative Party. Sir Ian Gilmour, later sacked from Mrs Thatcher's Cabinet, carefully distinguished between conservatism and liberalism in his book *Inside Right* (1978). William Waldegrave (1978), a future member of both the Thatcher and Major governments, attacked neo-liberalism and reasserted a conservative tradition involving the acceptance of state power. Several contributors to a generally sympathetic volume of *Conservative Essays* (ed. Cowling, 1978) were expressly critical of liberal ideas:

The urgent need today is for the State to regain control over 'the people', to re-exert its authority, and it is useless to imagine that this will be helped by some libertarian mishmash drawn from the writings of Adam Smith, John Stuart Mill, and the warmed up milk of nineteenth century liberalism. (Worsthorne, in Cowling, 1978, p. 149)

Yet Peregrine Worsthorne need not have worried about Mrs Thatcher's rhetorical commitment to 'set the people free'. She shared his belief in firm government and restoring the authority of the state. Her 'nineteenth-century liberalism' was distinctly partial; she never exhibited much sympathy for the libertarian implications of Mill's thought in the field of tastes and morality, nor John Bright's pacifist internationalism. The Falklands War, Mrs Thatcher's approach to Europe, firm controls on immigration, tough penal policies, and the National Curriculum in education were hardly inspired by free-market ideas. An influential radical Marxist critique of Thatcherism coined the term 'authoritarian populism' to describe its combination of free-market economics with some traditional conservative elements with popular appeal – patriotism, law and order, authority and strong government (Hall and Jacques, 1983; Edgar, 1984; Gamble, 1989). These moral, authoritarian and patriotic elements of New-Right thinking were clearly evident in other countries, particularly among Mrs Thatcher's right-wing Republican allies in the United States.

It is a confusing consequence of the elastic and ambiguous definition of key concepts in the study of ideology that Thatcherism can be interpreted as both a product of one form of liberalism and a reaction against another. Just as neo-liberalism involved a reaction against Keynesianism and the welfare state, so neo-conservativism involved a reaction against another dominant orthodoxy of the recent past – in this case the progressive 'liberal' permissiveness of the 1960s. The 1960s saw the abolition of capital punishment, the relaxation of censorship, divorce law reform and the legalization of abortion and homosexuality, advanced and supported by 'liberal' progressive politicians from all parties. These measures both reflected changes in public opinion and contributed to further changes in attitude and behaviour. Some critics, largely on the right, blamed the breakdown of marriage, family life and moral standards more generally on the 'permissive society'.

The 'family-values' reaction by the 'moral majority' against 'liberal permissiveness' was never as vocal or prominent an element in Thatcherism as it was in the Republicanism of Ronald Reagan. Although the moral campaigners believed she was sympathetic,

Mrs Thatcher herself generally avoided explicit commitments on issues of personal morality, and indeed showed a resigned tolerance towards the publicized sexual misdeeds of her male colleagues. Norman Tebbit was much less restrained, however, and blamed the 1960s for the breakdown of family life and traditional morality. His language found a strong answering chord in the rank and file membership of the Conservative Party, and this, to an extent, influenced the political agenda of Mrs Thatcher's successors, John Major and William Hague.

Tensions within Thatcherism

There are tensions and ambiguities in all ideologies and the contrasting neo-liberal and neo-conservative strands of Thatcherism have always provided a potential source of conflict (see Figure 9.1). To a degree, however, the two strands were compatible; both implied hostility to trade unionism, bureaucracy and corporatist tendencies in government. From a neo-liberal perspective trade-union practices, corporatist policies (such as incomes policy) and bureaucracy all involved unjustified interference with free-market forces. From a neo-conservative perspective, strikes and other union activities, concessions to powerful producer groups under corporatism and the entrenched influence of the higher civil service all posed a threat to the authority of the state and its elected government. Moreover, the free economy advocated by neo-liberals required a strong state to enforce competition, uphold contracts and resist the pressures and claims upon it from powerful sectional interests.

Yet there were also some obvious tensions. For example, on the environment neo-conservatives tended to be right-wing conservationists, while neo-liberals sought to remove controls on planning and development which interfered with market forces. There were also differences on a host of moral issues such as abortion, censorship and addiction issues (including alcohol, tobacco and drugs). Sunday trading involved a symbolically important clash of values. Neo-liberals wanted restrictions on Sunday trading abolished in the interests of free market forces. Neo-conservatives wished to 'keep Sunday special' in accordance with traditional values and also protect vulnerable small shopkeepers and shopworkers. It was on this issue that the Thatcher government suffered a rare and embarrassing defeat.

However, the most important divisions were over foreign policy and particularly Europe. Thus some Conservatives saw the European

Community (as it then was) in terms of their own free-market convictions, while others perceived a threat to national sovereignty and national interests. The European Community seemed to embody the free-market capitalist values dear to Mrs Thatcher, which is why she supported British entry and enthusiastically signed the Single European Act. Yet it was also associated with bureaucratic and corporatist tendencies which she opposed in Britain. More seriously, intensifying pressures towards closer political union apparently threatened Britain's national sovereignty and independence, a core Conservative value. Mrs Thatcher's personal schizophrenia over Europe reflected the tensions between the neo-liberal and neo-conservative elements in her own political philosophy. This schizophrenia has been bequeathed to her party, with damaging consequences.

Arguably, however, the tensions within Thatcherism reflect older tensions within the Conservative tradition. The neo-conservative authoritarian streak in Thatcherism involved a change in emphasis from the liberal progressive attitudes of Macmillan, Butler, Macleod, Boyle and Heath, but reflected the attitudes and demands which regularly surfaced from the rank and file at Conservative Party conferences throughout the postwar period. Also, the libertarian strand in conservatism was not new, as Greenleaf (1973) has demonstrated. Even in the supposed heyday of Tory collectivism there were strong pressures for competition. The Conservatives were reelected to the slogan 'Set the People Free' in 1951, and proceeded to dismantle rationing and controls, denationalize steel and road haulage, establish commercial television, and later commercial radio, relax rent controls, and abolish resale price maintenance. The sale of council houses, sometimes regarded as quintessential Thatcherism, was Conservative policy in the 1950s. Here Mrs Thatcher differed from her predecessors in her more ruthless application of policy.

Ideology and pragmatism

Even the ideological drive behind Thatcherism can be exaggerated. The forced sale of council houses at substantial discounts, and the privatization of the former nationalized industries perhaps had as much to do with pragmatic political objectives as free-market ideas. The extension of home ownership and share ownership gave more voters a stake in property and popular capitalism, while reducing Labour's traditional constituency of council tenants, public-sector employees and trade unionists. It can be seen in terms of the politics of statecraft, the con-

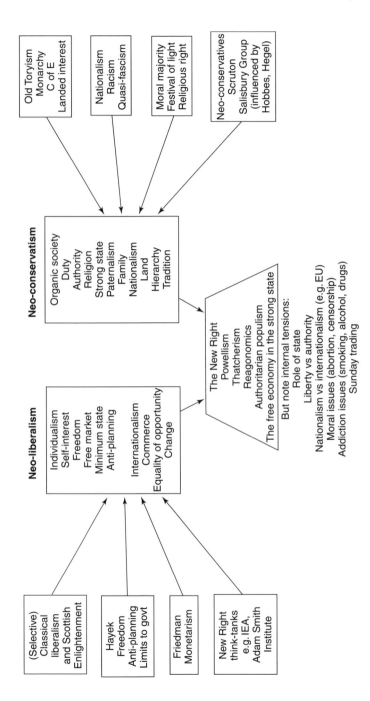

Figure 9.1   Tensions within Thatcherism and the New Right

struction of new coalitions of interests (Bulpitt, 1987). Mrs Thatcher, like Disraeli over a century before, was making a bid for the skilled working-class vote.

At another level it can be argued that Thatcherism was a response to altered circumstances. In the earlier postwar period it seemed that commitment to the welfare state and full employment was necessary to win elections, but by the 1970s both the economic assumptions behind those commitments and their political rationale were seen as questionable. Faith in Keynesian demand management was undermined by mounting economic problems, while a growing proportion of the electorate seemed disillusioned with both the benefits of the welfare state and its mounting cost, with adverse consequences for taxation and take-home pay. Thatcherism thus involved a response to the new mood; it was as much the politics of electoral calculation as the politics of conviction.

There is clearly something in such analysis. Mrs Thatcher was more pragmatic than some of her enthusiastic acolytes and advisers would have wished. Thus she declared that the National Health Service was safe in Conservative hands, and rejected rail and post-office privatization. However some of the policies of Mrs Thatcher's third term, most notably the poll tax, seemed to have a clearer ideological than electoral rationale (although it certainly appealed to the ideas of many Conservative Party activists).

A problem for any radical administration, of the right or the left, is whether to maintain the momentum of reform or seek to consolidate after initial objectives are achieved. Both Mrs Thatcher's government and Attlee's government after the Second World War had completed the more popular aspects of their programmes well before their end. The Attlee government chose consolidation, appeared politically and ideologically exhausted, and lost office. The Thatcher government preferred permanent revolution and moved on to the more controversial privatization of water and the decidedly unpopular poll tax, and broke up. Perhaps consolidation was never an option for Mrs Thatcher, because she was in the last analysis an ideological rather than a pragmatic politician. Ideas were clearly important to her, and she had argued that the Conservatives needed an ideology to counter socialism. She spurned the traditional civil service sources of policy advice, consulting ideologically sympathetic New Right think-tanks such as the Institute of Economic Affairs and the Adam Smith Institute, and, with Keith Joseph, founding the Centre for Policy Studies. Hers were the politics of conviction rather than pragmatism.

The legacy of Thatcherism

Ideologies are action-oriented and if they are scored in terms of their measurable impact, Thatcherism scores highly. The Thatcher governments did substantially transform Britain, more than any previous administration since Attlee's. Moreover, many of the changes, like those of the Attlee government, seem irreversible for the foreseeable future. Even a Labour government with a huge majority has not contemplated renationalizing privatized industries, and has modified rather than reversed Thatcher reforms in local government and the NHS. Mrs Thatcher's governments have altered the terms of political trade in ways which have affected her Labour as well as her Conservative successors.

Even so, 'Thatcherism' never really conquered the country (Crewe, in Skidelsky, 1988). It was the electoral system combined with the divisions within the opposition which delivered a series of impressive victories at the polls. Mrs Thatcher in three elections failed to achieve anything approaching the proportion of the popular vote won by Eden in 1955 or Macmillan in 1959. She won her biggest parliamentary majority in 1983 with a smaller proportion of the vote than that secured by the defeated Sir Alec Douglas Home in 1964. Moreover, between the peaks of the General Election years, there were deep troughs in which the party lost heavily in local elections and parliamentary by-elections. Neither Mrs Thatcher herself, nor her party, nor its policies and underpinning ideas were ever as popular as some commentators have suggested.

Yet if Thatcherism was never that popular it caught the mood for change. The old assumptions which had governed policy-making since the end of the Second World War until the early 1970s no longer appeared tenable. Keynesian remedies no longer seemed to work; the welfare state had failed to eradicate poverty; the public sector appeared insensitive and inefficient; and compromise in industrial relations had failed to deliver industrial peace. While Mrs Thatcher's abrasive style and particular remedies did not always inspire approval, her governments were tackling what were widely perceived as problems – high public spending and taxation, inflation, bureaucracy and waste, union power. Moreover, the acronym TINA ('There is no alternative') which was proclaimed by enthusiasts was also reluctantly conceded by many more. There did not seem to be a credible alternative in terms of ideas or policies. Thatcherism involved some nasty medicine but appeared necessary to many to purge the British state, society and economy of manifold weaknesses.

The legacy for the Conservative Party is mixed. If Mrs Thatcher can be credited with restoring the fortunes of her party to the extent of winning three successive General Elections and a long, almost unprecedented, period of unbroken Conservative rule, she also left a legacy of internal party division. Differences over policies and ideas were intensified by personal and factional rivalries, to the extent that dissecting the faultlines in modern Conservatism has already become something of an academic industry. In part these differences only mirror old tensions, between for example the libertarian and collectivist strands in Conservatism (Greenleaf, 1973, 1983). Yet they were exacerbated by Mrs Thatcher's own abrasive and uncompromising style. Divisions were not accommodated; dissenting colleagues (Gilmour, Prior, Pym, Heseltine) and even former allies (Tebbit, Lawson, Howe) were removed or provoked to resign. Thus a party for which unity was long said to be its secret weapon (Blake, 1997, p. 405) became deeply divided, while the embrace of ideology obstructed the party's former pragmatic flexibility in pursuit of power.

From Thatcher to Major

Mrs Thatcher's fall sparked off some speculation over the future direction of British conservatism. Yet too many leading Conservatives were implicated in Thatcherism to make total repudiation a credible option. Moreover, the victory of John Major, Mrs Thatcher's preferred successor, first in the leadership election of 1990 and then in the General Election of 1992, apparently confirmed that the Thatcher legacy was safe.

However, the particular circumstances of Mrs Thatcher's fall left a legacy of bitterness and internal recriminations within the Conservative Party. In retrospect it might have been better for the party had Mrs Thatcher been eventually repudiated by the electorate rather than by her own Cabinet and parliamentary colleagues; then the need for a change in leadership and direction might perhaps have been acknowledged. As it was, her numerous admirers both within the parliamentary party and the wider party in the country considered she had been betrayed, and they never forgave those deemed directly or indirectly responsible. John Major's government never acquired full legitimacy for those of the true Thatcherite faith, and only briefly from the wider public. The authority derived from the unexpected election victory in 1992 was swiftly followed by 'Black Wednesday', disastrous poll ratings and party splits. He was not helped by the slighting observations of his predecessor, 'the queen over the water', who soon became disillusioned with her anointed heir.

Although the Major government involved a marked change in political style, there were few significant differences in policy and ideas (Kavanagh and Seldon, 1994). The poll tax, incautiously described as the flagship of Thatcherism, was an early casualty, but this had become a political necessity. Otherwise the Major government energetically pursued the changes in education and health begun under Mrs Thatcher, and extended competition in public services. There was no slackening in the privatization programme. The politically contentious break-up of British Rail was forced through, while the government was only diverted from its intention to privatize the Royal Mail (which Mrs Thatcher had avoided) by the lack of a sufficient parliamentary majority. Major's only significant innovation was the Citizen's Charter, hailed by some as a new deal for the public services, but viewed by critics (not entirely fairly) as essentially cosmetic. Thus Major's government appeared more of an extended coda to his predecessor's than a new and distinctive administration (Kavanagh and Seldon, 1994).

In retrospect John Major had a difficult, perhaps impossible, role. He had to appease zealots of the 'No Turning Back' group that there was to be no retreat from the true Thatcherite faith, and yet at the same time satisfy the demands for change in the party and the country. His own personality and style was consensual, in marked contrast to Thatcher's, and circumstances required that he should strive to contain widening party divisions. Yet the tensions between the neo-liberal and neo-conservative elements of the New Right, evident within the party when Mrs Thatcher was still Prime Minister, became rather more apparent after she left office.

The divisions were most obvious over Europe. Initially John Major indicated that he was more sympathetic towards the European ideal than Mrs Thatcher, while still standing for British interests within Europe. Thus his conduct of the negotiations at Maastricht (in which he secured exemptions for Britain from the Social Chapter and from monetary union) was presented as a diplomatic triumph. Even so, a small hard-core of rebels opposed the Maastricht Treaty from the start, exploiting a growing general hostility to Europe following the disastrous 'Black Wednesday' when Britain was ignominiously forced out of the Exchange Rate Mechanism, and, even more, the escalating BSE crisis. Major faced a challenge to his leadership from John Redwood in 1995 and a threat to his party's electoral prospects from the newly-established Referendum Party and UK Independence Party. Yet he could not appease the Euro-sceptics without risking losing the support of the most powerful ministers within his own Cabinet (Major, 1999, pp. 342–85, 578–607).

Thus Conservatism appeared increasingly on the defensive during John Major's period as Prime Minister. Under Mrs Thatcher the party offered a radical challenge to the Butskellite consensus of the postwar era. The very success of that challenge had now transformed Conservatives into defenders of a new status quo, increasingly subject to criticism, particularly on the management of the reformed Health Service and the privatized utilities. Moreover, Conservatives were obliged to defend a chequered economic record. Two recessions, culminating in the effective forced devaluation of Black Wednesday had undermined their claims to economic competence. Tax rises after 1992, coupled with the collapse of the housing market, helped to alienate a substantial section of the middle classes on whom Conservatives relied for their core electoral support. It was also unfortunate that Major launched a 'back to basics' initiative, which was misinterpreted and subsequently undermined when his government became mired in sleaze, following a series of financial and sexual scandals involving ministers and backbenchers (Major, 1999, pp. 554–77).

Of course, it is also true that some of the problems with which Conservative governments had been grappling reflected changes both in British society and the wider world – demographic change, the breakdown of traditional families and communities, technological change and unemployment, resource depletion and pollution, and the changing relationships between the developed and the developing worlds. In such circumstances it is unsurprising that New Right prescriptions had failed to produce magic solutions. The free market was the 'big idea' which the New Right had claimed would transform the British economy and society, but following two decades of free-market orthodoxy some of the familiar problems of market failure were being rediscovered both in Britain and the wider world.

Conservatism for the twenty-first century – Hague and after

The reversal of Conservative political fortunes has been rapid and massive. After a fourth successive election victory in 1992 the party seemed unassailable and its opponents unelectable. In the space of a few years the roles have been reversed. The natural party of government has become a party of ineffective opposition.

Defeat was always going to be traumatic for the Conservatives; the 'natural party of government' had become accustomed to the fruits of office. The sheer scale of the 1997 defeat, even though predicted by the polls, was a worse shock – the heaviest defeat since 1906, or, some suggested, since 1832. A direct consequence was the removal from Parliament of some former Cabinet Ministers–including Malcolm Rifkind, Ian Lang and (for a time) Michael Portillo. This electoral cull of some of the party's leading lights was swiftly followed by the retirement to the back benches of the former Prime Minister, John Major, and Deputy Prime Minister, Michael Heseltine, and then as a consequence of the ensuing leadership election the departure from the shadow cabinet of Clarke, and soon afterwards Howard, Lilley, Dorrell and Redwood. Thus the 1997 election produced an almost unprecedented turnover of the party's collective leadership.

Like Thatcher and Major before him, William Hague won the subsequent leadership election for negative reasons. Relatively unknown, he was less tarnished by the perceived failures of the Major government and carried less baggage than his rivals. Fresh faces at the top of the party apparently offered the prospect of a clean break with the past, and there were early indications that Hague favoured a more inclusive, tolerant party. Indeed, he quickly moved to reform the party's internal organization and decision-making, with the expectation of creating a more modern democratic party with a wider popular appeal.

Yet giving more power and influence to the party's dwindling ageing membership (Whiteley *et al.*, 1994, p. 50) was hardly compatible with broadening its electoral appeal. While some leading Conservatives were aware of the need for change, it proved difficult to persuade constituency activists to accept the practical implications of gender equality, multiculturalism, toleration of different patterns of sexual behaviour and non-conventional families. A speech by Peter Lilley which sought to distance the party from Thatcherism disastrously backfired. Thus prospects for a softer, more inclusive conservatism receded. Subsequently, the party's uncompromising ideas on crime, asylum seekers, sex and drugs (articulated by Shadow Home Secretary Anne Widdecombe) were largely at one with those of (generally elderly) Conservative members.

So apart from some pragmatic post-election concessions to realism including the acceptance of devolution and the minimum wage, against which the party had campaigned fiercely, there was no real attempt to redefine or update the party philosophy, such as took place after the Conservative defeats of 1945, 1966 and 1974. Instead Hague concentrated on attacking the government, capitalizing on events and issues raised by others (such as the Countryside Alliance, or the fuel protest lobby) rather than seeking to win the battle of ideas by articulating an alternative vision of the future.

Indeed the ideological visions most widely canvassed related to the past rather than the future. Some advocated a return to One-Nation conservatism of the postwar era, but this had depended on a symbiotic relationship between a paternalist leadership and a deferential loyal party which enabled Conservative governments to pursue progressive welfare policies out of tune with the interests and values of Conservative supporters. Today the party in parliament and the constituencies has become less deferential, and less inclined to acquiesce in policies which run counter to their own gut instincts. Moreover, the old 'One-Nation' project has been transformed by changing class interests and loyalties, and the increasing political salience of ethnic, gender and other divisions. Thus the Conservative Party has lost a large slice of its previous core middle-class vote, without being able to reach out successfully to the new multi-ethnic, multi-faith nation containing a diversity of lifestyles and family groupings.

The favoured alternative for many Conservatives is thus a return to the moral certainties and electoral successes associated with Mrs Thatcher, who continues to cast a long shadow over her party. Thus John Major was effectively disowned for backsliding from the true faith, while William Hague was endorsed as Mrs Thatcher's legitimate successor. Significantly she campaigned hard for Hague in the 2001 election, having taken a back seat in 1992 and 1997. While she enthused party activists, many commentators thought her rhetoric alienated voters, for whom she belonged to the past rather than the future. Indeed, for the party, Mrs Thatcher's brand of conviction politics has become an ideological straitjacket, preventing any significant rethinking.

One imperative for the new Conservative opposition was to rethink its economic policies and particularly its approach to taxing and spending. This was never going to be easy. It was no longer true that state spending mainly benefited the working class and was paid for by taxes raised from the middle classes. While the middle classes gained substantially and disproportionately from some state spending (for example spending on higher education, subsidized rail transport, and the arts), taxation had become more regressive. Thus an increasing proportion of the middle classes (particularly those employed in the NHS and other public services) favoured tax and spend policies, while the old working class might be tempted by tax cuts. Attempting to respond to these diverse pressures, the Conservative opposition unconvincingly promised both improved public services and tax cuts. Their task was rendered much more difficult by Labour's apparently successful management of the economy between 1997 and 2001. The previous Conservative trump-card, proven economic competence, was now held by their Labour opponents. It was now Conservative sums which 'did not add up'.

Constitutional reform, particularly devolution, presented a bigger potential threat to traditional Conservative values. The party which has been the party of the Union for well over a century may no longer have a Union to defend, although there was little choice but to accept devolution once it was achieved. One possibility now is to try to make devolution work and thus preserve 'four nations in one'. Yet the Conservatives lost their links with the Ulster Unionists in the early 1970s and have been reduced to minor party status in Scotland and Wales (although ironically the proportional electoral system which they opposed has preserved a significant Conservative presence in the devolved assemblies). Thus, increasingly, they appear an English party and as such might benefit politically from the break-up of the Union which they have long sought to maintain. Elsewhere they have sought to exploit Labour's problems with Lords reform and the London mayoralty, but they have yet to develop a more comprehensive Conservative approach to constitutional reform.

Yet Conservative confusion on the constitution has probably not damaged them much politically. Europe is another matter; a running sore which has cost them their previous reputation for unity and moderation. Hague chose to adopt a harder Eurosceptic position which isolated the dwindling number of Conservative europhiles, and drove a few out of the party. It was assumed a clear line would banish the ambiguities of the Major years, and appeal to a Eurosceptic electorate. Thus Hague fought the 2001 election as a single-issue campaign to 'save the pound'. It is now almost universally recognized that this was a mistake. Although the majority of voters shared Conservative opposition to the euro, it was well down their list of priorities. Hague's obsession with Europe meant that Labour's general record and Conservative alternatives never received detailed scrutiny. His tough line with dissent meant that the party was perceived as 'dogmatic', and 'extreme' rather than united, particularly among those voters who recalled that all the main developments in the UK's relationship with Europe had been undertaken by previous Conservative Governments. The party was effectively denying its own past.

The 2001 election was in some respects more disastrous than that of 1997 for the Conservatives, as they had failed to make any significant recovery despite the problems and weakening popularity of the Blair government. The prompt resignation of Hague offered another opportunity for a fresh start, but the indications are that the party remains ill-equipped to take it, trapped as it is between the need to renew its appeal to a fast-changing wider electorate and the very different concerns of its own ageing activists. Significantly, Conservative MPs preferred to reject Michael Portillo, who had become the candidate of change, and give Conservative members a stark choice between two sharply contrasting candidates, the pro-Euro Kenneth Clarke and the Maastricht rebel Iain Duncan Smith. It seems unlikely that the resulting comfortable winner, Duncan Smith, who was the first choice of less than a third of Conservative MPs in their final ballot, will find it easy to reunite his divided party and restore its electoral fortunes. His early decisions, including his choice of a shadow cabinet, seem to have confirmed expectations that he will take the Conservatives further to the right.

Conservatives cannot rely on the mistakes of their opponents to be eventually restored to power. The Liberal Democrats' revival means it is not even certain that it will be the Conservatives who will eventually reap the benefit of any future Labour failure or unpopularity. The twentieth century was a 'Conservative Century' (Seldon and Ball, 1994) but they may not similarly dominate the twenty-first century unless they somehow manage to reinvent themselves, as they so often managed in the past. As one former Conservative minister has warned, 'the price of political complacency and intellectual stagnation is usually high' (Patten, 1995, p. 2).

Further reading

The literature is extensive and daunting. For the neo-liberal ideas which influenced Thatcherism see especially Hayek's classic neo-liberal text *Road to Serfdom* and Friedman (1962). There is a useful discussion of Powellism in Gamble (1974), and Powell's ideas are also explored in biographies (for example Cosgrave, 1989) and his own writings (1991). Joseph's ideas can be sampled in *Stranded in the Middle Ground* (1976). A neo-conservative perspective is to found in the collection of essays edited by Cowling (1978) and in Scruton (1980). On Thatcherism, Bosanquet (1983), Keegan (1984), Green (1987) and King (1987) concentrate largely on monetarism and the free-market aspects of the New Right, while Hall and Jaques (1983), Levitas (1986), Gamble (1988) and Skidelsky (1988) also acknowledge the importance of traditional conservative and neo-conservative themes.

Young's (1989) illuminating biography of Mrs Thatcher can be contrasted with her own account (1993) and that of other leading protagonists such as Gilmour (1992) and Lawson (1992). Ranelagh (1992) is useful on influences, while Kavanagh (1990) and Adonis and Hames (1994) provide a useful overall perspective.

Conservatism after Thatcher has been less exhaustively explored. Kavanagh and Seldon (1994) and Ludlam and Smith (1996) have both edited useful collections of essays on Major whose own autobiography (1999) is illuminating. Whiteley *et al.* (1994) is useful on Conservative Party members, while Patten (1995) has reviewed Conservative ideas. Post-1997 obituaries for Conservatism include Gilmour and Garnett (1997) and Gray and Willetts (1997). Recent developments are best explored on the Party website, http//www.conservatives.com/

10

From Old to New Labour

A new party with a new ideology?

Just as conservatism was transformed in the last quarter of the twentieth century, so it is claimed that the ideology of the Labour Party also has been fundamentally altered. New Labour is sometimes perceived as quite different from the old Labour Party from which it emerged; the ideas embraced by Blair's party and government have become linked with the concept of a 'Third Way', although there is some argument over both the nature of the Third Way and of the alternative routes which are implicitly rejected.

The extent of the change from the old to the new party can be dramatized by comparing Labour's programme under Blair with that on which it fought and lost the 1983 election. Then the party, led by the veteran Bevanite and unilateralist Michael Foot, was committed to unilateral nuclear disarmament, exit from the European Community and a massive expansion in public spending including further nationalization, in accordance with Clause IV of its constitution. By 1997 the commitments to nuclear disarmament and leaving the European Union had been overturned. Labour had agreed to keep within Conservative spending plans for two years and not only were proposals for further nationalization abandoned, but Labour had implicitly accepted the extensive privatization programme of the Thatcher and Major governments. Indeed, Clause IV of Labour's constitution which committed the party to public ownership had been completely rewritten. Critics argued that Blair had abandoned socialism, and even social democracy, and some accused him of being Thatcher's heir. John Major (1999, p. 593) has called him a 'political kleptomaniac', appropriating Conservative language and policies.

Even so, the extent of the transformation can be exaggerated. The Labour Party of the early 1980s was untypical and represented the high-tide of the left's advance (Seyd, 1987), and pragmatic reformism of Blair's government is not so very different from that of previous Labour governments. Blair's rhetoric, indeed, has some marked similarities with that of another Labour leader who came to power after a long period of Conservative rule, who also emphasized the themes of modernization, progress and a 'new Britain', Harold Wilson. So it is equally possible to argue that New Labour is not so very different from the ideas and practice of the old Labour Party.

Here, however, an intermediate position is taken. New Labour is different not so much because Blair has betrayed his party's (always contestable) socialism, but because Britain and the world has changed. Firstly British society has changed. The old manual working class with which Labour was identified is smaller and more fragmented. New cleavages on lines of ethnicity, nationality and gender now overlay and complicate old class divisions. Secondly, 18 years of Conservative government have changed the terms of political trade, far more so than the 13 years of Conservative rule from 1951–64. It is now scarcely politically feasible to put back the clock to before 1979; to that extent Blair's New Labour is inevitably influenced by the Thatcherism which preceded it. Thirdly, and most conclusively, the world has changed. The fashionable concept of globalization can be exaggerated, and indeed may be viewed as but the culmination of a trend evident for a century or more. Even so, British politics can no longer be immunized from global markets and global communications.

Old Labour, democratic socialism and social democracy

If the political ideas of the old Labour Party are characterized as more labourist than socialist, James Callaghan (Morgan, 1997) may be seen, perhaps, as the embodiment of that labourist tradition. He was the last Labour leader who had not attended university; he had emerged from a working-class and trade-union (albeit white-collar), background. As such he belonged neither socially nor intellectually to the old Bevanite left represented by Wilson, Crossman, Castle and Foot, nor to the revisionist Gaitskellite right around Crosland and Jenkins. Instead, Callaghan was, generally, the authentic voice of the old 'contentious alliance' with the trade unions (Minkin, 1991, p. 112). As such he led the opposition to Wilson and Castle's plans to reform industrial relations in 1969 and eagerly pursued incomes policy and the social contract with the unions when he became Prime Minister in 1976. He related to Labour's old male, working-class base. He was less inter-

ested in either the progressive liberal reforms over which Roy Jenkins
had presided as Home Secretary, or Barbara Castle's enthusiasm for
equal opportunities and child benefit. The collapse of his government in
1979 in the face of 'the winter of discontent' in retrospect marks the
death of old labourism. The future appeared to lie either with a more
committed left-wing socialism or with a revisionist social democracy.

The old tension between left and right, or between 'democratic
socialists' and 'social democrats', turned into open warfare within the
party after the 1979 election defeat. The breach was prefaced and apparently provoked by a swing to the left within Labour (Seyd, 1987; Shaw,
1994). This was symbolized by the election of the old Bevanite and unilateralist Michael Foot as leader, but also involved changes to the
party's constitution and a policy commitment to withdraw Britain from
the EEC (Bradley, 1981; Kogan and Kogan, 1982; Stephenson, 1982).
Four former Labour Cabinet ministers, Roy Jenkins, Shirley Williams,
Bill Rodgers and David Owen then set up a new party, the Social
Democratic Party, soon joined by another two dozen Labour MPs
(Jenkins, 1991; Crewe and King, 1995). 'Social democrat' had long
been a convenient label for describing reformist or revisionist Labour
politicians; Now the social democrats were effectively split between
those who joined the new party, and those like Healey and Hattersley
who stayed with Labour. Weakened by defections, social democrats
within the Labour Party had a difficult time. Healey came close to being
defeated in the deputy leadership contest by Tony Benn, heading a
broad left alliance. Despite this narrow setback the left seemed firmly in
control of the party's programme up to the 1983 election.

While Labour was weakened and divided, for a time the SDP
thrived. The new members they attracted were largely 'political
virgins' – not previously closely identified with any old political party,
and indeed enthusiastic about a wholly new party with a new style and
approach. Yet the SDP was never essentially new, but effectively a
'Mark II Labour Party' (Crewe and King, 1995, pp. 125–8). Indeed,
they claimed to be the true heirs of Attlee and Gaitskell. Their leaders
alleged that they had not left the Labour Party, but that the Labour
Party had left them, implying a marked ideological shift to the left by
Labour. However, most Labour 'moderates' in parliament, and the vast
bulk of Labour councillors, active members and trade unionists
declined to join the SDP, whose preoccupation with past battles within
the Labour Party bedevilled any project to establish a new party with a
new philosophy and programme. The SDP programme involved, critics
alleged, a 'new yesterday' – support for the EEC and NATO, modified

Keynesianism, the welfare state and incomes policy. The only essentially new policy proposal was constitutional reform, particularly electoral reform, a commitment which owed much to their Liberal allies. Although there was a considerable intellectual ferment, including a spate of new books by prominent Social Democrats, its only distinctive idea which appeared at all novel in the British context was the 'social market' which drew heavily on German experience (Williams, 1981; Owen, 1981; Marquand, 1988). Failing to capture the 'moderate' Labour faction or to forge a new political ideology, the SDP was eventually obliged to choose between submerging their identity within the Liberals, or political extinction (Crewe and King, 1995, pp. 385–410).

New Labour?

The left's apparent dominance within the Labour Party, which had provoked the SDP breakaway, proved short-lived (Seyd, 1987), although whether the formation of the SDP assisted or delayed the return of the Labour Party to 'moderate' consensus politics is contentious (Healey, 1989; Jenkins, 1991; Hattersley, 1995). However, a more potent influence on Labour was Mrs Thatcher's brand of conservatism. Four successive Conservative Party election victories from 1979 altered the political landscape and compelled some rethinking of Labour's philosophy and commitments. The party could no longer simply defend the Attlee inheritance. They could seek to restore it, or jettison parts no longer considered relevant, or forge new policy proposals, but preservation of the status quo was no longer an option. Realization of this compelled an extensive policy review (Shaw, 1994, pp. 81–107) and some ideological reassessment, beginning under the leadership of Kinnock, and continued by first Smith and then Blair (Ludlam and Smith, 2001).

Thus Labour has now abandoned virtually all the commitments which led to the establishment of the SDP. The 1983 manifesto commitment to withdraw from the European Community was among the first casualties of this new realism, and since then Labour has become positively enthusiastic about Europe. Following the 1987 defeat the commitment to nuclear disarmament, with which Kinnock had been closely associated, was quietly abandoned as part of the policy review. After the more unexpected 1992 defeat Labour has sought to avoid any commitment to raise spending and taxation. More fundamental to the party's ideology has been a rethinking of the relationship with the trade unions, largely carried through under the leadership of John Smith

(1992–94), and, most symbolic of all, a rewriting of Clause IV of the party constitution in 1994–95 under Blair.

While the importance of the union link has been reaffirmed, in practice the Labour leadership has increasingly distanced itself from the unions. It was soon clear that Labour would not reverse the bulk of the Conservative union reforms and, moreover, organizational reforms within the Labour Party, including the end of the trade union block vote, reduced union influence over party policy. This accentuated a trend away from Labour's past identification with trade unions and the manual working class which has been underway for over half a century. Thus, firstly, most of the parliamentary party and even the bulk of constituency activists have long ceased to be of the working class (Hindess, 1971). Secondly, and partly perhaps reflecting these social changes within the party, the policies pursued by Labour have not always appeared to benefit the old working class. Moreover, in recent years Labour has been represented as more interested in promoting equal opportunities for women, blacks or gays than defending the interests of their traditional (and formerly largely male) working-class clientele. Such perceptions may be exaggerated, but underline the extent to which the Labour Party is no longer automatically seen by many white, male, manual workers as 'their' party.

The manual working class is itself relatively smaller, and more divided – for example between public and private-sector employees, between council tenants and owner occupiers, and on gender and ethnic grounds. Some workers have become relatively affluent consumers and property owners, while others have lost jobs and seen their living standards eroded. Such changes have weakened working-class solidarity; As the working class appears less homogeneous it is not surprising that there is less of a common working-class culture. Labour began as an explicitly class party, with a programme pitched deliberately at the working class, although it always enjoyed some middle-class support and active involvement. The reduction in size and the fragmentation of the old manual working class meant that Labour had to broaden its appeal towards 'middle England'. This also implied some ideological revision away from labourism.

This ideological revision was symbolically secured through the rewriting of Clause IV, Labour's commitment to public ownership. Blair succeeded where Gaitskell had failed in 1960 partly because circumstances had changed. Most of the former nationalized industries had been privatized, and it was increasingly recognized that wholesale renationalization was politically and economically unrealistic. Yet Blair handled the issue more skilfully than Gaitskell. Labour's principles and values remained the same, he argued, but required updating because the world had changed. 'Let us say what we mean and mean what we say' (Blair Conference speech, 1994). The new clause, backed by a three to one majority, is broader but more anodyne and less memorable than the old. It symbolized the ideological transition of the party towards the mainstream European social democratic tradition (Sassoon, 1997; pp. 736–740).

Yet 'New Labour' is not a new party. Even the most controversial changes – the reform of the union link and the rewriting of Clause IV – are more to do with presentation than substance. The unions have never really exercised the power over the parliamentary party which the constitution apparently gave them, and Labour was never really committed to wholesale public ownership. Thus the reforms have more to do with the abandonment of what were perceived as electoral liabilities. Labour's proclaimed ideology has been adjusted to accord more closely with Labour practice.

The international context

The transition to New Labour cannot be explained simply in terms of domestic British politics, but has to be related also to the changing international context. Although Labour's ideology has long been peculiarly insular, influenced largely by British politicians and thinkers, it has inevitably been significantly affected by developments in the wider world. From 1945 the 'Cold War' between the west and the Soviet Union particularly shaped and constrained Labour's thinking.

The Cold War divided socialists. Labour, along with social democracy in Europe, was aligned with the USA the standard bearer of capitalism against the alternative 'really existing socialism' of the USSR. Indeed the Labour leadership remained as committed to Britain's presumed 'special relationship' with the USA as the Conservatives. This periodically caused severe strains within the broad labour movement, parts of which were never keen on NATO and the American alliance. Thus there was opposition to German rearmament in the 1950s, to the nuclear deterrent in the 1960s and to US policy in Vietnam and elsewhere in the 1960s and 1970s. Such issues split the party and also provoked Conservative accusations that Labour was 'soft on Communism'.

The end of the Cold War removed the presumed Soviet threat and marginalized Labour's previous problems with defence policy. Yet at the same time the collapse of the USSR confirmed the supremacy of the free market and discredited planning, for whatever its deficiencies in the eyes of western socialists, Soviet communism represented an apparently flourishing alternative to western capitalism – living proof that it was possible to organize an economy on different lines (Hobsbawm, 1994). Its collapse removed the alternative, and the constant threat it presented to capitalism. Socialism everywhere suffered a psychological defeat, while a triumphalist capitalism felt less obliged to make concessions to the interests of labour. Dahrendorf (1990) emphatically declared that socialism in all its variants (including social democracy) was dead. Socialists naturally refused to accept this verdict but recognized that they were now purveying their message in a 'sceptical age' (R. Miliband, 1994).

At the start of the new millennium the longer-term consequences of the fall of the Berlin wall seem less clear. The post-communist transition to a 'New World Order' has proved more problematic than neo-liberals anticipated, and the free market no longer appears the universal panacea they proclaimed. Social democracy has made something of a comeback in western Europe, suggesting that Dahrendorf's announcement of its death was at least premature. In the year 2000 the largest EU member states, Germany, France and Italy, as well as Britain, all had governments which might be described as social democrat (although the Italian 'Olive Tree' coalition lost power in 2001).

However, these governments had to recognize that they operated in a transformed global environment. Socialism in one country was no longer a feasible option (if it ever had been). Even the British Labour Party, with its long insular tradition, had to face up to the realities of the diminished power of nation states in the global economy and rethink its relations with the wider world. Among other developments this assisted a more positive evaluation of the European Union at the very time when Conservatives were becoming increasingly Euro-sceptic. More fundamentally, globalization was one of the crucial elements in the transition to 'New Labour' and the 'Third Way.'

The end or redefinition of socialism?

Some would argue that Blair's New Labour marks the end of socialism. The accusations of selling out on socialism have been levelled at past leaders, from MacDonald onwards, yet some critics would argue that the Labour Party is not and never has been a socialist party (see

Chapter 4). It all depends, of course, on what is meant by socialism. In the same speech in which Blair announced proposals for a new Clause IV he also talked of his socialism:

> A belief in society, working together, solidarity, cooperation, partnership – these are our words. This is my socialism – and we should stop apologising for using the word. It is not the socialism of Marx or state control. It is rooted in a straightforward view of society: in the understanding that the individual does best in a strong and decent community of people, with principles and standards and common aims and values. It is social-ism. We are the party of the individual because we are the party of the community. Our task is to apply those values to the modern world. (Blair, Labour Conference speech, 1994)

Critics would argue that Blair's rhetoric is short on specifics, and might further fairly allege that he has talked rather less of his socialism in recent years. Even so, Blair in this speech cleverly reemphasized key buzz words which had been part of Labour's vocabulary since the party's establishment: 'society', 'solidarity' 'cooperation' 'partnership' 'community'. He went on to talk about 'opportunity', 'responsibility' 'fairness' and 'trust'. Such a vocabulary would not have been out of place in the mouth of any of Labour's previous leaders, although, as always, there is considerable scope for argument over interpretation and application. Is there any theoretical substance behind the rhetoric? Three strands of thought associated with Blair's leadership while still in opposition might be emphasized – Christian socialism, communitarianism, and stakeholding.

Tony Blair, like his immediate predecessor John Smith, is a practising Christian who derives his socialist convictions from his Christianity, drawing on a long tradition of Christian and ethical socialism within the Labour Party which has been less in evidence in recent years. That tradition has involved strengths and weaknesses (see Chapter 4). While the moral conviction and sincere commitment of Christian socialists have added powerfully to the party's appeal, the implications for analysis and policy prescription are less clear. Moreover, there is an additional problem today which did not exist when Christian socialism was at its most influential, before the First World War. Then Britain was still substantially a Christian country. Today, Christian imagery no longer has the same resonance for the majority, and may alienate those attached to other faiths, or none.

Blair has also laid considerable emphasis on the concept of community which links closely with the socialist values of fraternity, solidarity and cooperation, and contrasts with the extreme individualism associated with the New Right. It also suggests an inclusive concern for all members of the community, rather than the divisive politics of class, which fits comfortably within the mainstream tradition of British socialism and broadens Labour's electoral appeal. Finally, it implies a concern with the small scale and a more decentralized, participative approach to socialism which is useful for a party trying to avoid its past association with bureaucratic centralized state socialism. Communitarianism has become intellectually fashionable on both sides of the Atlantic (Etzioni, 1995), and the manifold positive associations of the term 'community' makes it appealing to politicians. However, in the hands of both philosophers and politicians it remains imprecise, evoking almost any kind or size of human organization or association. Its common use as an all-purpose sanitizing term, promiscuously available across the political spectrum, renders 'community' a somewhat insubstantial foundation on which to base a remodelled socialist philosophy.

Another allied concept, 'stakeholding', became particularly fashionable following its advocacy by Will Hutton (1995, 1997), and its endorsement by Blair (speech to Singapore Business Community, 8 January 1996; John Smith Memorial Lecture, 7 February 1996), and by Tony Wright in the preelection publication *Why Vote Labour* (1997, pp. 53–4). The term has been used at the level of companies to emphasize the 'stake' workers, customers and the local community, as well as shareholders, have in the organization. At the level of society and the national economy, stakeholding similarly asserts the importance of employees, consumers and the wider public interest under capitalism. Hutton himself defines stakeholding in terms of 'a mutuality of rights and obligations, constructed around the notion of economic, social and political inclusion' (Hutton, in Kelly *et al.*, 1997: 3). Critics on the left suggest the term is at best imprecise and at worst involves too many concessions to capitalism. Indeed one sympathetic critic has described stakeholding as a capitalist rather than a socialist argument (Barnett, in Kelly *et al.* 1997, p. 83). On the right, by contrast, stakeholding appears similar to the discredited corporatism of the 1970s (Willetts in Kelly *et al.*, 1997), a point which Hutton (in Kelly *et al.* 1997) denies, although he does admit that it 'places limits on the operation of unfettered markets'.

In practice, however, the language of stakeholding has been employed rather sparsely after 1997. Favoured German and East Asian alternatives to the Anglo-American model of capitalism now seem less viable, and the broad inclusive agenda of stakeholding has been displaced by a renewed emphasis on 'shareholder value'. Thus, according to some observers, the dominance of the City and financial interests has been reasserted and 'Will Hutton's stakeholder economy seems more remote than ever' (Roberts and Kynaston, *New Statesman*, 17 September 2001, pp. 25–7).

A third way?

The ideas associated with stakeholding, Christian socialism and community all involve a critique of acquisitive individualism. They all emphazise the importance of obligations as well as rights, inclusion rather than exclusion, cooperation, collaboration and partnership in place of unfettered competition. As such they have all been absorbed into the broader, more embracing term, the 'third way.'

The term 'third way' has a long history, particularly if it is identified with a 'middle way'. Before the First World War both New Liberalism and Fabian socialism offered a political path between unrestrained free-market capitalism and revolutionary socialism. The threats to western political economies posed by the 1917 Bolshevik Revolution followed by the 1929 slump intensified the search for another way – fascism was briefly presented as such a middle way between Bolshevism and capitalism, while the Conservative rebel Macmillan offered his own democratic 'Middle Way' in the 1930s. After the Second World War social democracy provided a largely successful middle way between Stalinism and laissez-faire capitalism for a generation until overtaken by the problems of the 1970s, which for a time revived the appeal of the free market on the one hand and a more fundamental socialism on the other. Blair's 'third way' then may be seen as part of a continuing search for an alternative to free-market neo-liberalism and centralized state planning.

Critics on the left have viewed the third way as little more than Thatcherism with a smiling face, although much of the Labour government's agenda has been far from Thatcherite – for example, constitutional reform, the minimum wage and Brown's mildly redistributive budgets. Is it just a middle way? Blair himself sometimes talks in such terms. 'The solutions of neither the old Left nor the new Right will do. We need a radical centre in modern politics' (Blair 1996, p. 38). This is reminiscent of the appeal of the old SDP, and Blair has also spoken of the need to rebuild the centre – left coalition of Labour and the New Liberalism, citing approvingly Marquand's (1999) 'progressive dilemma'.

The Third Way can be seen as a revived and refined form of social democracy (Giddens, 1998). Heywood (1998), by contrast, sees the third way as involving the rejection of social democracy for liberal communitarianism, while Le Grand (1998) argues it is neither neo-liberal nor social democratic but a true 'Third Way'. Freeden (1999), finally, locates New Labour 'between the three great Western ideological traditions – liberalism, conservatism and socialism' but drawing on all three.

All this suggests a good dose of pragmatism. What matters is what works. Yet there have been attempts to put more theoretical flesh on the third way both at the micro level of institutions and policies at the sharp end, and at the macro level of global trends. Thus at the micro level, the reform of specific institutions around networks and partnership has been represented as an alternative to bureaucracy on the one hand and markets on the other. The New NHS White Paper claimed:

> There will be no return to the old centralised command and control system of the 1970s ... But nor will there be continuation of the divisive internal market of the 1990s ... [Instead there will be a] third way of running the NHS based on partnership and driven by performance.

The third way is also, particularly in housing and social services, often explicitly linked with the third or voluntary sector involving a not-for-profit alternative to free- market forces and public-sector bureaucracy. The third way sits comfortably within the new language of 'governance', of governments at all levels 'steering' rather than 'rowing', 'enabling' others to provide services rather than delivering services themselves (Rhodes, 1997; Le Grand, 1998).

Giddens (1998) takes a global perspective on the third way which links Blair's New Labour with Clinton's Democrat administration and Schröder's vision of social democracy in Germany. He sees it as a development within rather than an alternative to social democracy, to take account of a number of dilemmas and challenges including globalization, transformations in personal life and problems of the environment. He argues for 'a new relationship between the individual and community', a redefinition of rights and obligations. He emphasizes a number of buzz terms also employed by Christian socialists, communitarians and advocates of stakeholding, such as 'devolution', 'participation' 'partnership' an 'active civil society' 'inclusion' 'the third sector', 'the social investment state'.

At one level the third way seems to involve more rhetoric than substance, yet when attempts are made to clothe the fine words with illustrative detail it becomes too complex for simple elucidation. The attraction of the free market on the hand and central planning on the other is the simplicity of the models – the central idea is easy enough to grasp, even if implementation is more problematic. The third way, by contrast, involves a mass of contentious concepts and a wide variety of practices. While it is a useful umbrella term to describe Labour's current project, it seems unlikely to acquire much popular resonance.

New Labour in government

Blair's electoral triumph in 1997, reaffirmed in 2001, can be exaggerated. His landslide, like Mrs Thatcher's before him, was secured on around 43 per cent of the popular vote and was a consequence, like hers, of the electoral system and a divided opposition. Yet he managed to reach parts of the country, 'middle England', which had rejected old Labour. His appeal transcends that of his party. Indeed, he initially sought cooperation and even coalition with the Liberal Democrats (Ashdown, 2000), showed his readiness to work with pro-Europe Conservatives, and welcomed defectors into his 'big tent'. Thus he has taken over not so much the Thatcher free-market project as the 'One-Nation' approach of her Conservative predecessors. Yet in so doing he has not departed markedly from the pragmatic, gradualist route laid down by previous Labour prime ministers, allowing for the differing domestic and international circumstances in which he achieved power. His 'socialism' remains contestable, but so was theirs. Two things about Blair's first term stand out, firstly its radical constitutional reform programme, and secondly its cautious but initially successful stewardship of the economy.

Some enthusiasts for constitutional reform have been disappointed by Labour's programme, citing the shortcomings of specific reforms (electoral reform, open government, Lords reform) or the apparent absence of a coherent vision beyond particular initiatives; thus (in New Labour terminology) the constitutional reform programme is insufficiently 'joined up'. Yet the rapid implementation of devolution to Scotland, Wales, Northern Ireland and London, the reform of the Lords, the introduction of new electoral systems for the European Parliament and devolved assemblies, and the incorporation into UK law of the European Convention on Human Rights amounts to little less than a constitutional revolution, although one which is still in progress and where the final outcome is far from clear. Although parts of this radical reform programme springs from unfinished business of previous Labour governments (notably Lords reform and devolution), constitutional reform in the past has been more a Liberal (and Liberal Democrat) cause than a Labour one. Moreover, problems in implementing devolution, particularly in Wales and London, the compromises involved with Lords reform and the unfavourable outcomes of Labour's electoral reforms have ensured that the government has secured little credit for its radicalism in the country or the party.

By contrast, its early cautious stewardship of the economy has generally been judged a success. This was important for Labour. All previous Labour governments have encountered economic crises, not always of their own making, yet contributing to a record of cumulative failure. Thus although Labour's social policies were widely supported, its central failure in economic management repeatedly proved a massive electoral liability. Here, the contrasting records of the Major and Blair governments have produced a remarkable reversal in party fortunes. The Conservatives' reputation for economic competence was destroyed by the ERM debacle of 'Black Wednesday' in 1992, while Labour's second landslide majority in 2001 reflected its own successful economic management, delivering growth, low inflation and reduced unemployment. Sceptics might doubt how far the successful record was down to Labour. Perhaps they were simply lucky with world trends from which the economy benefited (just as previous Labour governments might be adjudged unlucky). Yet in politics perceptions are important.

However, Labour's very success in managing the economy (until 2001) has removed its previous alibi for failing to satisfy the hopes of its supporters. Extra money for health and education has come too little too late, while Gordon Brown's tax reforms to benefit families and the low paid (for example through the New Deal) have appeared too complex and sometimes too reminiscent of the means tests previously attacked by Labour politicians to secure the wholehearted approval of socialists. Thus Labour's support (ironically like that of the Conservatives in the 1980s) rests more on antipathy towards the Conservative opposition rather than positive enthusiasm. Labour scores because of what it is not rather than what it is, despite all the rethinking which took place under the leadership of Kinnock, Smith and Blair.

New Labour in the new millennium

Blair's remarkable second landslide victory at the polls in 2001 was a feat which had eluded not only previous Labour governments but the reforming Liberal administrations of Gladstone and Asquith. Left of centre administrations in the past had represented relatively brief interruptions to normal Conservative dominance, so the prospect of a long period of Labour rule takes British politics into hitherto uncharted territory.

Yet, despite this unprecedented second landslide, the failure of the so-called 'Peoples Party' to engage with or enthuse the people remains evident. For all Labour's rhetorical emphasis on community, devolution, participation and inclusion, the reality is falling electoral turnout and, apparently, the increased alienation of the public from the political process. This is not a problem confined to Britain, nor within Britain is it confined to Labour, although it is particularly problematic for a party which has always placed a strong emphasis on an active engaged membership and citizenry.

It remains to be seen whether the government becomes more confident and radical, or continues with the pragmatic caution which characterized much of its first term. One key issue facing Labour is its future relations with the European Union and especially its strategy on the single European currency. Blair wants Britain to be at the heart of Europe, but it is difficult to see how this will be possible if Britain remains outside the euro zone. Yet the immediate problems of economic adjustment and the difficulties in winning the political argument in the face of an increasingly Eurosceptic electorate present formidable obstacles. Even so, Blair's 2001 Conference speech suggests that his government is prepared to take on the argument, perhaps sooner rather than later.

An equally important question is how far Labour will be able to deliver the 'world-class public services' ambitiously promised in their manifesto. In the past Labour has been closely identified with public provision of services, and Blair reaffirmed the commitment to public services both in the undelivered speech to the TUC Conference and his Labour Conference speech in 2001. Critics within the party, however, are particularly concerned about the Private Finance Initiative and the increased role of the private sector in the delivery of some services (for example the privatization of air traffic control, and the plans for the London underground). The continuing problems on the privatized railways, culminating in the collapse of Railtrack, has provided further ammunition for critics. Yet almost regardless of the issue of

'Public–Private Partnerships' it is widely reckoned that Labour's plans for the public services will require very substantial continuing increases in public spending, with awkward implications for taxation. Much will depend here on Labour's continued successful management of the UK economy, although this is always liable to external shocks outside the control of the British Treasury, a point confirmed by the economic fallout from the attack on the World Trade Centre in September 2001, and the ensuring 'war against terrorism'.

These dramatic events have marginalized domestic issues, although normal politics will presumably return eventually. The immediate consequence, however, has been to transform Blair into a politician of global significance. His new world vision, articulated in his party conference speech, has provoked a range of reactions from ecstatic endorsement to dire warnings of hubris. He has been freely compared with Gladstone or Churchill (Shannon, *Guardian*, 4 October 2001). His vision has even been related to the philosopher Kant's dream of international order and perpetual peace, yet he has also been accused of hypocrisy, imperialism and warmongering (see Cowley and Pilger, *New Statesman*, 15 October 2001). Blair's words and actions cannot but affect and perhaps profoundly reshape perceptions of New Labour's ideology. Beyond that, the stakes have suddenly become frighteningly high, not just for Blair himself, his party, or even his country.

Further reading

Minkin (1991) remains indispensable on the *Contentious Alliance* with the trade unions, while Morgan (1997) is illuminating on Callaghan, in retrospect the last 'Old Labour' leader. For the internal problems of the Labour Party in the 1980s Seyd (1987) and Shaw (1994) provide an overview. Benn's diaries (1990, 1994) provide an insider's view from the left, and Healey's autobiography (1989) one from the right. Crewe and King (1995) provide the most authoritative account of the rise and fall of the SDP, although early accounts by Bradley (1981) and Stephenson (1982) capture the atmosphere of the time, while Jenkins (1991) and Owen (1991) provide contrasting personal reminiscences. Williams (1982), Owen (1981, 1984) and Rodgers (1982) all contributed to the debate on social democracy from an SDP perspective, and Hattersley (1987) from Labour's ranks.

On the emergence of New Labour, see Blair's (1996) collection of speeches, insider accounts by Mandelson and Liddle (1996), and Gould

(1998), and other perspectives from Anderson and Mann (1997) Brivati and Bale (1997), and Driver and Martell (1998). Freeden (1999), Bevir (2000), Ludlam (2000), Temple (2000) and Wickham Jones (2000) have all written useful journal articles. See Marquand (1999) for his interpretation of the *Progressive Dilemma* and subsequent observations on the 'Blair paradox'. Hutton (1995, 1997) and Kelly *et al.* (1997) are essential reading on stakeholding, and Giddens (1998) on the Third Way, but on the latter see also Rhodes (1997) and Le Grand (1998). For communitarianism see Etzioni's (1995) influential populist interpretation. Interim judgements on New Labour in government are appearing thick and fast. See particularly Ludlam and Smith (2001). Speeches, policy statements and so on can be found on the party website http://www.lab.org.uk/. Further information on the Labour government can be obtained from Departmental websites.

11

Conclusion: The Future of British Politics

British politics and the wider world

It is difficult to consider soberly the future of British politics amidst apocalyptic visions of a Third World War, involving, some suggest, a projected struggle between rival civilizations. A world crisis inevitably diminishes the importance of domestic concerns. Questions which recently dominated British political debate, such as the single European currency, Lords reform, devolution, and even the future of public services, seem somehow relatively trivial set against the issues surrounding terrorism and war. However, it is hardly new for issues of domestic politics to be overtaken by an international crisis. Political ideologies forged principally on domestic issues are periodically forced to confront wider moral dilemmas. War has proved particularly divisive and difficult for British liberalism, and has often forced Labour to make some painful choices. It can have awkward political consequences, including the curtailing of normal civil liberties and reduced tolerance for those perceived as different and thus potentially unreliable and dangerous. Thus in the Second World War anti-Nazi German refugees were interned. Following the September 2001 attack on the Twin Towers in New York and the ensuing allied response, it is already feared that progress towards a multicultural society in Britain has been damaged, perhaps irreparably, by heightened fears of Muslims and Arabs and Asians generally.

Yet history suggests that normal politics will eventually resume. Thus familiar concerns over public services, employment and inflation, law and order, women's rights, pollution and the environment will again be at the centre of political debate. Moreover, one perhaps surprising consequence of international conflict has often been a renewed concern for domestic social reform and reconstruction. War can concentrate the mind on the prospects for a different social and political order once peace is restored.

Is it possible to make any more substantial predictions about the future for British politics? Prophecy is hazardous, and it is safer to indicate possibilities. Five different scenarios are lightly sketched below. The first suggests that the future could closely resemble the past – a continuation of the Labour–Conservative duopoly. The second examines the prospects for some party and ideological realignment in either a reformed two-party system or a multiparty system. The third considers the end of British politics as we know it, through either the absorption of Britain into a European superstate or through the break-up of Britain as a result of separatist nationalism. The fourth looks at a range of other radical alternative futures. The fifth considers a more humdrum but depressing future, with the growth of political ignorance, apathy and alienation leading to a widening gap between the political elite and the mass.

More of the same? The continuation of two party duopoly

The future could closely resemble the past. What is striking about British politics compared with that of Britain's continental neighbours is its continuity, moderation and stability. Britain's history over the previous century compared with the history over the same period of other European states such as France, Germany, Italy, Spain or Greece, is characterized by an absence of deep ideological divisions, sharp breaks and regime changes. Occasional political crises, as in 1909–11, 1926 and 1931, did not lead to political breakdown, but were ultimately resolved fairly peacefully. While social and industrial unrest either side of the First World War appeared serious enough it never reached the levels of political violence in many other western countries (although Ireland was, of course, a different matter). Although the Bolshevik Revolution and the rise of fascism both had massive implications for British foreign policy, both ultimately made relatively little impact on domestic British politics. Neither communism nor fascism ever took off in Britain. British politics has thus avoided the extremes of left and right and involved a limited choice between parties and ideologies generally grouped around the moderate centre of the political spectrum. Despite periods of three or four-party competition, normally two major parties have contended for the support of the mass of the electorate by seeking to occupy the middle ground of politics, roughly in accordance with Downs 'economic theory of democracy' (1957).

In practice the two-party duopoly of the twentieth century was always uneven. In terms of control of government it was largely a Conservative century. One obvious possibility in view of the party's past capacity to recover rapidly from electoral disaster is that Conservative hegemony will be sooner or later restored. Alternatively, as some commentators are already predicting, Britain could face a long period of Labour hegemony. The second Labour landslide of 2001 was unprecedented, not just in terms of previous Labour history; the Liberals never managed a similar feat when they were the alternative governing party. The mould of Conservative dominance may have been broken and the twenty-first century, in contrast with the twentieth, could be a Labour century.

Party and ideological realignment?

There could, however, be a significant realignment of party forces in Britain, reflecting new ideological divisions. Although the mainstream political ideologies of conservatism, liberalism and socialism have been closely associated with major UK political parties, ideological divisions between parties have sometimes appeared less deep than those within them. Examples include the historical differences within the Liberal Party over Irish Home Rule, imperialism and the New Liberalism, the differences within the Conservatives over protection, over appeasement, over 'Thatcherism', and most recently over Europe, and the long-running divisions within Labour between socialists and social democrats. Thus at various times there has appeared to be more ideological common ground among politicians across parties than within them, and this has suggested the need for some party realignment which would lead to a closer match between party and ideological divisions in British politics.

Despite the assumption of two-party normalcy, the nineteenth century saw a series of significant party realignments culminating in the Liberal split over Irish Home Rule in 1886 which led to what proved a permanent political alliance between the Conservatives and the Liberal Unionists. The only really successful party realignment of the twentieth century involved the rapid replacement of the Liberals by Labour as the main opposition party to the Conservatives in the decade after the end of the First World War. Other projected realignments either failed to get off the ground (Rosebery's middle party, the fusion of the Conservatives and Lloyd George coalition Liberals) or proved partial and short-term (MacDonald's 1931 National coalition).

From the 1960s towards the end of the 1980s it was divisions within the Labour Party which fuelled most of the speculation over a realignment which might ultimately take in also Liberals and moderate Conservatives. Tony Benn (1989, p. 324) told Roy Jenkins in early 1971 that he could see 'the Labour Party actually splitting, resulting in a broad centre party which was European, flanked by a Powellite right and a Michael Foot–Tribune left.' Yet when the split eventually occurred in 1981, the SDP with their Liberal allies failed to 'break the mould' of British politics, in part because some leading social democrats such as Healey and Hattersley preferred to stay with Labour, but more substantially because the Conservative 'wets' opposed to Mrs Thatcher declined to join the new party (Jenkins, 1991, pp. 553–5).

More recently the prospects for party realignment have centred on a Labour–Liberal Democrat rapprochement. Labour's return to moderation meant that the two parties moved closer on constitutional reform, Europe and economic policy and worked together on devolution. Speculation was assisted by a persuasive reinterpretation of twentieth-century British political history which argued that Conservative dominance had been assisted by the breakdown of the progressive alliance between Liberal and Labour in the early years of the century (Marquand, 1999). Blair was substantially persuaded, and according to some interpretations it was only the size of Labour's majority which put paid to the project of a formal coalition, leading ultimately perhaps to merger (Ashdown, 2000). It could still happen, but appears increasingly unlikely.

Today the prospects for realignment seem more dependent on divisions within the Conservatives. Already leading pro-European Conservatives have shared a platform with Tony Blair, and they appear to have more in common with most of the Labour front bench than they do with some of their own party. To that extent realignment seems logical – and could yet be triggered by a referendum on British entry to the single European currency. Past precedent, however, suggests that such a major Conservative Party split is unlikely to happen, although individual defections may continue. Perhaps a more feasible alternative is that Conservative internal divisions could help the Liberal Democrats replace them as the main opposition, as Labour replaced the divided Liberals in the 1920s, and as the Liberal–SDP Alliance came close to overtaking Labour in 1983. It could happen, although it depends substantially on the capacity of the Conservatives to successfully reinvent themselves once more.

Party realignment may often appear to make sense in ideological terms, uniting those in substantial agreement on values and issues, and marking off those who think differently. Even so, British history suggests that projected realignments are rarely realized. The strength of party loyalties despite intra-party ideological differences can be variously explained, but the first-past-the-post electoral system has been a significant factor in inhibiting the emergence of breakaway and new parties.

This could change. Indeed, already the different electoral systems employed for the election of devolved assemblies and the European Parliament have assisted the development of multiparty politics, and the representation of a somewhat wider range of political thinking. It could ultimately lead to a more significant change in the style and content of politics in Britain, particularly if electoral reform is eventually extended to Westminster. Multiparty Britain could become reality, and British party politics might resemble more closely its continental neighbours.

The end of British politics as we know it?

The party realignments discussed in the previous section hardly involve more than a reshuffling of a familiar political pack. Indeed they are substantially premised upon the need for a logical reordering of existing ideological divisions rather than a new kind of politics articulating new issues and values.

It is an obvious point, but the whole notion of 'British' politics is founded on the presumption of the continuation of the British state. This can no longer be taken for granted. One possibility, famously touted by William Hague in his 'foreign land' speech to the Conservative Party Conference, is that Britain could be submerged in a European superstate. If that happened, existing party politics and associated ideological divisions would be completely transformed. British parties would be subsumed within European parties, perhaps largely in line with the existing parties represented in the European Parliament. It is one possible scenario, but for all the talk of closer European integration and Euro-federalism, it is the institutions representing member states such as the Council of Ministers which call the shots in decision-making rather than the pan-European institutions such as the Commission and European Parliament. Enlargement of the European Union is further likely to impede closer integration.

Separatist nationalism presents a more potent and immediate threat to the survival of British politics. Conservatives and a few Labour dissidents predicted that devolution endangered the union and could lead to separation, the aspiration of Scottish and Welsh nationalists. Indeed some observers treat the break-up of the United Kingdom as a virtually accomplished fact (Nairn, 2000, 2001). A disintegration of the British state would clearly profoundly affect existing political forces, and might stimulate new political formations based on different ideological cleavages. If the British state does break up it may be assumed that it will be the consequence of the increased political salience of Scottish and Welsh nationalism, which might in turn provoke an English nationalist reaction, and these various nationalisms would almost certainly continue to loom large for a time after separation to consolidate new political units and encourage new political allegiances and identities. Even if the break-up of Britain does not take place in the immediate future, devolution seems irreversible and within the emerging more complex system of multilevel governance, nationalism seems likely to remain a significant ideological force. Nationalism could take the inclusive civic republican form favoured by socialists and liberals, although it might alternatively be more exclusively ethnic, and narrowly chauvinist.

Radical alternatives?

Outside the political mainstream there are all kinds of radical alternative political futures which are passionately and sometimes vociferously advocated. It is only possible here to lightly sketch some of the possibilities. Some clearly relate to ideas discussed in earlier chapters on racism and multiculturalism (Chapter 6), feminism (Chapter 7) and the Greens (Chapter 8), and it is unnecessary to rehearse the arguments again in any detail. The political agenda of ethnic minorities on the one hand and racists on the other cuts across much of mainstream British party politics. The women's movement and radical feminists in particular argue for a very different style and content of politics to the 'malestream' political tradition. Taken together, the politics of nation, race and gender are bound up with issues of identity, culture and allegiance which cut across the old politics of economic class differences and 'left and right'. The global concerns of the Greens seek to transcend all these divisions. Although all these alternative agendas can certainly be related to economic divisions and economic disadvantage and deprivation, this is not what they claim to be about. They would all reject the mantra of the Clinton Democrats – 'It's the economy stupid! – subsequently taken up by New Labour.

Yet although it is possible to imagine all kind of radical alternative futures in which politics might take a very different shape, it is more difficult to envisage how they might come about. It is possible that the increased presence of women in representative and governmental institutions will incrementally transform the style and substance of politics, although the impact of those condescendingly dubbed 'Blair's babes' after the 1997 election have so far rather disappointed radical feminists. Equally, a richer more diverse multicultural politics could take shape over time as different groups participate more fully in the political system.

Yet it is difficult to see how political protest can bring about the radical changes which the protesters demand. While demonstrations against global capitalism have certainly captured the attention of conventional political leaders and the world's media, it is difficult to see how the protesters can bring about the end of the system they so passionately oppose. More realistically, perhaps, some form of crisis might be the catalyst for change. Economic prosperity has been a major factor in maintaining political stability over most of the western world since the Second World War, which can be contrasted with the marked political instability which characterized the interwar period when economic crises were a major factor in the collapse of liberal democratic regimes. One important question is how and in what ways politics might be transformed by a serious economic recession or possibly an ecological crisis. Could the current liberal democratic consensus survive a severe economic downturn? Might such a downturn lead to the reemergence of left-wing socialist or quasi-fascist alternatives, or would a major shock to the system lead to the kind of reassessment of lifestyles and values which Greens seek?

Global terrorism has already had serious implications for the world economy, and has aroused renewed concerns over biological warfare which could unleash serious and perhaps irreversible environmental effects. Crisis and instability, if prolonged, could clearly have serious implications not just for domestic British politics but for liberal democracy everywhere

The growth of alienation and apathy?

The real danger to the future of liberal democracy and elsewhere may come from a rather more mundane source – growing popular apathy and alienation from politics generally. The growth of representative democracy from the nineteenth century offered the prospect of connecting the masses to governing elites. To a degree it seemed to happen with the establishment of a full adult franchise, high levels of participation in elections and the growth of mass political parties. Active citizens and an active membership of democratic mass parties appeared to create a functioning democratic system. Yet in the years after the Second World War some aspects of political participation in Britain began to weaken. Party membership, and more particularly active party membership, went into steep decline. Today active participation in political parties is confined to a small minority, and the internal deliberations of what are no longer mass parties hardly contribute to the healthy functioning of a democratic political system. Electoral turnout began to decline from a high point in the early 1950s and low turnouts became particularly marked in local and European elections. Politicians could comfort themselves that general-election turnout, though declining gradually over a period, remained at reasonably high levels. The marked drop in turnout in 2001, despite a concerted effort to improve electoral registration and make voting easier, was a nasty shock. Blair's massive landslide was secured with the active support in the polling booths of only a quarter of the total electorate. However, the decline in turnout in Britain substantially matches trends over most of the western world.

Poll evidence indicates considerable political ignorance and shows a marked lack of interest in conventional parliamentary and party politics. Elections are a turn-off for the majority of the voters, who long since abandoned attending political meetings and reading party campaign literature, but who are now switching off television election coverage. Politics seems to bore people, particularly young people. Television soaps and game shows attract far more involved engagement.

Some would argue that this reflects an absence of genuine opportunities for citizen participation. An active engaged citizenry would be required to do far more than make a very limited choice between rival teams of leaders every four or five years. Anarchists are fond of holding up a card with ten or so crosses on it – the extent of the average person's participation in politics in a lifetime. People do not think that the votes they cast in the ballot box can make a real difference to their lives and that's why they stay away from the polling stations and find parliamentary politics a turn-off. There is something in the argument, although it is difficult to believe that more people would become involved if they were given increased opportunities to participate. The opposite could be the case as active participation takes time and energy and may prove frustrating.

Critics would point to a vibrant alternative politics of pressure and protest – the campaigners against new roads or airport extensions, against the export of veal calves, against GM crops and nuclear power, and above all in recent years against global capitalism and war. Their passionate commitment contrasts with the apathy of the electorate. Yet the protesters are in many cases much less representative of public opinion than the political elites they rail against. Indeed, the causes which have apparently attracted most vocal popular support have not been those of the radical alternative left, but the thoroughly conservative Countryside Alliance, and the fuel protesters in Autumn 2000.

Conservatives have indeed only rarely in the past endorsed the politics of pressure and protest, generally when they are (historically exceptionally) excluded from power. The more familiar conservative line is to regard a lack of preoccupation with politics as normal and healthy; ordinary people have more interesting things to do (Hogg, 1947, Oakeshott, 1962). Indeed, even when the Conservative Party was a mass party, the bulk of members seemed content to defer to the leadership on political issues, while deriving primarily social benefits from participation in the Young Conservatives and local constituency parties. Yet such social activities no longer seem to appeal, and a sharply declining and ageing active membership poses enormous difficulties for a party which in the past relied substantially on unstinted voluntary activity for its successful election campaigns.

There is a real fear that a continuing fall in even the most basic political participation could further disconnect political elites from the masses they are supposed to represent and create a crisis of legitimacy for governments. Political leaders in Britain and elsewhere are conscious of the problem and seek to address it, but solutions will not be easy. However, unless the mass of the people reengage with the political process, it is not just the future of specific ideologies which is brought into question, but the future of liberal democracy itself.

Bibliography

Abrams, M., Rose, R. and Hinden, R. (1960) *Must Labour Lose?* (Harmondsworth: Penguin).

Adams, I. (1993) *Political Ideology Today* (Manchester: Manchester University Press).

Adams, I. (1998) *Ideology and Politics in Britain Today* (Manchester: Manchester University Press).

Adelman, P. (1970) *Gladstone, Disraeli and Later Victorian Politics* (Harlow: Longman).

Adelman, P. (1986) *The Rise of the Labour Party*, 2nd edn (London: Longman).

Adonis, A. and Hames, T. (1994) *A Conservative Revolution? The Thatcher–Reagan Decade in Perspective* (Manchester: Manchester University Press).

Alter, P. (1994) *Nationalism*, 2nd edn (London: Arnold).

Anderson, B. (1983) *Imagined Communities* (London: NLB/Verso).

Anderson, P. and Mann, N. (1997) *Safety First: The Making of New Labour* (London: Granta Books).

Arblaster, A. (1984) *The Rise and Decline of Western Liberalism* (Oxford: Blackwell).

Ashdown, P. (2000) *The Ashdown Diaries, volume 1, 1988–1997* (London: Allen Lane).

Ashford, N. (1989) 'Market Liberalism and the Environment: A Response to Hay', *Politics*, vol. 9, no. 1.

Ayer, A. J. (1988) *Thomas Paine* (London: Faber & Faber).

Bacchi, C. L. (1990) *Same Difference: Feminism and Sexual Difference* (London: Allen & Unwin).

Back, L. and Solomos, J. (2000) *Theories of Race and Racism: A Reader* (London: Routledge).

Ballard, J. (2000) 'What is the Future of the Liberal Democrats?', *Talking Politics*, vol. 12(2).

Barker, R. (1978) *Political Ideas in Modern Britain* (London: Methuen).

Barker, R. (1994) *Politics, Peoples and Government* (Basingstoke: Macmillan – now Palgrave).

Barker, R. (2000) 'Hooks and Hands, Interests and Enemies: Political Thinking as Political Action', *Political Studies,* vol. 48(2).

Barrett, M. (1980) *Women's Oppression Today: Problems in Marxist Feminist Analysis* (London: Verso).

Barrett, M. and Phillips, A. (eds) (1992) *Destabilizing Theory: Contemporary Feminist Debates* (Cambridge: Polity Press).

Barry, B. (2001) 'Multicultural Muddles' *New Left Review*, March/April 2001.

Barry, N. P. (1986) *On Classical Liberalism and Libertarianism* (London: Macmillan – now Palgrave).

Beer, S. H. (1982) *Modern British Politics* (London: Faber & Faber).

Behrens, R. (1989) 'Social Democracy and Liberalism' in L. Tivey and A. Wright (eds), *Party Ideology in Britain* (London: Routledge).

Bell, D. (1960) *The End of Ideology* (Free Press).

Benewick, R. (1972) *The Fascist Movement in Britain*, 2nd edn (London: Allen Lane).

Benn, T. (1979) *Arguments for Socialism* (London: Jonathan Cape).

Benn, T. (1989) *Office without Power: Diaries 1968–1972, (*London: Arrow).

Benn, T. (1990) *Conflicts of Interest: Diaries 1977–80* (London: Arrow).

Benn, T. (1994) *The End of an Era: Diaries 1980–90* (London: Arrow).

Bentley, M. (1984) *Politics without Democracy* (London: Fontana).

Bentley, M. (1987) *The Climax of Liberal Politics: British liberalism in theory and practice, 1869–1918* (London: Edward Arnold).

Berlin, I. (1969) 'Two Concepts of Liberty', in *Four Essays on Liberty* (Oxford: Oxford University Press).

Bernstein, G. L. (1986) *Liberalism and Liberal Politics in Edwardian England* (London: Allen & Unwin).

Bevir, M. (2000) 'New Labour: A Study in Ideology' *The British Journal of Politics and International Science*, vol 2, no. 3, October 2000.

Birch, A. H. (1977) *Political Integration and Disintegration in the British Isles* (London: Allen & Unwin).

Blair, T. (1996) *My Vision of a Young Country* (London: Fourth Estate).

Blake, R. (1966) *Disraeli* (London: Eyre & Spottiswoode).

Blake, R. (1997) *The Conservative Party from Peel to Major* (London: Heinemann).

Bookchin, M. (1982) *The Ecology of Freedom*, (Palo Alto: Cheshire Books).

Bosanquet, N. (1983) *After the New Right* (London: Heinemann).

Bottomore, T. (1991) *A Dictionary of Marxist Thought* (Oxford: Blackwell).

Bradley, I. (1981) *Breaking the Mould: the birth & prospects of the Social Democratic Party* (Oxford: Martin Robertson).

Bradley, I. (1985) *The Strange Rebirth of Liberal Britain* (London: Chatto & Windus).

Branson, N. (1979) *Poplarism 1919–1925* (London: Lawrence & Wishart).

Breuilly, J. (1993) *Nationalism & the State*, 2nd edn (Manchester: Manchester University Press).

Brittan, S. (1968) *Left or Right – the bogus dilemma* (London: Secker & Warburg).

Brockway, F. (1977) *Towards Tomorrow* (London: Hart-Davis MacGibbon).

Brownmiller, S. (1977) *Against Our Will* (Harmondsworth: Penguin).

Bruley, S. (1999) *Women in Britain since 1900* (Basingstoke: Macmillan – now Palgrave).

Bryson, V. (1992) *Feminist Political Theory: an Introduction* (Basingstoke: Macmillan – now Palgrave).

Bryson, V. (1999) *Feminist Debates: Issues of Theory and Political Practice* (Basingstoke: Macmillan – now Palgrave).

Bryson, V. (2000) 'Men and Sex Equality' *Politics,* vol. 20, no. 1.

Buck, P. W. (1975) *How Conservatives Think* (Harmondsworth: Penguin).

Bullock, A. and Stallybrass, O. (eds) (1977) *The Fontana Dictionary of Modern Thought* (London: Fontana/Collins).

Bulmer, M & Solomos, J. (eds) (1999) *Racism* (Oxford: Oxford University Press).

Bulpitt, J. (1987) 'Thatcherism as Statecraft', in M. Burch and M. Moran (eds), *British Politics: A Reader* (Manchester: Manchester University Press).

Burke, E. (1790) *Reflections on the Revolution in France*, edited by Hill, B. W. (1975) (Fontana/Harvester Press).

Butler, D. & King, A (1965) *The British General Election of 1964* (London: Macmillan – now Palgrave).

Butler, D. & Kavanagh, D. (1997) *The British General Election of 1997* (Basingstoke: Macmillan – now Palgrave).

Butler, D. & Butler, G. (1994) *British Political Facts 1900–1994*, 7th edn (London: Macmillan – now Palgrave).

Caine, B. (1997) *English Feminism 1780–1980* (Oxford: Oxford University Press).

Calhoun, C. (1997) *Nationalism* (Buckingham: Open University Press).

Callaghan, J. (1987) *The Far Left in British Politics* (Oxford: Basil Blackwell).

Callaghan, J. (1990) *Socialism in Britain* (Oxford: Basil Blackwell).

Carson, R. (1965) *Silent Spring* (Harmondsworth: Penguin).

Carsten, F. L. (1967) *The Rise of Fascism* (London: Batsford).

Carter, A. (1988) *The Politics of Women's Rights* (Harlow: Longman).

Carter, N. (2001) 'The Environment' in *Developments in Politics* (ed. Lancaster) (Ormskirk: Causeway Press).

Challinor, R. (1977) *The Origins of British Bolshevism* (London: Croom Helm).

Clarke, J., Cochrane, A. and Smart, C. (1987) *Ideologies of Welfare* (London: Hutchinson).

Clarke, P. F. (1971) *Lancashire and the New Liberalism (Cambridge:* Cambridge University Press).

Coates, D. (1980) *Labour in Power?* (Harlow: Longman).

Cole, J. (1995) *As It Seemed To Me: Political Memoirs* (London: Weidenfeld & Nicolson).

Coole, D. H. (1988) *Women in Political Theory* (London: Wheatsheaf Books).

Cornford, F. M. (1945) *The Republic of Plato* (Oxford: Oxford University Press).

Cosgrave, P. (1989) *The Lives of Enoch Powell* (London: Bodley Head).

Cowley, P and Fisher, J. (2000) 'The Conservative Party', *Politics Review*, vol. 10 (2).

Cowling, M. (ed.) (1978) *Conservative Essays* (London: Cassell).

Crewe, I. and King, A. (1995) *SDP: The Birth, Life and Death of the Social Democratic Party* (Oxford: Oxford University Press).

Crick, B. (1987) *Socialism* (Buckingham: Open University Press).

Crick, B (ed.) (1991) *National Identities* (Oxford: Blackwell).

Crick, B. (1993) *In Defence of Politics*, 4th edn (Harmondsworth: Penguin).

Crosland, C. A. R. (1956) *The Future of Socialism* (London: Jonathan Cape).

Dahrendorf, R. (1990) *Reflections on the Revolution in Europe* (London: Chatto & Windus).

Dangerfield, G. (1966) *The Strange Death of Liberal England* (London: MacGibbon & Kee).

Davies, N. (1999) *The Isles: A History* (London: Macmillan – now Palgrave).

Dearlove, J. and Saunders, P. (2000) *Introduction to British Politics*, 3rd edn (Cambridge: Polity Press).

Deutsch, K. W. *Nationalism and Social Communication* (New York: MIT Press).

Dinwiddy, J. (1989) *Bentham* (Oxford: Oxford University Press).

Disraeli, B. (1844, 1983 ed.) *Coningsby* (Harmondsworth: Penguin).

Disraeli, B. (1845, 1980 ed.) *Sybil* (Harmondsworth: Penguin).

Dobson, A. (1995) *Green Political Thought*, 2nd edn (London: Routledge).

Dobson, A. (ed.) (1991) *The Green Reader* (London: Andre Deutsch).

Donald, J. and Hall, S. (eds) (1986) *Politics and Ideology* (Buckingham: Open University Press).

Downs, A. (1957) *An Economic Theory of Democracy* (New York: Harper & Row).

Driver, S. and Martell, L. (1998) *New Labour: Politics after Thatcherism* (Cambridge: Polity Press).

Dunn, J. (1969) *The Political Thought of John Locke* (Cambridge: Cambridge University Press).

Dworkin, A. (1981) *Pornography* (London: Women's Press).

Eatwell, R. (1995) *Fascism: A History* (London: Chatto & Windus).

Eatwell, R. and Wright, A. (eds) (1999) *Contemporary Political Ideologies*, 2nd edn (London: Continuum).

Eccleshall, R. (1977) 'English Conservatism as Ideology', *Political Studies*, vol. xxv, no. 1.

Eccleshall, R. (1986) *British Liberalism: Liberal Thought from the 1640s to the 1980s* (Harlow: Longman).

Eccleshall, R. (1990) *English Conservatism since the Reformation: An introduction and anthology* (London: Unwin Hyman).

Eccleshall, R., Geoghegan, V., Jay R., Kenny, M., MacKenzie, I and Wilford R. (1994) *Political Ideologies, an Introduction*, 2nd edn (London: Routledge).

Eckersley, R. (1992) *Environmentalism and Political Theory: Towards an Ecocentric Approach* (London: UCL Press).

Edgar, D. (1984) 'Bitter Harvest' in Curran, J. (ed.) *The Future of the Left* (London: Polity Press/New Socialist).

Etzioni, A. (1995) *The Spirit of Community* (London: Fontana Press).

Evans, B. (1984) 'Political ideology and its role in recent British politics' in Robins, L. (ed.), *Updating British Politics* (The Politics Association).

Evans, J. (1995) *Feminist Theory Today* (London: Sage).

Evans, J., Hills, J., Hunt, K., Meehan, E. Tuscher, T, Vogel, U. and Waylen, G. (1986) *Feminism and Political Theory* (London: Sage Publications).

Evans, M. (1982) *The Woman Question* (London: Fontana).

Evans, M. (1997) *Introducing Contemporary Feminist Thought* (Cambridge: Polity Press).

Eysenck, H. J. (1957) *Sense and Nonsense in Psychology* (Harmondsworth: Penguin).

Figes, E. (1978) *Patriarchal Attitudes* (London: Virago).

Finer, S. E. (ed.) (1975) *Adversary Politics and Electoral Reform* (London: Wigram).

Firestone, S. (1979) *The Dialectic of Sex* (London: The Women's Press).

Flew, A. (ed.) (1979) *A Dictionary of Philosophy* (London: Pan/Macmillan).

Foot, M. and Kramnick, I. (eds) (1987) *The Thomas Paine Reader* (Harmondsworth: Penguin).

Foote, G. (1986) *The Labour Party's Political Thought* (London: Croom Helm).

Franklin, B. (1994) *Packaging Politics* (London: Edward Arnold).

Fraser, D. (1984) *The Evolution of the British Welfare State* (London: Macmillan – now Palgrave).

Freeden, M. (1978) *The New Liberalism: An Ideology of Social Reform* (Oxford: Oxford University Press).

Freeden, M. (1986) *Liberalism Divided: A Study in British Political Thought 1914–1939* (Oxford: Oxford University Press).

Freeden, M. (1996) *Ideology and Political Theory* (Oxford: Clarendon Press).

Freeden, M. (1998) 'Is Nationalism a Distinct Ideology?', *Political Studies*, vol. 46, no. 4.

Freeden, M. (1999) 'The Ideology of New Labour', *The Political Quarterly*, vol. 70, 1.

Freely, M. (1995) *What About Us? An Open Letter to the Mothers Feminism Forgot* (London: Bloomsbury).

Friedan, B. (1965) *The Feminine Mystique* (Harmondsworth: Penguin).

Friedan, B. (1977) *It Changed my Life* (London: Victor Gollancz).

Friedan, B. (1982) *The Second Stage* (London: Michael Joseph).

Fukuyama, F. (1989) 'The End of History?' *The National Interest*, no. 16, Summer 1989.

Fukuyama, F. (1992) *The End of History and the Last Man* (London: Hamish Hamilton).

Gamble, A. (1974) *The Conservative Nation* (London: Routledge & Kegan Paul).

Gamble, A. (1988) *The Free Economy and the Strong State* (London: Macmillan – now Palgrave).

Garner, R. (1995) *Environmental Politics* (London: Harvester Wheatsheaf).

Gellner, E. (1983) *Nations and Nationalism* (Oxford: Basil Blackwell).

George, V. and Wilding, P. (1985) *Ideology and Social Welfare* (London: Routledge & Kegan Paul).

Giddens, A. (1994) *Beyond Left and Right: the Future of Radical Politics* (Cambridge: Polity Press).

Giddens, A. (1998) *The Third Way: the Renewal of Social Democracy* (Cambridge: Polity).

Giddens, A. (1999) 'Better than warmed over porridge', *New Statesman*, 12 February.

Gilmour, I. (1978) *Inside Right* (London: Quartet Books).

Gilmour, I. (1992) *Dancing with Dogma: Britain under Thatcherism* (London: Simon & Schuster).

Gilmour, I. and Garnett, M. (1997) *Whatever Happened to the Tories? The Conservatives since 1945* (London: Fourth Estate).

Goldsmith, E. (ed.) (1972) *A Blueprint for Survival* (Harmondsworth: Penguin).

Goodin, R (1992) *Green Political Theory* (Cambridge: Polity Press).

Goodwin, B. (1997) *Using Political Ideas*, 4th edn (Chichester: John Wiley & sons).

Gould, P. (1998) *The Unfinished Revolution* (London: Abacus).

Grant, J. (1993) *Fundamental Feminism* (London: Routledge).

Gray, J. (1986) *Liberalism* (Buckingham: Open University Press).

Gray, J. and Willetts, D. (1997) *Is Conservatism Dead?*(London: Profile Books).

Gray, R. (1981) *The Aristocracy of Labour in Nineteenth-Century Britain c. 1850–1914* (London: Macmillan – now Palgrave).

Green, D. G. (1987) *The New Right* (Brighton: Wheatsheaf).

Green, T. H. (1881, ed. Harris, P. and Morrow, J. 1986) *Lectures on the Principles of Political Obligation* (Cambridge: Cambridge University Press).

Greenfeld, L. (1992) *Nationalism: Five Roads to Modernity* (Cambridge Ma.: Harvard University Press).

Greenleaf, W. H. (1973) 'The character of modern British conservatism' in Benewick, R. Berkhi, R. N. and Parekh, B. (eds), *Knowledge and Belief in Politics* (London: Allen & Unwin).

Greenleaf, W. H. (1983) *The British Political Tradition, Vol. 1, The Rise of Collectivism, Vol. 2, The Ideological Heritage* (London: Methuen).

Greer, G. (1970) *The Female Eunuch* (London: MacGibbon & Kee).

Hall, S. and Jacques, M. (eds) (1983) *The Politics of Thatcherism* (London: Lawrence & Wishart).

Hamilton, M. B. (1987) 'The elements of the concept of ideology' *Political Studies*, vol. xxxv, no. 1, March.

Hampsher-Monk, I. (1992) *A History of Modern Political Thought: Major Political Thinkers from Hobbes to Marx* (Oxford: Blackwell).

Hardin, G. (1968) 'The tragedy of the commons', *Science*, vol. 162.

Harvie, C. (1994) *Scotland and Nationalism* (London: Routledge).

Hattersley, R. (1987) *Choose Freedom: The future of democratic socialism* (London: Michael Joseph).

Hattersley, R. (1995) *Who goes home?* (London: Little, Brown).

Hay, J. R. (1983) *The Origins of the Liberal Welfare Reforms*, 1906–1914 (London: Macmillan – now Palgrave).

Hay, P. R. (1988) 'Ecological values and the western political traditions from anarchism to fascism', *Politics*, vol. 8, no. 1.

Hayek, F. (1975) 'The Principles of a Liberal Social Order' in Crespigny, A. and Cronin, J. (eds), *Ideologies of Politics* (Oxford: Oxford University Press).

Hayek, F. A. (1976) *The Road to Serfdom* (London: Routledge & Kegan Paul).

Healey, D. (1989) *The Time of My Life* (London: Michael Joseph).

Heywood, A. (1997) *Political Ideologies: An Introduction*, 2nd edn (Basingstoke: Macmillan – now Palgrave).

Heywood, A. (1998) 'Its the culture, stupid! Deconstructing the Blair project' *Talking Politics,* vol. 11, 1.

Hindess, B. (1971) *The Decline of Working Class Politics* (London: MacGibbon & Kee).

Hobhouse, L. T. (1911, 1964) *Liberalism* (Oxford: Oxford University Press).

Hobsbawm, E. J. (1969) *Industry and Empire* (Harmondsworth: Penguin).

Hobsbawm, E. J. (1992) *The Age of Revolution 1789–1848* (London: Abacus).

Hobsbawm, E. J. (1988) *The Age of Capital 1848–1875* (London: Cardinal).

Hobsbawm, E. J. (1989) *Politics for a Rational Left* (London: Verso).

Hobsbawm, E. J. (1990) *Nations and Nationalism since 1780* (Cambridge: Cambridge University Press).

Hobsbawm, E. J. (1994) *The Age of Empire 1875–1914* (London: Abacus).

Hobsbawm, E. J. (1994) *Age of Extremes: The Short Twentieth Century 1914–1991* (London: Michael Joseph).

Hobsbawm, E. J. (1996) 'The Cult of Identity Politics', *New Left Review*, 217, May/June, 1996.

Hogg, Q. (1947) *The Case for Conservatism* (West Drayton: Penguin).

Holland, S. K. (1975) *The Socialist Challenge* (London: Quartet Books).

Honderich, T. (1990) *Conservatism* (London: Hamish Hamilton).

Hume, L. J. (1981) *Bentham and Bureaucracy* (Cambridge: Cambridge University Press).

Humm, M. (ed.) (1992) *Feminisms: A Reader* (London: Harvester Wheatsheaf).

Hutchinson, J. (1994) *Modern Nationalism* (London: Fontana Press).

Hutchinson, J. and Smith, A. D. (eds) (1994) *Nationalism* (Oxford: Oxford University Press).

Hutton, W. (1995) *The State We're In* (London: Jonathan Cape).

Hutton, W. (1997) *The State to Come* (London: Vintage).

Jackson, S. et al. (eds) (1993) *Women's Studies: A Reader* (London: Harvester Wheatsheaf).

Jenkins, R. (1991) *A Life at the Centre* (London: Macmillan – now Palgrave).

Joll, J. (1979) *The Anarchists*, 2nd edn (London: Methuen).

Joseph, K. (1976) *Stranded on the Middle Ground* (London: Centre for Policy Studies).

Kavanagh, D. (ed.) (1982) *The Politics of the Labour Party* (London: Allen & Unwin).

Kavanagh, D. (1990) *Thatcherism and British Politics*, 2nd edn (Oxford: Oxford University Press).

Kavanagh, D. and Morris, P. (1994) *Consensus Politics*, 2nd edn (Oxford: Blackwell).

Kavanagh, D. and Seldon, A. (1994) *The Major Effect* (London: Macmillan – now Palgrave).

Kedourie, E, (1993) *Nationalism*, 4th edn (Oxford: Blackwell).

Keating, M. (1998) *The New Regionalism in Western Europe* (Cheltenham: Edward Elgar).

Keegan, W. (1984) *Mrs Thatcher's Economic Experiment* (London: Allen Lane).

Kellas, J. G. (1991) *The Politics of Nationalism and Ethnicity* (Basingstoke: Macmillan – now Palgrave).

Kelly, R. (2001) 'Conservatism under Hague: The Fatal Dilemma', *Talking Politics*, vol. 13, no. 2.

Kershaw, I. (1993) *The Nazi Dictatorship: problems and perspectives in inter-pretation* (London: Edward Arnold).

King, D. S. (1987) *The New Right* (Basingstoke: Macmillan – now Palgrave).

Kingdom, J. (1999) *Government and Politics in Britain* (Cambridge: Polity Press)

Kirk, R. (1982) *The Portable Conservative Reader* (Harmondsworth: Viking Penguin).

Kitchen, M. (1976) *Fascism* (London: Macmillan – now Palgrave).

Kogan, D and Kogan, M. (1982) *The Battle for the Labour Party* (London: Kogan Page).

Laqueur, W. (ed.) (1979) *Fascism: A Reader's Guide* (Harmondsworth: Penguin Books).

Lawson, N. (1992) *The View from No. 11: Memoirs of a Tory Radical* (London: Bantam).

Laybourn, K. (2000) *A Century of Labour* (Stroud: Sutton Publishing).

Leach, R. (1995) *Turncoats: Changing Party Allegiance by British Politicians* (Aldershot: Dartmouth).

Leach, R. (1996) *British Political Ideologies* (Hemel Hempstead: Prentice-Hall/Harvester Wheatsheaf).

Le Grand, J. (1998) 'The Third Way begins with Cora', *New Statesman*, 6 March.

Levitas, R. (ed.) (1986) *The Ideology of the New Right* (London: Polity Press).

Lichtheim, G. (1970) *A Short History of Socialism* (London: Weidenfeld & Nicolson).

Locke, J (ed. Gough, 1966) *A Letter Concerning Toleration*, with *Second Treatise of Civil Government* (Oxford: Basil Blackwell).

Lovell, T. (ed.) (1990) *British Feminist Thought: A Reader* (Oxford: Basil Blackwell).

Lovelock, J. E. (1979) *Gaia: A new look at life on Earth* (Oxford: Oxford University Press).

Lovenduski, J. and Randall, V. (1993) *Contemporary Feminist Politics* (Oxford: Oxford University Press).

Ludlam, S. (2000) 'New Labour: what's published is what counts', *British Journal of Political Science*, vol 2, no. 2, June 2000

Ludlam, S. and Smith, M. (eds) (1996) *Contemporary British Conservatism* (Basingstoke: Macmillan – now Palgrave).

Ludlam, S. and Smith, M. (eds) (2001) *New Labour in Government* (Basingstoke: Macmillan – now Palgrave).

Mac an Ghaill, M. (1999) *Contemporary Racisms and Ethnicities* (Buckingham: Open University Press).

McCormick, J. (1991) *British Politics and the Environment* (London: Earthscan Publications Ltd).

McCrone, D. (1992) *Understanding Scotland* (London: Routledge).

MacDonald, J. R. (1911) *The Socialist Movement* (London: Home University Library).

Mackenzie, J. M. (ed.) (1986) *Imperialism and Popular Culture* (Manchester: MUP).

McKenzie, R. T. (1963) *British Political Parties*, 2nd edn (London: Heinemann).

McKenzie, R. T. and Silver, A. (1968) *Angels in Marble* (London: Heinemann).

MacKinnon, C. (1989) *Towards a Feminist Theory of the State* (London: Harvard University Press).

McLellan, D. (1976) *Karl Marx* (London: Paladin, Granada Publishing).

McLellan, D. (1979) *Marxism after Marx* (London: Macmillan – now Palgrave).

McLellan, D. (1995) *Ideology*, 2nd edn (Buckingham: Open University Press).

Macpherson, C. B. (1962) *The Political Theory of Possessive Individualism* (Oxford: Oxford University Press).

Macpherson, Sir W. (1999) *The Stephen Lawrence Inquiry* (Cm 4262) (London: The Stationery Office Ltd).

Maddox, J. (1972) *The Doomesday Syndrome* (London: Macmillan – now Palgrave).

Major, J. (1999) *The Autobiography* (London: HarperCollins).

Malthus, T. (1970) *An Essay on the Principle of Population* (ed. Flew) (Harmondsworth: Penguin).

Mannheim, K. (1960) *Ideology and Utopia* (London: Routledge & Kegan Paul).

Manning, D. J. (1976) *Liberalism* (London: Dent).

Marquand, D. (1977) *Ramsay MacDonald* (London: Jonathan Cape).

Marquand, D. (1988) *The Unprincipled Society* (London: Fontana).

Marquand, D. (1999) *The Progressive Dilemma* (London: Phoenix).

Marr, A. (1992) *The Battle for Scotland* (Harmondsworth: Penguin Books).

Martell, L. (1994) *Ecology and Society: An Introduction* (Cambridge: Polity Press).

Marx, K. (1977, ed. McLellan, D.) *Selected Writings* (Oxford: Oxford University Press).

Marx, K. and Engels, F. (1962) *Selected Works* (two vols) (London: Lawrence and Wishart).

Meadows, D. H., Meadows, D. L., Randers, D.L. and Behrens III, W. (1974) *The Limits to Growth* (London: Pan).

Michels, R. (1962) *Political Parties* (Free Press).

Middlemas, K. (1979) *Politics in Industrial Society: the experience of the British system since 1911* (London: Deutsch).

Mies, M. and Shiva, V. (1993) *Ecofeminism* (London: Fernwoood Publications, Zed books).

Miles, R. (1989) *Racism* (London: Routledge).

Miles, R. (1993) *Racism after 'Race Relations'* (London: Routledge).

Miliband, D. (ed.) (1994) *Re-inventing the Left* (Cambridge: Polity Press

Miliband, R. (1972) *Parliamentary Socialism*, 2nd edn (London: Merlin Press).

Miliband, R. (1994) *Socialism for a Sceptical Age* (Cambridge: Polity Press).

Mill, J. S. (ed. Warnock, 1962) *Utilitarianism, On Liberty*, with introduction by M. Warnock (1962) (London: Fontana/Collins).

Mill, J. S. (ed. Acton, H. B., 1972) *Utilitarianism, On Liberty, Representative Government* (London: J. M. Dent).

Mill, J. S. (ed. Okin, S., 1988) *The Subjection of Women* (Indianapolis: Hackett Publishing Company).

Mill, J. S. and Bentham, J. (ed. Ryan, A., 1987) *Utilitarianism and Other Essays* (Harmondsworth: Penguin).

Millett, K. (1977) *Sexual Politics* (London: Virago).

Minkin, L. (1978) *The Labour Party Conference* (London: Allen Lane).

Minkin, L. (1991) *The Contentious Alliance: Trade Unions and the Labour Party* (Edinburgh: Edinburgh University Press).

Minogue, K. (1967) *Nationalism* (London: Batsford).

Minogue, K. (1985) *Alien Powers: The Pure Theory of Ideology* (London: Weidenfeld & Nicholson).

Mirza, H. S. (ed.) (1997) *Black British Feminism* (London: Routledge).

Mitchell, J. (1974) *Psychoanalysis and Feminism* (Harmondsworth: Penguin).

Mitchell, J. and Oakley, A. (1986) *What is Feminism?* (Oxford: Blackwell).

Morgan, K. R. (1997) *Callaghan: A Life* (Oxford: Oxford University Press).

Morris, W. (1962) *Selected Writings and Designs* (ed. Briggs, A.) (Harmondsworth: Penguin).

Nairn, T. (1981) *The Break-up of Britain* (London: NLB & Verso).

Nairn, T. (2000) *After Britain: New Labour and the Return of Scotland* (London: Granta Books).

Nairn, T. (2001) 'Post Ukania', *New Left Review*, 7, Jan/Feb 2001.

Nisbet, R. (1986) *Conservatism* (Buckingham: Open University Press).

Nozick, R. (1974) *Anarchy, State and Utopia* (Oxford: Blackwell).

Oakeshott, M. (1962) *Rationalism in Politics and other Essays* (London: Methuen).

Okin, S. M. (1990) *Justice, Gender and the Family* (New York: Basic Books).

O'Riordan, T. (1976) *Environmentalism* (London: Pion Ltd).

O'Sullivan, N. (1976) *Conservatism* (London: Dent).

Owen, D. (1981) *Face the Future* (Oxford: Oxford University Press).

Owen, D. (1991) *Time to Declare* (London: Michael Joseph).

Owen, R. (1991) *A New View of Society and Other Writings*, edited by G. Claeys (Harmondsworth: Penguin).

Paine, T. (1791–2, ed. Collins, 1969) *The Rights of Man* (Harmondsworth: Penguin).

Parekh, B. (2000a) *The Future of Multi-Ethnic Britain: Report of the Commission on Multi-Ethnic Britain* (London: Profile Books in association with Runnymede Trust).

Parekh, B. (2000b) *Rethinking Multiculturalism: Cultural Diversity and Political Theory* (Basingstoke: Macmillan – now Palgrave).

Patten, J. (1995) *Things to Come: The Tories in the 21st Century* (London: Sinclair-Stevenson).

Paxman, J. (1998) *The English* (London: Michael Joseph).

Pearson, R. and Williams, G. (1984) *Political Thought and Public Policy in the Nineteenth Century* (London: Longman).

Pelling, H. (1965) *The Origins of the Labour Party* (Oxford: Oxford University Press).

Pepper, D. (1993) *Eco-Socialism: From Deep Ecology to Social Justice* (London: Routledge).

Perryman, M. (ed.) (1994) *Altered States: Postmodernism, Politics, Culture* (London: Lawrence and Wishart).

Phizacklea, A. and Miles, R. (1980) *Labour and Racism* (London: Routledge & Kegan Paul).

Pierre, J. and Peters, B. G. (2000) *Governance, Politics and the State* (Basingstoke: Macmillan – now Palgrave).

Pierson, S. (1973) *Marxism and the Origins of British Socialism* (Cornell University Press).

Pimlott, B. (1977) *Labour and the Left in the 1930s* (Cambridge: Cambridge University Press).

Pimlott, B. (1992) *Harold Wilson* (London: HarperCollins).

Plamenatz, J. P. (1963) *Man and Society: a critical examination of some important social and political theories from Machiavelli to Marx*, two vols (London: Longmans).

Plant, J. (ed.) (1989) *Healing the Wounds: The Promise of Ecofeminism* (Green Print, The Merlin Press).

Pois, R. A. (1986) *National Socialism and the Religion of Nature* (London: Croom Helm).

Popper, K. R. (1962) *The Open Society and its Enemies*, 4th edn, 2 vols, (London: Routledge & Kegan Paul).

Porrit, J. and Winner, D. (1988) *The Coming of the Greens* (London: Fontana/Collins).

Pyle, A. (1995) *The Subjection of Women: Contemporary Responses to John Stuart Mill* (Bristol: Thoemmes Press).

Quinton, A. (1978) *The Politics of Imperfection* (London: Faber & Faber).

Ramazanoglu, C. (1989) *Feminism and the Contradictions of Oppression* (London: Routledge).

Randall, V. (1987) *Women and Politics* (London: Macmillan – now Palgrave).

Ranelagh, J. (1992) *Thatcher's People* (London: Fontana).

Rawls, J. (1971) *A Theory of Justice* (Oxford: Oxford University Press).

Rawnsley, A. (2001) *Servants of the People; The Inside Story of New Labour* (Harmondsworth: Penguin).

Regan, T. (1988) *The Case for Animal Rights* (London: Routledge & Kegan Paul).

Rex, J. (1986) *Race and Ethnicity* (Buckingham: Open University Press).

Rhodes, R. A. W. (1997) *Understanding Governance* (Buckingham: Open University Press).

Richards, J. R. (1982) *The Sceptical Feminist* (Harmondsworth: Penguin).

Riddell, P. (1983) *The Thatcher Government* (Oxford: Martin Robertson).

Robertson, D. (1993) *The Dictionary of Politics* (Harmondsworth: Penguin).

Robinson, M. (1992) *The Greening of British Party Politics* (Manchester: Manchester University Press).

Rubinstein, D. (2000) 'A New Look at New Labour' *Politics,* vol. 20,3.

Rushdie, S. (1998) *The Satanic Verses* (London: Viking)

Russell, C. (1999) *An Intelligent Person's Guide to Liberalism* (London: Duckworth).

Saggar, S. (1992) *Race and Politics in Britain* (London: Harvester Wheatsheaf).

St John-Stevas, N. (1982) 'Tory philosophy – a personal view' in *Three Banks Review*, June, no. 134.

Sandbach, F. (1980) *Environment, Ideology and Policy* (Oxford: Basil Blackwell).

Sargent, L (ed.) (1981) *The Unhappy Marriage of Marxism and Feminism: a Debate on Class and Patriarchy* (London: Pluto Press).

Sassoon (1997) *One Hundred Years of Socialism* (London: Fontana Press).

Saville, J. (1988) *The Labour Movement in Britain* (London: Faber & Faber).

Scarman, Lord (1981) *The Brixton Disorders 10–12 April 1981: Special Report* (London: HMSO).

Schultz, H. J. (1972) *English Liberalism and the State: Individualism or Collectivism?* (Lexington, Mass.: Heath).

Schumacher, E. F. (1973) *Small is Beautiful* (London: Sphere Books).

Schumpeter, J. A. (1943) *Capitalism, Socialism and Democracy* (London: Allen & Unwin).

Schwarzmantel, J. (1991) *Socialism and the Idea of the Nation* (London: Harvester Wheatsheaf).

Scruton, R. (1980) *The Meaning of Conservatism* (London: Macmillan – now Palgrave).

Scruton, R. (1983) *A Dictionary of Political Thought* (London: Macmillan – now Palgrave/Pan).

Seldon, A. and Ball, S. (1994) *Conservative Century: The Conservative Party since 1900* (Oxford: Oxford University Press).

Seliger, M. (1976) *Ideology and Politics* (London: Allen & Unwin).

Seyd, P. (1987) *The Rise and Fall of the Labour Left* (London: Macmillan – now Palgrave).

Seymour-Ure, C. (1974) *The Political Impact of the Mass Media* (Constable).

Shaw, E. (1994) *The Labour Party since 1979: Crisis and Transformation* (London: Routledge).

Singer, P. (1990) *Animal Liberation* (London: Cape).

Skellington, R. (1996) *'Race' in Britain Today* (London: Sage).

Skidelsky, R. (1967) *Politicians and the Slump* (Harmondsworth: Penguin).

Skidelsky, R. (1990) *Oswald Mosley*, 3rd edn (London: Macmillan – now Palgrave).

Skidelsky, R. (ed.) (1988) *Thatcherism* (London: Chatto & Windus).

Skinner, Q. (1978) *The Foundations of Modern Political Thought*, 2 vols (Cambridge: Cambridge University Press).

Smith, A. (1776) *The Wealth of Nations*, edited with an introduction by E. Cannan (1976) (University of Chicago Press).

Smith, A. D. (1991) *National Identity* (Harmondsworth: Penguin Books).

Smith, P. (1967) *Disraelian Conservatism and Social Reform* (London: Routledge).

Solomos, J. and Back, L. (1995) *Race, Politics and Social Change* (London: Routledge).

Solomos, J. and Back, L. (1996) *Racism and Society* (Basingstoke: Macmillan – now Palgrave).

Stephenson, H. (1982) *Claret and Chips: the rise of the SDP* (London: Michael Joseph).

Tawney, R. H. (1961) *The Acquisitive Society* (London: Fontana).

Tawney, R. H. (1964) *Equality* (London: Unwin).

Taylor, S. (1982) *The National Front in English Politics* (London: Macmillan – now Palgrave).

Temple, M. (2000) 'New Labour's Third Way: pragmatism and governance' *The British Journal of Politics and International Relations*, vol. 2, no. 3, October 2000.

Thatcher, M. (1977) *Let Our Children Grow Tall* (London: Centre for Policy Studies).

Thatcher, M. (1993) *The Downing Street Years* (London: HarperCollins).

Thompson, E. P. (1980) *The Making of the English Working Class* (Harmondsworth: Penguin).

Thompson, K. (1986) *Beliefs and Ideology* (London: Ellis Horwood & Tavistock Publications).

Thomson, D. (1966) *Political Ideas* (Harmondsworth: Penguin).

Thurlow, R. C. (1987) *Fascism in Britain: A History 1918–1985* (Oxford: Basil Blackwell).

Tivey, L. (ed.) (1981) *The Nation State* (Oxford: Martin Robertson).

Tivey, L. and Wright, A. (1989) *Party Ideology in Britain* (London: Routledge).

Tong, R. (1992) *Feminist Thought: A Comprehensive Introduction* (London: Routledge).

Vincent, A. (1995) *Modern Political Ideologies*, 2nd edn (Oxford: Blackwell).

Vincent, J. (1966) *The Formation of the Liberal Party, 1857–1868* (London: Constable).

Waldegrave, W. (1978) *The Binding of Leviathan* (London: Hamish Hamilton).

Walter, N. (1999) *The New Feminism* (London: Virago).

Walker, M. (1977) *The National Front* (London: Fontana).

Wallace, W. (1997) *Why vote Liberal Democrat?* (Harmondsworth: Penguin Books).

Warren, K. J. (ed.) (1994) *Ecological Feminism* (London: Routledge).

Watson, J. S. (1960) *The Reign of George III* (Oxford: Oxford University Press).

Weale, A. (1992) *The New Politics of Pollution* (Manchester: Manchester University Press).

Whiteley, P. (1983) *The Labour Party in Crisis* (London: Methuen).

Whiteley, P., Seyd, P. and Richardson, J. (1994) *True Blues: The Politics of Conservative Party Membership* (Oxford: Clarendon Press).

Willetts, D. (1997) *Why Vote Conservative?* (Harmondsworth: Penguin Books).

Williams, R. (1976) *Keywords: A Vocabulary of Culture and Society* (London: Fontana/Croom Helm).

Williams, S. (1981) *Politics is for People* (Harmondsworth: Penguin).

Wilson, D. (1984) *Pressure: The A to Z of Campaigning in Britain* (London: Heinemann).

Wollstonecraft, M. (1792, ed. Tauchert, 1995) *A Vindication of the Rights of Women* (London: Dent, Everyman).

Wright, A. (1983) *British Socialism* (London: Longman).

Wright, A. (1987) *Socialisms: Theories and Practices* (Oxford: Oxford University Press).

Wright, D. G. (1970) *Democracy and Reform, 1815–1885* (Harlow: Longman).
Wright, T. (1997) *Why vote Labour?* (Harmondsworth: Penguin Books).
Young, H. (1989) *One of Us* (London: Macmillan – now Palgrave).
Young, H. (1998) *This Blessed Plot: Britain and Europe, from Churchill to Blair* (London: Macmillan – now Palgrave).

Index